D.J. Herrmann
R. Chaffin
Editors

Memory in
Historical Perspective

*The Literature
Before Ebbinghaus*

D0843122

Springer-Verlag

WITHDRAWN

Recent Research in Psychology

Douglas J. Herrmann   Roger Chaffin
Editors

Memory in
Historical Perspective

The Literature Before Ebbinghaus

Springer-Verlag
New York Berlin Heidelberg
London Paris Tokyo

Douglas J. Herrmann
Department of Psychology
Hamilton College
Clinton, New York 13323, USA

Roger Chaffin
Department of Psychology
Trenton State College
Trenton, New Jersey 08650, USA

With 9 Illustrations.

Library of Congress Cataloging-in-Publication Data
Herrmann, Douglas J.
  Memory in historical perspective.
  (Recent research in psychology)
  Bibliography: p.
  Includes indexes.
  1. Memory—Early works to 1800.   I. Chaffin, Roger.
II. Title.   III. Series.
BF371.H48   1988   153.1′2′09   88-1993

Camera-ready text prepared by the editors using Nota Bene software.
Printed and bound by Edwards Brothers, Inc., Ann Arbor, Michigan.
Printed in the United States of America.

9 8 7 6 5 4 3 2 1

ISBN 0-387-96705-2 Springer-Verlag New York Berlin Heidelberg
ISBN 3-540-96705-2 Springer-Verlag Berlin Heidelberg New York

"Psychology has a long past, but only

a short history."

Hermann Ebbinghaus (1908)

FOREWORD

Memory researchers today are well acquainted with the recent literature, but know less about pre-scientific accounts of memory. We do not expect the scholars of previous centuries to be able to contribute directly to our understanding of the current issues in memory research. The ideas of the past have, however, shaped the issues of today and can often provide a useful perspective on current debates. Certainly, memory researchers need to be aware of the origins of their field. As Herrmann and Chaffin point out in their introduction, many of the issues of today are foreshadowed in the discussions of earlier scholars.

Memory in Historical Perspective provides researchers, teachers and students with ready access to the major works that represent the history of the field. The collection fills an important gap in the memory literature and should help to repair the neglect of the early scholarship on memory. I have found most of the selections to be readable and stimulating. Scholars before Ebbinghaus were not experimentalists, but they faced many of the same issues that we do today about the nature of memory and its relation to other psychological processes. In addition many of the early writers on memory were keen observers and describe a wide range of memory phenomena. I recommend the collection to all who want to deepen their understanding of human memory and cognition.

Richard C. Atkinson

Chancellor, University of
California at San Diego

PREFACE

We first became aware of the value of the literature on memory from before the 20th century during the debate over the semantic/episodic distinction. One of us (Doug Herrmann) looked at the pre-Ebbinghaus literature for precedents for the distinction. A quick search was sufficient to show that the issues involved in this debate had arisen with surprising frequency in the discussions of previous centuries. The pre-Ebbinghaus literature was clearly relevant to current debates in memory research. Another lesson from this search was that the memory literature of previous centuries is difficult to find. These early works are not cited by memory researchers today, and the writings are in different volumes, in different libraries. Reading the pre-Ebbinghaus literature required frequent use of inter-library loan, long delays, and travel to distant libraries. The inaccessibility of the literature and its clear relevance to contemporary concerns led us to compile the present collection to make the early literature on memory more accessible to memory researchers.

The sources that pointed us to the writings collected here are described in the appendix. The collection has several limitations. The foremost of these is a consequence of the fact that we are memory researchers, not classical or medieval scholars. All the works included were already in print in English. We were unable to include some substantial works that have not been translated, e.g., those of Albertus Magnus. The collection is limited to the Graeco-Roman-Christian tradition out of which the present-day experimental approach to the study of memory emerged. We regret that the work contains no work by the women scholars of this tradition. Recent scholarship has added considerably to the number of classical and medieval woman whose work has been translated or collected, but the number is still very small, and does not include discussions of memory. In spite of these limitations, we hope that the writings will challenge, provoke, reassure and inspire you, as they have us.

Douglas J. Herrmann

Roger J. S. Chaffin

ACKNOWLEDGEMENTS

We thank the many people who have contributed to the development of this book. Richard Atkinson, Mary Crawford, Bob Hoffman, and David Murray advised us about content. Mary Ellen Whipple served as researcher, translator, and typist. Jessie Cryer typed the initial draft of the manuscript. Shirley Knop copy-edited the manuscript.

The first author thanks the Applied Psychology Unit of the Medical Research Council in Cambridge, England, for providing a congenial atmosphere in 1982-83 when much of the source material was located in the Cambridge University Libraries. Editorial work and final preparation of the manuscript were completed while the second author was on a post-doctoral fellowship at the Educational Testing Service (ETS). We thank ETS for its generous support of the preparation of the manuscript and are grateful for the support and encouragement we received from the late Bill Turnbull.

We thank the publishers, editors, translators and writers who have given permission for their works to be reproduced in this volume.

The passage by Hesiod is reprinted from *Hesiod*, translated by R. Lattimore, by permission of the University of Michigan Press.

The passages from the following works, originally published by Heinemann, are reprinted by permission of the current publishers, Harvard University Press, and the Loeb Classical Library: The Clouds in *Aristophanes: Works*, translated by B. B. Rogers; Mnemosyne from *Lyra Graeca*, volume III, *Other Scolia*, edited and translated by J. M. Edmonds; *De Oratore* by Cicero, translated by E. W. Sutton, completed with an introduction by H. Rackham; *Tusculan Disputations* by Cicero, translated by J. E. King; *(Cicero) Ad. G. Herennium*, translated by H. Caplan; *Natural History* II, *Libri III-VII* by Pliny the Elder, translated by H. Rackham; *Institutio Oratoria of Quintillian*, translated by H. E. Butler.

Dialexeis is reprinted from *The Art of Memory*, by Frances Yates by permission of Routledge and Kegan Paul.

Passages from *The Dialogues of Plato*, translated by B. Jowett, and from *The Works of Aristotle Translated into English,* edited by W. D. Ross, are reprinted by permission of Oxford University Press.

Passages from the following works are also reprinted with permission of the publishers.

Plotinus: The Enneads. Translated by Stephen MacKenna, third edition revised by B. S. Page. Published by Faber and Faber, London, 1962.

Augustine: Confessions and Enchiridion. Translated and edited by A. C. Outler. Library of the Christian Classics, Vol. VII. Published by the Westminster Press, Philadelphia, 1955.

Augustine: Later Works. Translated and selected by J. Burnaby. Library of the Christian Classics, Vol. VIII. Published by the Westminster Press, Philadelphia, 1955.

Martianus Capella and the Seven Liberal Arts. Vol. II, *The Marriage of Philology and Mercury*. Translated by W. H. Stahle and R. Johnson, with E. L. Burge. Published by Columbia University Press, New York, 1977.

Truth. Vol. 2, Questions X-XX, by Aquinas. Translated by J. V. McGlynn. Published by Henry Regnery, Chicago, 1953.

Summa Theologiae by Aquinas. Translated and edited by T. Gilby, K. Foster, and L. Bright. Published by Blackfriars, in conjunction with McGraw-Hill, New York and Eyre & Spottiswoode, London, 1964.

Commentary on the Metaphysics of Aristotle by Aquinas. Translated by J. P. Rowan. Published by Henry Regnery, Chicago, 1961.

The Literary Works of Leonardo da Vinci. Compiled and edited by Jean Paul Richter. Published by Phaidon Press, London, 1981.

Essays by Montaigne. Translated by J. M. Cohen. Published by Penguin Books, Harmondsworth, 1958.

The Philosophic Works of Francis Bacon. Translated by R. C. Ellis and J. Spedding; edited by J. M. Robertson. Published by Routledge, London, 1905.

The Essays on the Intellectual Powers of Man by Thomas Reid. Published by M.I.T. Press, Cambridge, 1969.

Immanuel Kant's Critique of Pure Reason. Translated by Norman Kemp Smith. Published by MacMillan, London, 1961.

CONTENTS

INTRODUCTION

In this book we have collected the classic writings on memory from the period before introduction of the scientific method to memory scholarship by Hermann Ebbinghaus in 1885. The collection has been developed to promote awareness of these writings and to facilitate their integration with modern scholarship on memory. The writings come from different sources, making it difficult to examine and study them. Many cannot be readily obtained in most college libraries.

There are at least three reasons why a knowledge of the classic writings on memory might facilitate modern scholarship in psychology, philosophy, and other disciplines (Herrmann & Chaffin, 1987). First, a knowledge of these writings may give a better appreciation of the current *Zeitgeist* in the study of memory, its origins, its rivals, and its potential for change. Second, these writings offer insights into the varied phenomena of memory. Third, knowledge of these writings will help a scholar to avoid duplication of past discoveries, to build on the work of earlier scholars, and to recognize questions about memory that are truly new. We will discuss each point in turn.

Awareness of the *Zeitgeist*

It is difficult to be fully aware of the extent to which one's own work is a product of the prevailing climate of opinion or *Zeitgeist*. Greater awareness of these influences allows a researcher to make more informed judgments about the direction that an inquiry might take. One way that a researcher may understand the *Zeitgeist* better is through the study of the development of thought about an issue or phenomenon.

Memory scholarship before Ebbinghaus may be classified in terms of four approaches. The *pragmatic* approach sought ways to improve a person's ability to learn and remember. The *empirical* approach documented the existence and nature of memory phenomena. Scholars taking a *theoretical* approach attempted to explain the mechanisms of memory. The *pre-theoretical* approach characterized memory in an intuitive and informal manner. Our perception of the approaches taken by the authors of the writings presented in this text is shown in Table 1. It is possible that the reader will differ with us about the approach taken by some of the scholars. Nevertheless, it is clear that different scholars used different approaches and that certain approaches were more prominent in some periods than in others.

The popularity of the different approaches to memory has shifted over the centuries and this continues today. Consider the recent enthusiasm over "everyday memory". Discussion of the value of the "new" approach of looking at the functioning of memory in natural settings has sometimes grown quite heated during the past decade. Much of the discussion has assumed that the issue is a new one. This is not the case; the everyday memory movement is a resurgence of the practical approach to memory. Bahrick (1985) has pointed out

Table 1

Selected Sources on Memory
before Ebbinghaus Classified by Approach to the Subject

Century	Source	Approach
8th B.C.	Hesiod	Pre-theoretical
5th B.C.	Anonymous (*Dialexis*)	Practical
	Anonymous (*Mnemosyne*)	Pre-theoretical
	Heraclitus	Practical
4th B.C.	Aristophanes	Pre-theoretical
	Plato	Empirical, Theoretical
3rd B.C.	Aristotle	Empirical, Theoretical
1st B.C.	Cicero	Practical
	Anonymous (*Ad Herennium*)	Practical
1st A.D.	Quintillian	Practical
	Pliny	Empirical, Pre-theoretical
3rd A.D.	Plotinus	Empirical, Theoretical, Practical
5th A.D.	Augustine	Theoretical
6th A.D.	Martianus Capella	Empirical, Pre-theoretical, Practical
13th A.D.	Thomas Aquinas	Theoretical
14th A.D.	Leonardo da Vinci	Practical
16th A.D.	Michel Eyquen de Montaigne	Empirical
17th A.D.	Francis Bacon	Theoretical
18th A.D.	David Hume	Theoretical
	Immanuel Kant	Theoretical
	Thomas Reid	Theoretical
	Samuel Rogers	Empirical, Theoretical
19th A.D.	Thomas Brown	Theoretical
	William Burnham	Theoretical

2

that the shift from a theoretical/empirical focus to a practical focus has occurred twice in this century. Similar shifts have also occurred in earlier eras. We believe that debates about the *Zeitgeist*, such as the one about everyday memory research, would be more productive if we were more mindful of the different approaches to memory that have occurred throughout our history.

Insights about Memory

The ideas of scholars of earlier ages have insights to offer us today about the nature of memory. We will give one example from our own research into memory in natural settings. During the late 1970's an interest developed in the use of external memory aids (thanks largely to the work of John Harris, 1980). One question that was raised at early conferences on memory aids had to do with their potentially reactive nature. It was proposed that memory aids may lessen a person's memory ability by leading the person to rely more on the memory aid and less on memory itself. We recall the nods of enlightenment when this point about reactivity was raised. Comments were made for and against this "new" idea, i.e., that an aid might actually have deleterious effects.

The notion that an aid may lessen ability is not, however, a new idea. Plato, as well as some of his followers, held strong reservations about the widespread teaching of writing because writing (a memory aid) would allow a person to avoid relying on memory and, hence, lessen memory ability. Quintillian similarly objected to Cicero's internal memory aids because their use might lessen a person's understanding of the material memorized. Now suppose that the researchers at conferences concerned with memory aids in the late '70's had read the scholarship before Ebbinghaus pertaining to memory aids; they would have had already developed an understanding of the reactivity issue. This insight would surely have facilitated and elevated discussions about memory aids; and progress in the field would have been more rapid. The issue of memory aid reactivity is one small point in the universe of questions about memory. But the resolution of many small points facilitates the development of sound theories.

Original Contributions to Memory Knowledge

It might be thought that the work done on memory before the introduction of the scientific method by Ebbinghaus could not be of value to empirical researchers because this work relied on informal observation and theoretical analysis. Since the experiment is a more powerful tool than natural observation, the argument runs, the pre-Ebbinghaus work should not be trusted by modern researchers. This argument is, of course, faulty. While the power of the experimental method cannot be denied, a reading of the pre-Ebbinghaus literature demonstrates that natural observation and intuition successfully identified, without the use of experiment, many of the phenomena of memory that we study today. Since many modern investigations of memory are concerned with the same topics that concerned the pre-Ebbinghaus scholars, the early scholarship does have a contribution to make to the understanding of the basic phenomena and mechanisms of memory.

3

Knowledge of pre-Ebbinghaus scholarship allows the student of memory to place a question about memory in its historical context and to distinguish those questions that are really new from those that have been debated for centuries. Scholars who are ignorant of history may pursue intractable approaches or may rediscover phenomena and theoretical constructs that have been thoroughly discussed in earlier eras. Rediscoveries are undesirable because they do an injustice to the work of past scholars, and because rediscovery does not advance knowledge when research that was more informed might have done so (Boring, 1950; Crutchfield & Krech, 1963; Watson, 1960).

In the present state of ignorance about pre-Ebbinghaus scholarship, however, rediscovery is usually preferable to continued neglect. If a phenomenon has been lost to a scientific community, it is necessary for it to be rediscovered for the scientific community to regain the lost work. Nevertheless, this rediscovery also entails a duplication of effort that would have been avoided had past work not been forgotten.

Rediscovery is not a rare event in psychology (see Cole & Rudnicky, 1983), or in other disciplines. To illustrate the point, imagine what most memory psychologists would say when asked to name the major phenomena of memory and the people who discovered them. For example, who discovered: abstract/concrete memory codes, attributes of encoding, levels of processing, and the semantic-episodic distinction. The typical answer would likely be the names of twentieth-century psychologists; yet all of these phenomena were discussed by pre-Ebbinghaus scholars.

At this point we must offer a caveat about the credit for these rediscoveries. Numerous studies could have been selected (including some of our own work) to illustrate rediscovery. The instances examined here were selected only because of their prominence in the recent research literature. Scholars who made the rediscoveries deserve credit for their work because without the rediscovery the phenomena would have remained unknown. Rediscoveries are made necessary by the prevailing conventions of scholarship in our discipline. The problem lies with the discipline rather than with the individuals making the rediscoveries. The field has followed a standard of scholarship that does not require the citation of work before Ebbinghaus or, for that matter, of work more than twenty years old.

Some instances in which pre-Ebbinghaus ideas have been rediscovered by post-Ebbinghaus scholars in psychology are presented in Table 2.

Table 2

Rediscoveries by Post-Ebbinghaus Scholars of Constructs

Discussed by Pre-Ebbinghaus Scholars

Construct	Post-Ebbinghaus Scholars	Pre-Ebbinghaus Scholars
Abstract/concrete	Paivio (1969)	Cicero, Augustine, Aquinas[1]
Attributes of memory	Bower (1967) Underwood (1969) Wickens (1970)	Brown (Aristotle, Reid and others)
Levels of processing	Craik and Lockhart (1972)	Bacon[1,2]
Retrieval failure	Shiffrin (1970) Tulving (1983)	Aristotle, Quintillian, Bacon, J.S. Mill
Semantic/episodic memory types	Tulving (1972)	Aristotle, Augustine, Aquinas, Brown, Abercrombie, Bain[3]

For additional scholars see :
  [1] - Marshall and Fryer (1978)
  [2] - Murray (1978)
  [3] - Herrmann (1982)

These instances involve memory constructs and attendant phenomena that are commonly held to be the discoveries of our era. The modern scholars who have investigated and written about each construct are listed in the center column of the table. The scholars before Ebbinghaus who wrote about these constructs are listed in the right-hand column. Some of the modern scholars in the table pointed out in their seminal works the connection between their research and the ideas of one or more pre-Ebbinghaus scholars: Paivio (1969, 1971) indicated in considerable detail the pre-Ebbinghaus sources that are important to dual coding theory; Shiffrin (1970) quoted William James's (1890) distillation of James Mill's views on retrieval. It is not our purpose to determine to what extent the modern constructs were anticipated by scholars before Ebbinghaus. The important point is that at least the germ of the modern construct was available to post-Ebbinghaus researchers had they consulted the pre-Ebbinghaus literature.

It is interesting to speculate about how research involving the constructs in Table 2 would have developed had post-Ebbinghaus scholars been aware of the pre-Ebbinghaus literature. Had the field of human memory been aware of pre-Ebbinghaus scholarship, debate about these constructs might have been more focused to begin with, research would have moved more quickly from demonstration experiments to functional experiments, and the present level of knowledge about these constructs would be higher today. Marshall and Fryer (1978) in their brief history of memory research lamented the fact that modern psychological theories of memory appeared not to have advanced much over the theories of early scholars. Tulving (1983) recently expressed a similar view. But how can a discipline expect to rise above past scholarly achievements if it ignores them?

In summary, we have given three reasons for regarding work on memory before Ebbinghaus as part of the literature that researchers should know and cite (Herrmann & Chaffin, 1987). Knowledge of this literature may make a researcher more sensitive to the *Zeitgeist*, may foster insights about research issues, and may direct attention to little-explored research questions. It is unfortunate that the scholarship before Ebbinghaus has been ignored in recent times (see Boring, 1950; Crutchfield & Krech, 1963; Watson, 1960). This collection has been assembled as a first step toward redressing the balance.

A Brief History of Memory Before Ebbinghaus

The value that early societies placed on memory is expressed by the gods and goddesses that governed affairs involving memory. In Egypt (circa 4000 B.C.) the god Thoth, shown in Figure 1a, had this responsibility. In Greece (circa 1000 B.C.) the goddess Mnemosyne, shown in Figure 1b, dealt with memory, as conveyed by Hesiod's account of Greek mythology. There are good reasons for believing that writings on memory existed before Hesiod, but none have survived (Yates, 1966). Mnemosyne was one of Zeus's wives and the mother of the Muses, the spiritual source of the Arts. An anonymous riddle, titled, *Mnemosyne*, from around 300 B.C. appears to express the view that memory defies logical analysis.

The first practical writing on how to improve memory is a fragment from the 5th century B.C., titled *Dialexeis*; the fragment advises that attentiveness and rehearsal aids learning (Yates, 1966). In the same century, Heraclitus also made practical observations; for example, he noted that "the eyes are more exact witnesses than the ears." A little later Aristophanes pointed out the role of motivation in memory when he remarked that he remembered what was owed him, but not what he owed.

Plato and Aristotle were the first memory theorists. Plato gives several metaphors for memory that can be seen as the first models of memory. The wax tablet model represents memory traces as impressions in wax; the aviary model represents each memory as a bird of a different species; and the scribe model represents memory as a record of experience written down according to the whims of a scribe. Aristotle, shown in Figure 1c teaching young Alexander the Great, set forth the basic "laws" of associationism, advanced fundamental analyses of memory retrieval, and also pointed out various memory phenomena, e.g., the decline of memory with age.

Interest in the pragmatic aspects of memory grew in the Roman period. Cicero, shown in Figure 1d, and the anonymous author of Ad Herennium championed the use of the "method of loci" in memorization. Quintillian also taught Cicero's methods but with a note of skepticism about the value of complex mnemonic techniques. In particular, Quintillian feared that the method of loci would slow remembering because the loci and the to-be-remembered information imposed a "double task" on memory.

Augustine, shown in Figure 1e, was the third major theoretician of memory. He wrote about a wide variety of issues, especially about the different kinds of memory. Like Plato, Augustine suggested metaphorical models of memory, likening acquisition to the digestive processes of the stomach and remembering to the exploration of caverns. Additionally, Augustine discussed the relationship between memory and emotions, noting that the knowledge of the emotion held during an experience "clung to my memory so that I can call it to mind." Also in the fifth century, Martianus Capella wrote a mythology that, like the earlier mythology described by Hesiod, represented memory and its relationship to the other psychological faculties. Cappella characterized Memory as a god whose role was to make Psyche behave in a more realistic manner.

During the dark ages work on memory (and all other topics) decreased. Interest in memory from the 5th century into the medieval period was very rare (or the works have since been lost; Yates, 1966). In the 13th century, Aquinas brought Aristotle's views on memory into prominence again. However, theoretical interests were unusual for Aquinas's time. In the Renaissance to follow, the focus was primarily on the practical use of the visual arts for the improvement of memory, although Bacon made some empirical observations about the nature of memory. Interest in visual memory aids peaked in the 16th century in the work of Giordano Bruno, Peter Ramus and others and this was followed in the late 17th century by the publication of numerous memory aids (Yates, 1966).

During the 17th century the approach to memory scholarship shifted from the practical to the theoretical, a shift that led to a new spurt of work on memory. Scholars such as Francis Bacon, David Hume, and Immanuel Kant (shown in Figures 1f-h respectively), as well as Thomas Reid, Thomas Brown, and many others, paid a great deal of attention to memory. Interest in memory was so great in this period that even poets (Samuel Rogers and Robert Merry) wrote poems to express their views about the relation of memory and the emotions. In 1885 Ebbinghaus (see also Ebbinghaus 1908, 1913) opened a new chapter in the inquiry into memory with the publication of his monograph describing his empirical studies of memory. Memory became the object of experimental, as well as philosophical, study.

Figure 1a
THOTH, THE EGYPTIAN GOD OF LEARNING,

MEMORY, AND WISDOM
(*c. 3000 B.C.*)

Figure 1b
MNEMOSYNE

Thou fill'st from the winged
    chalice of the soul
Thy lamp, O Memory free winged
    to its goal

*This conception of Mnemosyne, and the lines above, are the work of
Dante Gabriel Rossetti (1828-1882), done between 1876 and 1881.*

Figure 1c

ARISTOTLE TEACHING ALEXANDER THE GREAT
From the painting by J. L. G. Ferris

Figure 1d
MARCUS TULLIUS CICERO
(Bettmann Archive)

Figure 1e
ST. AUGUSTINE
(From the painting by Fra Filippo Lippi)

Figure 1f
FRANCIS BACON
(From a painting)

Figure 1g
DAVID HUME
(*Bettmann Archive*)

Figure 1h
IMMANUEL KANT
(*From a painting*)

NOTE TO THE READER

Selection of the Writings

Memory in Historical Perspective contains passages about memory from twenty-four sources. The sources were selected to represent the thought on memory of each era. We included almost everything that we are aware of that has been translated into English from before the Renaissance. We gave priority to these early works because they were seminal for scholars of the Renaissance and those that followed and because the works of more recent writers are more accessible. For these early writers we have tried to include almost everything that they wrote on the subject of memory. Seven writers are included to represent the period from the Renaissance to 1885. No works on the visual arts as an aid to memory were included since Yates (1966) has already thoroughly reviewed this topic.

The number of different scholars in each century whose discussions of memory survives today is shown in Figure 2. The figure provides a count of the memory scholars cited in Yates' (1966) history of the arts of memory and Young's (1961) bibliography of memory. The count did not include scholars who produced special purpose publications like pamphlets on how to learn historical information. The figure shows the expected exponential increase in the number of scholars over the centuries. There is a gap in the record corresponding to the long period of transition from the hegemony of the Roman Empire to the development of the stable feudal kingdoms of the Middle Ages. For additional information about pre-Ebbinghaus scholarship on memory the reader may consult several excellent sources (Beare, 1906; Burnham, 1888; Edgell, 1924; Marshall & Fryer, 1978; Mitchell, 1911; Murray, 1976; Yates, 1966).

Format of the Writings

The excerpts are presented in a common format. The source for each passage is given first, followed by a brief account of the author's background and significance. A table of contents is given next for those excerpts long enough to require such a guide, followed by a description of the organization of the works excerpted. The writings selected for each author follow, with each passage labelled by author, work, and section.

For the table of contents we have used, where possible, the author's own headings. Where these were not available, we have used terms from the current psychological literature. Use of current terms to describe ideas proposed in a very different context will normally tend to misrepresent the writer's ideas. We use current terminology, not to suggest that ancient writers were thinking in modern terms, but to help present-day experimental psychologists locate material that would be relevant to a particular issue of present-day concern.

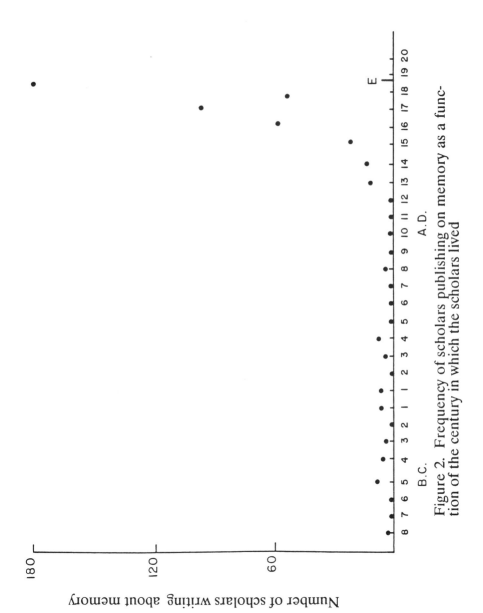

Figure 2. Frequency of scholars publishing on memory as a function of the century in which the scholars lived

Number of scholars writing about memory

The explanation of the organization of the author's works is intended to be of help to those who wish to locate the excerpted passages in the original work. For some authors (Plato and Aristotle) there is a standard system for referencing which will allow the reader to locate a passage in any modern translation of these works. For other authors the reader will find it easiest to locate the passage in the edition and translation from which the passage was taken rather than from a different edition or translation. We have tried to select editions that are standard or commonly available.

We have provided three indexes, a *subject index*, a *keyword index*, and a *name index*. The subject index lists topics discussed in the readings using current psychological terminology. This index is intended to help memory researchers to identify passages relevant to current concerns. For example, although Aquinas does not use the term "semantic memory", his discussion of the distinction between intellectual and sense memory is indexed under this heading because it appears to involve a closely related issue. The subject index should be used in conjunction with the keyword index which simply lists the occurrence of relevant words in the text. Finally, the name index lists the occurrence of names of people.

The passages provided are, in most cases, exhaustive of what each author wrote that is directly relevant to the topic of memory. References to memory for purposes that were extrinsic to memory (such as proofs of the existence of God in the case of Augustine and Aquinas) were not included unless they contained a direct assertion about memory function or theoretical statement about memory mechanisms. Where an author said essentially the same thing in two places we have provided only one of the passages.

The decision about where to begin and end each passage was dictated first by the relevance of the material to the subject of memory and, second, by the value of the material as a context for the rest of the passage. We believe that the context provided will be adequate for most readers to appreciate the points made by the writer. Readers requiring a wider context are referred to the work from which the excerpt was taken and to the supplementary readings listed for each author. The original texts should also be consulted for the editors' footnotes which have not been reproduced here. In the few cases where the information in a footnote seemed essential we have inserted it into the text in brackets.

The reader will find that, across the centuries, the later writers repeat the opinions and anecdotes of earlier writers. These redundancies are included because they are an integral part of the development of ideas about memory. Each age chose to repeat some points of earlier authors, to disagree with some points, and to ignore others. Those ideas and anecdotes that are repeated are used in new contexts and facilitate the comparison of approaches of the different writers.

HESIOD

8th Century B.C.

From: *Hesiod.* Translated by R. Lattimore. Published by the University of Michigan Press, 1959.

Hesiod was one of the earliest Greek poets. He was born, and spent most of his life, near Mt. Helicon in central Greece where he was first a shepherd and later a poet. Hesiod presents a gloomier and less glamorous view of life than Homer. Of the two complete epics which survive, the *Theogony*, excerpted here, describes the power struggles of the gods; the other is an exhortation to a life of hard work. The relationships between the gods described in the *Theogony* may be seen as a metaphorical description of the world order. Mnemosyne's position as goddess of memory and mother of the Muses appears to express a recognition of the dependence of the emotions -- the province of the Muses -- on memory.

Supplementary reading:

Brown, A. R. (1966). *The World of Hesiod.* New York: B. Bloom.

Theogony, lines 36 - 55

Come you then, let us begin from the Muses,
    who by their singing
delight the great mind of Zeus, their father,
    who lives on Olympos,
as they tell of what is, and what is to be,
    and what was before now
with harmonious voices, and the sound
    that comes sweet from their mouths
40   never falters, and all the mansion of Zeus
    the father
of the deep thunder is joyful
    in the light voice of the goddesses
that scatters through it, and the peaks
    of snowy Olympos re-echo
and the homes of the immortals, and they
    in divine utterance
sing first the glory of the majestic race
    of immortals
45   from its beginning, those born
    to wide Ouranos and Gaia,
and the gods who were born to these in turn,
    the givers of blessings.

Then next they sing of Zeus, the father
    of gods and of mortals,
and they begin this strain and end
    this strain singing of him,
how greatly he surpasses all gods,
    and in might is the strongest.
50   And then again the Olympian Muses,
    daughters of aegis-
wearing Zeus, delight his mind that dwells
    on Olympos
by singing the race of human kind,
    and the powerful Giants.
Mnemosyne, queen of the Eleutherian hills,
    bore them
in Pieria, when she had lain
    with the Kronian Father;

Theogony lines 93 - 104

As such a one walks through an assembly,
    the people adore him
like a god, with gentle respect;
    he stands out among all assembled.
Such is the holy gift the Muses
    give to humanity.
So it is from the Muses, and from Apollo
    of the far cast,
95   that there are men on earth who are poets,
    and players on the lyre.
The lords are from Zeus; but blessed
    is that one whom the Muses
love, for the voice of his mouth runs
    and is sweet, and even
when a man has sorrow fresh
    in the troublement of his spirit
and is struck to wonder over the grief
    in his heart, the singer,
100   the servant of the Muses singing
    the glories of ancient
men, and the blessed gods
    who have their homes on Olympos,
makes him presently forget his cares,
    he no longer remembers
sorrow, for the gifts of the goddesses
    soon turn his thoughts elsewhere.

Hail, then, children of Zeus:
  grant me lovely singing.

HERACLITUS

c. 540 B.C. - c. 480 B.C.

From: A Further Study of Heraclitus. By G. T. W. Patrick. Published in the *American Journal of Psychology*, 1888, *1*, 557-690.

Heraclitus of Ephesus was a Greek philosopher remembered for his view that the superficial variety of the world is the result of a fundamental formal unity. He taught that fire, water, earth, and air are in a state of dynamic equilibrium which provides the hidden connections between the apparent chaotic events of the world. His ideas are known only through fragments quoted and attributed to him by later writers.

Supplementary reading:

Kahn, C. H. (1979). *The Art and Thought of Heraclitus*. Cambridge: Cambridge University Press.

Heraclitus on Memory

II. ... And some men are as ignorant of what they do when awake as they are forgetful of what they do when they are asleep.

V. The majority of people have no understanding of the things with which they daily meet, nor, when instructed, do they have any right knowledge of them, although to themselves they seem to have.

XIII. Whatever concerns seeing, hearing, and learning, I particularly honor.

XV. The eyes are more exact witnesses than the ears.

ARISTOPHANES

c. 450 B.C. - c. 388 B.C.

From: The Clouds. In *Aristophanes: Works*. Translated by B. B. Rogers. The Loeb Classical Library, published by William Heinemann, 1962.

Aristophanes was the greatest of the ancient Greek dramatists. He satirized the society, philosophy, literature, and foreign policy of Athens where he lived. He wrote about 40 plays of which 11 survive. The lines below are among the most often quoted passages about memory.

Oh! as for that,
>My memory is of two sorts, long and short:
>With them who owe me aught it never fails;
>My creditors, indeed, complain of it
>As mainly apt to leak and lose its reckoning.

ANONYMOUS

Dialexeis

c. 400 B.C.

From: *The Art of Memory.* By Frances Yates. London: Routledge & Kegan Paul, 1966.

According to Yates, this *dialexeis* is believed to have had its origins among the sophists in ancient Greece, particularly Hippias of Elis who apparently excelled in memory (mentioned in Plato).

A great and beautiful invention is memory, always useful both for learning and for life.

This is the first thing: if you pay attention (direct your mind), the judgment will better perceive the things going through it (the mind).

Secondly, repeat again what you hear; for by often hearing and saying the same things, what you have learned comes complete into your memory.

Thirdly, what you hear, place on what you know. For example, *Chrysippus* is to be remembered; we place it on *gold* and *horse*. Another example: we place *glow-worm* on *fire* and *shine*. So much for names. For things (do) thus: for courage (place it) on Mars and Achilles; for metal-working, on Vulcan; for cowardice, on Epeus.

ANONYMOUS

Mnemosyne (memory)

c. 300 B.C.

From: *Lyra Graeca.* Volume III, *Other Scolia.* Edited and translated by J. M. Edmonds. Published by William Heineman, 1927.

Scolia were songs that were sung over wine at dinners in ancient Greece. The lyrics of this song, like Mnemosyne, represent a riddle, a conception of memory equally apt today.

O mild-eyed Mother of the Muses, follow thou a pure offspring of thy children. Freshly blooming is the song we bring, made motley with new-fashioned skill. [The Ship] is wet with the dews of Achelous. Pass thou no further by the shore, man, let go the sheet, slacken thy linen wings, make haste to the smooth-pebbled beach. 'Tis well. Look at the sea; escape ashore from the sore and awful frenzy of the ocean-ranging Southwind.

PLATO

c. 427 B.C. - 347 B.C.

From: *The Dialogues of Plato*. Translated by B. Jowett. Fourth edition, published by Oxford University Press, 1953.

Born into an aristocratic Athenian family, Plato was a close associate of Socrates, whose teachings he recorded in his early dialogues, dramatically posed debates that illustrated the Socratic method. His later work was more expository, systematic, and directed towards a more sophisticated audience, presumably the students of his Academy. The Academy which Plato founded in Athens was the first to provide a continuous and varied education for young men of the upper classes and served as a model in succeeding generations.

Plato was interested in necessary truths, like those of mathematics. These were, he proposed, stored in memory. This led to his most renowned proposal in the area of memory, the doctrine of recollection, first propounded in the Meno. All enduring truths can be elicited from the untutored by careful questioning and so they must be recollected from an earlier existence of the soul. An adequate explanation of the problems that led to this proposal required a distinction between performance and ability. Plato himself made many contributions in this direction, particularly in the *Theaetetus*; Aristotle continued the work and rejected the doctrine of recollection (e.g., in *Analytica Priora*).

Supplementary readings:

Allen, R. E., Ed. (1965). *Studies in Plato's Meta-physics*. Atlantic Highlands, NJ: Humanities Press.

Bluck, R. S. H. (1949). *Plato's Life and Thought*. London: Routledge & Kegan Paul.

PLATO

Table of Contents

Explanation of contents: The order of the dialogues follows that of Jowett and reflects the probable order of their composition. Reference to passages is made by Arabic numbers and letters (a-e). This standard citation form, used by Jowett, refers to pages and their subdivisions in the Stephanus edition. Stephanus page numbers and subdivisions that appear in Jowett are included in the text [in brackets]. Roman numerals given for excerpts from the Republic refer to books into which that work is divided. The table of contents refers to the beginning of each passage in which a topic is covered.

Soc. The soul, then, as being immortal and having been born again many times, and having seen all things that exist, whether in this world or in the world below, has knowledge of them all; and it is no wonder that she should be able to call to remembrance all that she ever knew about virtue, and about everything; for as all nature is akin, and the soul has learned [81d] all things, there is no difficulty in a man eliciting out of a single recollection all the rest--the process generally called 'learning'--if he is strenuous and does not faint; for all inquiry and all learning is but recollection. And therefore we ought not to listen to this eristic argument about the impossibility of inquiry: for it will make us idle, and it is sweet to the sluggard; but the [81e] other doctrine will make us active and inquisitive. In that confiding, I will gladly inquire with you into the nature of virtue.

Men. Yes, Socrates; but what do you mean by saying that we do not learn, and that what we call learning is only a process of recollection? Can you teach me how this is?

Soc . I told you, Meno, just now that you were a rogue, and [82a] now you ask whether I can·teach you, when I am saying that there is no teaching, but only recollection; and thus you imagine that you will expose me in a contradiction.

Men. Indeed, Socrates, I protest that I had no such intention. I only asked the question from habit; but if you can prove to me that what you say is true, I wish that you would.

Soc. Do you see, Meno, what advances he has made in his power of recollection? He did not know at first, and he does not know now, what is the side of a figure of eight feet: but then he thought that he knew, and answered confidently as if he knew, and felt no difficulty; now he feels a difficulty, and [84b] neither knows nor fancies that he knows.

Men. True.

Soc. Is he not better off in knowing his ignorance?

Men. I think that he is.

Soc. If we have made him doubt, and given him the 'torpedo's shock', have we done him any harm?

Men. I think not.

Soc. We have certainly, as would seem, assisted him in some degree to the discovery of the truth; and now he will wish to remedy his ignorance, but then he would have been ready to [84c] tell all the world again and again that the double space should have a double side.

Men. True.

Soc. But do you suppose that he would ever have started to inquire into or to learn what he fancied that he knew, though he was really ignorant of it, until he had fallen into perplexity under the idea that he did not know, and had desired to know?

Men. I think not, Socrates.

Soc. Then he was the better for the torpedo's touch?

Men. I think so.

Soc. Mark now the further development. I shall only ask him, and not teach him, and he shall share the inquiry with me: and [84d] do you watch and see if you find me telling or explaining anything to him, instead of eliciting his opinion. Tell me, boy, is not this a square of four feet which I have drawn?

Boy. Yes.

Soc. And now I add another square equal to the former one?

Boy. Yes.

Soc. And a third, which is equal to either of them?

Boy. Yes.

Soc. Suppose that we fill up the vacant corner?

Boy. Very good.

Soc. Here, then, there are four equal spaces?

Boy. Yes. [84e]

Soc. And how many times larger is this space than this other?

Boy. Four times.

Soc. But we wanted one only twice as large, as you will remember.

Boy. True.

Soc. Now, does not this line, reaching from corner to corner, bisect each of these spaces?[85a]

Boy. Yes.

Soc. And are there not here four equal lines which contain this space?

Boy. There are.

Soc. Look and see how much this space is.

Boy. I do not understand.

Soc. Has not each interior cut off half of the four spaces?

Boy. Yes.

Soc. And how many such spaces are there in this section?

Boy. Four.

Soc. And how many in this?

Boy. Two.

Soc. And four is how many times two?

Boy. Twice.

Soc. So that this space is of how many feet?

Boy. Of eight feet. [85b]

Soc. And from what line do you get this figure?

Boy. From this.

Soc. That is, from the line which extends from corner to corner of the figure of four feet?

Boy. Yes.

Soc. And that is the line which the learned call the diagonal. And if this is the proper name, then you, Meno's slave, are prepared to affirm that the double space is the square of the diagonal?

Boy. Certainly, Socrates.

Soc. What do you say of him, Meno? Were not all these answers given out of his own head? [85c]

Men. Yes, they were all his own.

Soc. And yet, as we were just now saying, he did not know?

Men. True.

Soc. But still he had in him those notions of his--had he not?

Men. Yes.

Soc. Then he who does not know may still have true notions of that which he does not know?

Men. Apparently.

Soc. And at present these notions have just been stirred up in him, as in a dream; but if he were frequently asked the same questions, in different forms, he would know as accurately as [85d] anyone at last?

Men. I dare say.

Soc. Without anyone teaching him he will recover his knowledge for himself, if he is merely asked questions?

Men. Yes.

Soc. And this spontaneous recovery of knowledge in him is recollection?

Men. True.

Soc. And this knowledge which he now has must he not either have acquired at some time, or else possessed always?

Men. Yes.

Soc. But if he always possessed this knowledge he would always have known; or if he has acquired the knowledge he [85e] could not have acquired it in this life, unless he has been taught geometry. And he may be made to do the same with all geometry and every other branch of knowledge; has anyone ever taught him all this? You must know about him, if, as you say, he was born and bred in your house.

Men. And I am certain that no one ever did teach him.

Soc. And yet he has these notions?

Men. The fact, Socrates, is undeniable.

Soc. But if he did not acquire them in this life, then he must [86a] have had and learned them at some other time?

Men. Clearly he must.

Soc. Which must have been the time when he was not a man?

Men. Yes.

Soc. And if there are always to be true notions in him, both while he is and while he is not a man, which only need to be awakened into knowledge by putting questions to him, his soul must remain always possessed of this knowledge; for he must always either be or not be a man.

Men. Obviously. [86b]

Soc. And if the truth of all things always exists in the soul, then the soul is immortal. Wherefore be of good cheer, and try to discover by recollection what you do not now know, or rather what you do not remember.

Men. I feel, somehow, that I like what you are saying.

Soc. And I too like what I am saying. Some things I have said of which I am not altogether confident. But that we shall be better and braver and less helpless if we think that we ought to inquire, than we should have been if we thought that there was no knowing and no duty to seek to know what we do not know;--that is a belief for which I am ready to fight, in word [86c] and deed, to the utmost of my power.

Yes, said Cebes interposing, your favourite doctrine, Socrates, that our learning is simply recollection, if true, also necessarily implies a previous time in which we have learned that which we now recollect. But this would be impossible unless our soul had been somewhere before existing in this form of man; here [73a] then is another proof of the soul's immortality. But tell me, Cebes, interrupted Simmias, what arguments are urged in favour of this doctrine of recollection. I am not very sure at the moment that I remember them.

One excellent proof, said Cebes, is afforded by questions. If you put a question to a person properly, he will give a true answer of himself, but how could he do this unless there were knowledge and a right account of the matter already in him? Again, this is most clearly shown when he is taken to a diagram [73b] or to anything of that sort.

But if, said Socrates, you are still incredulous, Simmias, I would ask you whether you may not agree with me when you look at the matter in another way;--I mean, if you are still incredulous as to whether what is called learning is recollection?

Incredulous I am not, said Simmias; but I want to have this doctrine of recollection brought to my own recollection, and, from what Cebes has started to say, I am beginning to recollect and be convinced: but I should still like to hear you develop your own argument.

This is what I would say, he replied:--We should agree, if [73c] I am not mistaken, that what a man is to recollect he must have known at some previous time.

Very true.

And do we also agree that knowledge obtained in the way I am about to describe is recollection? I mean to ask, Whether a person who, having seen or heard or in any way perceived anything, knows not only that, but also thinks of something else which is the subject not of the same but of some other kind of knowledge, may not be fairly said to recollect that of which he [73d] thinks?

How do you mean?

I mean what I may illustrate by the following instance:--The knowledge of a lyre is not the same as the knowledge of a man?

Of course not.

And yet what is the feeling of lovers when they recognize a lyre, or a cloak, or anything else which the beloved has been in the habit of using? Do not they, from knowing the lyre, form in the mind's eye an image of the youth to whom the lyre belongs? And this is recollection. In like manner anyone who sees Simmias may often remember Cebes; and there are endless examples of the same thing.

Endless, indeed, replied Simmias. [73e]

And is not this sort of thing a kind of recollection--though the word is most commonly applied to a process of recovering that which has been already forgotten through time and inattention?

Very true, he said.

Well; and may you not also from seeing the picture of a horse or a lyre recollect a man? and from the picture of Simmias, you may be led to recollect Cebes?

31

True.

Or you may also be led to the recollection of Simmias himself?

[74a] Quite so.

And in all these cases, the recollection may be derived from things either like or unlike?

It may be.

And when the recollection is derived from like things, then another consideration is sure to arise, which is--whether the likeness in any degree falls short or not of that which is recollected?

Certainly, he said.

Now consider this question. We affirm, do we not, that there is such a thing as equality, not of one piece of wood or stone or similar material thing with another, but that, over and above this, there is absolute equality? Shall we say so?

Say so, yes, replied Simmias, and swear to it, with all the [74b] confidence in life.

And do we know the nature of this absolute existence?

To be sure, he said.

And whence did we obtain our knowledge? Did we not see equalities of material things, such as pieces of wood and stones, and conceive from them the idea of an equality which is different from them? For you will acknowledge that there is a difference? Or look at the matter in another way:--Do not the same pieces of wood or stone appear to one man equal, and to another unequal?

That is certain.

But did pure equals ever appear to you unequal? or equality [74c] the same as inequality?

Never, Socrates.

Then these equal objects are not the same with the idea of equality?

I should say, clearly not, Socrates.

And yet from these equals, although differing from the idea of equality, you obtained the knowledge of that idea?

Very true, he said.

Which might be like, or might be unlike them?

Yes.

But that makes no difference: so long as from seeing one thing you conceive another, whether like or unlike, there must surely [74d] have been an act of recollection?

Very true.

But what would you say of equal portions of wood or other material equals? and what is the impression produced by them? Are they equals in the same sense in which absolute equality is equal? or do they fall short of this perfect equality in a measure?

Yes, he said, in a very great measure too.

And must we not allow, that when a man, looking at any object, reflects 'the thing which I see aims at being like some other thing, but falls short of and cannot be like that other [74e] thing, and is inferior', he who so reflects must have had a previous knowledge of that to which the other, although similar, was inferior?

Certainly.

And has not this been our own case in the matter of equals and of absolute equality?

Precisely.

Then we must have known equality previously to the time [75a] when we first saw the material equals, and reflected that they all strive to attain absolute equality, but fall short of it?

Very true.

And we recognize also that we have only derived this conception of absolute equality, and can only derive it, from sight or touch, or from some other of the senses, which are all alike in this respect?

Yes, Socrates, for the purposes of the present argument, one of them is the same as the other.

From the senses then is derived the conception that all sensible [75b] equals aim at an absolute equality of which they fall short?

Yes.

Then before we began to see or hear or perceive in any way, we must have had a knowledge of absolute equality, or we could not have referred to that standard the equals which are derived from the senses?--for to that they all · aspire, and of that they fall short.

No other inference can be drawn from the previous statements.

And did we not begin to see and hear and have the use of our other senses as soon as we were born?

Certainly. [75c]

Then we must have acquired the knowledge of equality at some previous time?

Yes.

That is to say, before we were born, I suppose?

It seems so.

And if we acquired this knowledge before we were born, and were born having the use of it, then we also knew before we were born and at the instant of birth not only the equal or the greater or the less, but all other such ideas; for we are not [75d] speaking only of equality, but of beauty, goodness, justice, holiness, and of all which we stamp with the name of absolute being in the dialectical process, both when we ask and when we answer questions. Of all this we affirm with certainty that we acquired the knowledge before birth?

We do.

But if, after having acquired, we have not on each occasion forgotten what we acquired, then we must always come into life having this knowledge, and shall have it always as long as life lasts--for knowing is the acquiring and retaining knowledge and not losing it. Is not the loss of knowledge, Simmias, just what we call forgetting?

Quite true, Socrates. [75e]

But if this knowledge which we acquired before birth was lost by us at birth, and if afterwards by the use of the senses we recovered what we previously knew, will not the process which we call learning be a recovering of knowledge which is natural to us, and may not this be rightly termed recollection?

Very true.

33

[76a] So much is clear--that when we perceive something, either by the help of sight, or hearing, or some other sense, that perception can lead us to think of some other thing like or unlike which is associated with it but has been forgotten. Whence, as I was saying, one of two alternatives follows:--either we all have this knowledge at birth, and continue to know through life; or, after birth, those who are said to learn only recollect, and learning is simply recollection.

Yes, that is quite true, Socrates.

And which alternative, Simmias, do you prefer? Have we the knowledge at our birth, or do we recollect afterwards things [76b] which we knew previously to our birth?

I cannot decide at the moment.

At any rate you can decide whether he who has knowledge will or will not be able to render an account of his knowledge? What do you say?

Certainly, he will.

But do you think that every man is able to give an account of the matters about which we were speaking a moment ago?

Would that they could, Socrates, but I much rather fear that tomorrow, at this time, there will no longer be anyone alive who is able to give an account of them such as ought to be given. [76c]

Then you are not of opinion, Simmias, that all men know these things?

Certainly not.

They are in process of recollecting that which they learned before?

Certainly.

But when did our souls acquire this knowledge?--clearly not since we were born as men?

Certainly not.

And therefore, previously?

Yes.

Then, Simmias, our souls must also have existed without bodies before they were in the form of man, and must have had intelligence.

Unless indeed you suppose, Socrates, that all such knowledge is given us at the very moment of birth; for this is the only time which remains. [76d]

Yes, my friend, but if so, when, pray, do we lose it? for it is not in us when we are born--that is admitted. Do we lose it at the moment of receiving it, or if not at what other time?

No, Socrates, I perceive that I was unconsciously talking nonsense.

Then may we not say, Simmias, that if there do exist these things of which we are always talking, absolute beauty and goodness, and all that class of realities; and if to this we refer all our sensations and with this compare them, finding the realities [76e] to be pre-existent and our own possession--then just as surely as these exist, so surely must our souls have existed before our birth? Otherwise our whole argument would be worthless. By an equal compulsion we must believe both that these realities exist, and that our souls existed before our birth; and if not the realities, then not the souls.

Plato: Greater Hippias 285d - e

Soc. What then are the subjects on which they listen to you with pleasure and applause? Pray enlighten me; I cannot see.

Hip. They delight in the genealogies of heroes and of men and in stories of the foundations of cities in olden times, and, to put it briefly, in all forms of antiquarian lore; so that because [285e] of them, I have been compelled to acquire a thorough comprehension and mastery of all that branch of learning.

Soc. Bless my soul, you have certainly been lucky that the Lacedaemonians do not want to hear a recital of the list of our Archons, from Solon downwards; you would have had some trouble to learn it.

Hip. Why? I can repeat fifty names after hearing them once.

Soc. I am sorry: I quite forgot about your mnemonic art. Now I understand how naturally the Lacedaemonians enjoy your multifarious knowledge, and make use of you as children do of old women, to tell them agreeable stories.

Plato: Republic VI. 485d - 487a

The true lover of learning then must from his earliest youth, as far as in him lies, desire all truth?   Assuredly.

But then again, as we know by experience, he whose desires are strong in one direction will have them weaker in others; they will be like a stream which has been drawn off into another channel.

True.

He whose desires are drawn towards the sciences and other studies will be absorbed in the pleasures of the soul, and his eagerness for bodily pleasure will decline--I mean, if he be a [485e] true philosopher and not a sham one.

That is most certain.

Such a one is sure to be temperate and the reverse of covetous; for the motives which make another man desirous of wealth and lavish spending have no place in his character.

Very true.

Here [486a] is another criterion of the philosophical nature, which has also to be considered.

What is that?

There should be no secret corner of illiberality; nothing can be more antagonistic than meanness to a soul which is ever longing after the whole of things both divine and human.

Most true, he replied.

Then how can he who has magnificence of mind and is the spectator of all time and all existence, think human life to be a great thing?

He cannot.

Or can such a one account death fearful?

No indeed. [486b]

Then the cowardly and mean nature has no part in true philosophy?

Certainly not.

Or again: can he who is harmoniously constituted, who is not covetous or mean, or a boaster, or a coward--can he, I say, ever be unjust or hard in his dealings?

Impossible.

Then you have another sign which distinguishes even in youth the philosophical nature from the unphilosophical; you will observe whether a man is just and gentle, or rude and unsociable.

True. [486c]

There is another point which should be remarked.

What point?

Whether he has or has not facility in learning; for you must not expect him to find entire satisfaction in a study which gives him pain, and in which after much toil he makes little progress.

Certainly not.

And again, if he can retain nothing of what he learns, will he not be full of forgetfulness and devoid of knowledge?

That is certain.

Labouring in vain, he must end in hating himself and his fruitless occupation?

Yes.

Then a forgetful soul can never be ranked among genuine [486d] philosophic natures; we must insist that the philosopher should have a good memory?

Certainly.

And once more, the inharmonious and unseemly nature can only tend to disproportion?

Undoubtedly.

And do you consider truth to be akin to proportion or to disproportion?

To proportion.

Then, besides other qualities, we must try to find a naturally well-proportioned and gracious mind, which will be easily led to the vision of the true being of everything.

Certainly.

I hope you do not doubt that all these qualities, which we [486e] have been enumerating, go together, and are necessary to a soul which is to have a full and perfect participation of being.

They are absolutely necessary, he replied. [487a]

And must not that be a blameless occupation which he only can pursue who has the gift of a good memory, and is quick to learn,--noble, gracious, the friend of truth, justice, courage, temperance, who are his kindred?

Plato: Republic VII. 535a - c

You remember, I said, the character which was preferred in our former choice of rulers?

Certainly, he said.

I would have you think that, in other respects, the same natures must still be chosen, and the preference again given to the surest and the bravest, and, if possible, to the fairest; but [535b] now we must look for something more than a noble and virile temper; they should also have the natural gifts which accord with this higher education.

And what are these?

Such gifts as keenness and ready powers of acquisition; for the mind more often faints from the severity of study than from the severity of gymnastics: the toil is more entirely the mind's own, and is not shared with the body.

Very true, he replied.

Further, he of whom we are in search should have a good [535c] memory, and be an unwearied solid man who is a lover of labour in any line; or he will never be able, besides enduring some bodily exercise, to go through all the intellectual discipline and study which we require of him.

Plato: Phaedrus 248c - e

And there is a law of Destiny, that the soul which attains any vision of truth in company with a god is preserved from harm until the next period, and if attaining always is always unharmed. But when she is unable to follow, and fails to behold the truth, and through some ill-hap sinks beneath the double load of forgetfulness and vice, and her wings fall from her and she drops to the ground, then the law ordains that this soul shall at her first birth pass, not into any other [248d] animal, but only into man; and the soul which has seen most of truth shall be placed in the seed from which a philosopher, or artist, or some musical and loving nature will spring; that which has seen truth in the second degree shall be some righteous king or warrior chief; the soul which is of the third class shall be a politician, or economist, or trader; the fourth shall be a lover of gymnastic toils, or a physician; the fifth shall lead the life of a prophet or hierophant; to the sixth the character of a poet or [248e] some other imitative artist will be assigned; to the seventh the life of an artisan or husbandman; to the eighth that of a sophist or demagogue; to the ninth that of a tyrant;--all these are states of probation, in which he who does righteously improves, and he who does unrighteously deteriorates, his lot.

Plato: Phaedrus 249b - 250c

[249b] But the soul which has never seen the truth will not pass into the human form. For a man must have intelligence by what is called the Idea, a unity gathered together by reason from [249c] the many particulars of sense. This is the recollection of those things which our soul once saw while following God--when regardless of that which we now call being she raised her head up towards the true being. And therefore the mind of the philosopher alone has wings; and this is just, for he is always, according to the measure of his abilities, clinging in recollection to those things in which God abides, and in beholding which He is what He is. And he who employs aright these memories is ever being initiated into perfect mysteries and alone becomes truly perfect. But, as he [249d] forgets earthly interests and is rapt in the divine, the vulgar deem him mad, and rebuke him; they do not see that he is inspired.

Thus far I have been speaking of the fourth and last kind of madness, which is imputed to him who, when he sees the beauty of earth, is transported with the recollection of the true beauty; he would like to fly away, but he cannot;

he is like a bird fluttering and looking upward and careless of the world below; and he is therefore thought to be mad. And I have shown this of all [249e] inspirations to be the noblest and highest and the offspring of the highest to him who has or shares in it, and he who loves the beautiful is called a lover because he partakes of it. For as has been already said, every soul of man has in the way of nature beheld true being; this was the condition of her passing into the [250a] form of man. But all souls do not easily recall the things of the other world; they may have seen them for a short time only, or they may have been unfortunate in their earthly lot, and, having had their hearts turned to unrighteousness through some corrupting influence, they may have lost the memory of the holy things which once they saw. Few only retain an adequate remembrance of them; and they, when they behold here any image of that other world, are rapt in amazement; but they are ignorant of what this rapture means, because they do not clearly [250b] perceive. For there is no radiance in our earthly copies of justice or temperance or those other things which are precious to souls: they are seen through a glass dimly; and there are few who, going to the images, behold in them the realities, and these only with difficulty. But beauty could be seen, brightly shining, by all who were with that happy band,-- we philosophers following in the train of Zeus, others in company with other gods; at which time we beheld the beatific vision and were initiated into a [250c] mystery which may be truly called most blessed, celebrated by us in our state of innocence, before we had any experience of evils to come, when we were admitted to the sight of apparitions innocent and simple and calm and happy, which we beheld shining in pure light, pure ourselves and not yet enshrined in that living tomb which we carry about, now that we are imprisoned in the body, like an oyster in his shell. Let me linger over the memory of scenes which have passed away.

Plato: Phaedrus 274e - 275b

It would take a long time to repeat all that Thamus said to Theuth in praise or blame of the various arts. But when they came to letters, Theuth said: O king, here is a study which will make the Egyptians wiser and give them better memories; it is a specific both for the memory and for the wit. Thamus replied: O most ingenious Theuth, the parent or inventor of an art is not always the best judge of the utility or inutility of his own inventions to [275a] the users of them. And in this instance, you who are the father of letters, from a paternal love of your own children have been led to attribute to them a quality which they cannot have; for this discovery of yours will create forgetfulness in the learners' souls, because they will not use their memories; they will trust to the external written characters and not remember of themselves. And so the specific which you have discovered is an aid not to memory, but to reminiscence. As for wisdom, it is the reputation, not the reality, that you have to offer to those who learn from you; they will have heard many things and yet received no teaching; they will appear to be omniscient and will generally [275b] know nothing; they will be tiresome company, having acquired not wisdom, but the show of wisdom.

38

Soc. And the way will be to ask whether perception is or is not the same as knowledge; for this was the real point of our argument, and with a view to this we raised (did we not?) those many strange questions. [163b]

Theaet. Certainly.

Soc. Shall we admit that we at once know whatever we perceive by sight or hearing? for example, shall we say that not having learned, we do not hear the language of foreigners when they speak to us? or shall we say that we hear and therefore know what they are saying? Or again, in looking at letters which we do not understand, shall we say that we do not see them? or shall we aver that, seeing them, we must know them?

Theaet. We shall say, Socrates, that we know what we actually see and hear of them--that is to say, we see, and hence know, the [163c] figure and colour of the letters, and we hear and know the elevation or depression of the sound; but we do not perceive by sight and hearing, and hence do not know, that which grammarians and interpreters teach about them.

Soc. Capital, Theaetetus; and about this there shall be no dispute, because I want you to grow; but look! there is another difficulty coming, and you must advise how we shall repulse it.

Theaet. What is it?

Soc. Some one will say, Can a man who has ever known any- [163d] thing, and still has and preserves a memory of that which he knows, not know that which he remembers at the time when he remembers? I have, I fear, a tedious way of putting a simple question, which is only, whether a man who has learned, and remembers, can fail to know?

Theaet. Impossible, Socrates; the supposition is monstrous.

Soc. Am I talking nonsense, then? Think: is not seeing perceiving, and is not sight perception?

Theaet. True.

Soc. And if our recent definition holds, every man knows that [163e] which he has seen?

Theaet. Yes.

Soc. And now, you would admit that there is such a thing as memory?

Theaet. Yes.

Soc. Is this memory of something or of nothing?

Theaet. Of something, surely.

Soc. Of things learned and perceived, that is?

Theaet. Certainly.

Soc. Often a man remembers that which he has seen?

Theaet. True.

Soc. Even if he closes his eyes? Or would he then forget?

Theaet. Who, Socrates, would dare to say so? [164a]

Soc. But we must say so, if the previous argument is to be maintained.

Theaet. What do you mean? I am not quite sure that I understand you, though I have a strong suspicion that you are right.

Soc. As thus: he who sees knows, as we say, that which he sees; for perception and sight and knowledge are admitted to be the same.

Theaet. Certainly.

Soc. But he who saw, and has knowledge of that which he saw, remembers, when he closes his eyes, that which he no longer sees.

Theaet. Yes.

Soc. But seeing is knowing, and therefore not-seeing is not- [164b] knowing?

Theaet. True.

Soc. Then the inference is, that a man who has attained the knowledge of something, though he still remembers this, may not know it since he does not see it; and this has been affirmed by us to be a monstrous supposition.

Theaet. Most true.

Soc. Thus, then, the assertion that knowledge and perception are one, seems to involve an impossible consequence.

Theaet. Yes.

Soc. Then they must be distinguished?

Theaet. I suppose that they must. [164c]

Soc. It seems that we must go back to our original question, What is knowledge?--But hold! Theaetetus, whatever are we proposing to do?

Theaet. About what?

Soc. Like a good-for-nothing cock, without having won the victory, we spring away from the argument and crow.

Theaet. How do you mean?

Soc. After the manner of disputers, we were satisfied with mere verbal consistency, and were well pleased if in this way we could gain an advantage. Although professing not to be mere eristics, [164d] but philosophers, I suspect that we have unconsciously fallen into the error of that ingenious class of persons.

Theaet. I do not as yet understand you.

Soc. Then I will try to explain myself: just now we asked the question, whether a man who had learned and remembered could fail to know, and we showed that a person who had seen might remember when he had his eyes shut and could not see, and then he would at the same time remember and not know. But this was an impossibility. And so the Protagorean fable came to nought, and yours also, who maintained that knowledge is the [164e] same as perception.

Theaet. So it seems.

Soc. And yet, my friend, I rather suspect that if Protagoras, who was the father of the first of the two brats, had been alive, he would have had a great deal to say on their behalf. But he is dead, and we insult over his orphan child; and even the guardians whom he left, and of whom our friend Theodorus is one, are unwilling to give any help, and therefore I suppose that we must take up his cause ourselves and see justice done?

Theod. Not I, Socrates, but rather Callias, the son of Hipponicus [165a], is his executor. For my part, I was too soon diverted from the abstractions of dialectic to geometry. Nevertheless, I shall be grateful to you if you assist him.

Soc. Very good, Theodorus; you shall see how I will come to the rescue. If a person does not attend to the meaning of terms as they are commonly used in argument, he may be involved even in greater paradoxes than these. Am I to explain this matter to you or to Theaetetus?

Theod. To both of us, and let the younger answer; he will incur less disgrace if he is discomfited. [165b]

Soc. Then now let me ask the awful question, which is this:--Can the same man know and also not know that which he knows?

Theod. How shall we answer, Theaetetus?

Theaet. He cannot, I should say.

Soc. He can, if you maintain that seeing is knowing. When you are imprisoned in a well, as the saying is, and the self-assured adversary closes one of your eyes with his hand, and asks whether you can see his cloak with the eye which he has closed, how will [165c] you answer the inevitable man?

Theaet. I should answer, 'Not with that eye but with the other'.

Soc. Then you see and do not see the same thing at the same time.

Theaet. Yes, in a certain sense.

Soc. None of that, he will reply; I do not ask or bid you answer in what sense you know, but only whether you know that which you do not know. You have been proved to see that which you do not see; and you have already admitted that seeing is knowing, and that not-seeing is not-knowing: I leave you to draw the inference.

Theaet. Yes; the inference is the contradictory of my assertion. [165d]

Soc. Yes, my marvel, and there might have been yet worse things in store for you, if an opponent had gone on to ask whether you can have a sharp and also a dull knowledge, and whether you can know near, but not at a distance, or know the same thing with more or less intensity, and so on without end. Such are the questions which might have been fired at you by a light-armed mercenary, who argued for pay. He would have lain in wait for you, and when you took up the position that sense and knowledge are the same, he would have made an assult upon hearing, smelling, and the other senses; he would have pressed the [165e] attack, until, in your envy and admiration of his wisdom, you were taken captive; and once he had got you into his net, you would not have escaped until you had come to an understanding about the sum to be paid for your release. Well, you ask, and how will Protagoras reinforce his position? Shall I answer for him?

Theaet. By all means.

Soc. He will repeat all those things which we have been urging [166a] on his behalf, and then he will close with us in disdain, and say:--The worthy Socrates asks a little boy, whether the same man could at once remember and not know the same thing; and when the boy, because he is frightened and unable to see what is coming, says No, he thinks, it appears, that he has held me up to ridicule. The truth is, O slatternly Socrates, that when you ask questions about any assertion of mine, and the person asked is found tripping, if he has answered as I should have answered, [166b] then I am refuted, but if he answers something else, then he is refuted and not I. For firstly do you really suppose that any one would admit the memory which a man has of an impression which has passed away to be similar to that which he experienced at the time? Assuredly not. Or would he hesitate to acknowledge that the same man may know and not know the same thing? Or, if he is afraid of making this admission, would he ever grant that one who is becoming unlike is the same as before he became unlike? Or rather would he admit that a man is one at all, and not many and infinite as the changes which take place in him? But must we speak by the card in order to guard [166c] against precise criticism of each other's words? No, my good sir, he will say, examine my view itself in a more generous spirit; and either show, if you can, that our sensations are not private to each individual, or, if you admit them to be so, prove that this does not involve the consequence that the appearance becomes, or, if you will have the word, is, to the individual only.

Plato: Theaetetus 191c - 198d

Soc. Let us make the assertion in another form, which may or [191c] may not have a favourable issue; but as we are in a great strait, every argument should be turned over and tested. Tell me, then, whether I am right in saying that you may learn a thing which at one time you did not know?

Theaet. Certainly you may.

Soc. And another and another?

Theaet. Yes.

Soc. I would have you imagine, then, that there exists in the mind of man a block of wax, which is of different sizes in different men; harder, moister, and having more or less of purity in one [191d] than another, and in some of an intermediate quality.

Theaet. I see.

Soc. Let us say that this tablet is a gift of Memory, the mother of the Muses; and that when we wish to remember anything which we have seen, or heard, or thought in our own minds, we hold the wax to the perceptions and thoughts, and in that material receive the impression of them as from the seal of a ring; and that we remember and know what is imprinted as long as the image lasts; but when the image is effaced, or cannot be taken, then we forget and do not know. [191e]

Theaet. Very good.

Soc. Now, when a person has this knowledge, and is considering something which he sees or hears, may not false opinion arise in the following manner?

Theaet. In what manner?

Soc. When he thinks what he knows, sometimes to be what he knows, and sometimes to be what he does not know. We were wrong before in deny-ing the possibility of this.

Theaet. And how would you amend the former statement?

Soc. I should begin by making a list of the impossible cases [192a] which must be excluded. (1) No one can think one thing to be another when he does not perceive either of them, but has the memorial or seal of both of them in his mind; nor can any mistaking of one thing for another occur, when he only knows one, and does not know, and has no impression of the other; nor can he think that one thing which he does not know is another thing which he does not know, or that what he does not know is what he knows; nor (2) that one thing which he perceives is another thing which he perceives, or that something which he perceives is something which he does not perceive; or that something which he does not perceive is something else which he does [192b] not per-ceive; or that something which he does not perceive is something which he perceives; nor again (3) can he think that something which he knows and per-ceives, and of which he has the impression coinciding with sense, is something

42

else which he knows and perceives, and of which he has the impression coinciding with sense;--this last case, if possible, is still more inconceivable than the others; nor (4) can he think that something which he knows and perceives, and of which he has the memorial in good order, is something else which he knows; nor if his mind is thus furnished, can he think that a thing which he knows and perceives is another thing which he perceives; or that a thing [192c] which he does not know and does not perceive, is the same as another thing which he does not know and does not perceive;--nor again, can he suppose that a thing which he does not know and does not perceive is the same as another thing which he does not know; or that a thing which he does not know and does not perceive is another thing which he does not perceive:--All these utterly and absolutely exclude the possibility of false opinion. The only cases, if any, which remain, are the following.

Theaet. What are they? If you tell me, I may perhaps understand you better; but at present I am unable to follow you.

Soc. A person may think that some things which he knows, or which he perceives and does not know, are some other things which he [192d] knows and perceives; or that some things which he knows and perceives, are other things which he knows and perceives.

Theaet. I understand you less than ever now.

Soc. Hear me once more, then:--I, knowing Theodorus, and remembering in my own mind what sort of person he is, and also what sort of person Theaetetus is, at one time see them, and at another time do not see them, and sometimes I touch them, and at another time not, or at one time I may hear them or perceive them in some other way, and at another time not perceive you, but still I remember you, and know you in my own mind. [192e]

Theaet. Very true.

Soc. Then, first of all, I want you to understand that a man may or may not perceive sensibly that which he knows.

Theaet. True.

Soc. And that which he does not know will sometimes not be perceived by him and sometimes will be perceived and only perceived?

Theaet. That is also true.

[193a] Soc. See whether you can follow me better now: Socrates can recognize Theodorus and Theaetetus, but he sees neither of them, nor does he perceive them in any other way; he cannot then by any possibility imagine in his own mind that Theaetetus is Theodorus. Am I not right?

Theaet. You are quite right.

Soc. Then that was the first case of which I spoke.

Theaet. Yes.

Soc. The second case was, that I, knowing one of you and not knowing the other, and perceiving neither, can never think him whom I know to be him whom I do not know.

Theaet. True. [193b]

Soc. In the third case, not knowing and not perceiving either of you, I cannot think that one of you whom I do not know is the other whom I do not know. I need not again go over the catalogue of excluded cases, in which I cannot form a false opinion about you and Theodorus, either when I know both or when I am in ignorance of both, or when I know one and not the other. And the same of perceiving: do you understand me?

Theaet. I do.

Soc. The only possibility of erroneous opinion is, when knowing you and Theodorus, and having on the waxen block the impression of both of you given as by a seal, but seeing you imperfectly [193c] and at a distance, I am eager to assign the right impression of memory to the right visual impression, and to fit this into its own print, in order that recognition may take place; but if I fail and transpose them, putting the foot into the wrong shoe--that is to say, putting the vision of either of you on to the wrong impression, or if my mind, like the sight in a mirror, which is transferred [193d] from right to left, err by reason of some similar affection, then 'heterodoxy' and false opinion ensues.

Theaet. Yes, Socrates, you have described the nature of opinion with wonderful exactness.

Soc. Or again, when I know both of you, and perceive as well as know one of you, but not the other, and my knowledge of him does not accord with perception--that was the case put by me just now which you did not understand.

Theaet. No, I did not.

Soc. I meant to say, that when a person knows and perceives one of you, and his knowledge coincides with his perception, he [193e] will never think him to be some other person, whom he knows and perceives, and the knowledge of whom coincides with his perception--for that also was a case supposed.

Theaet. True.

Soc. But there was an omission of the further case, in which as we now say, false opinion may arise, when knowing both, and [194a] seeing, or having some other sensible perception of both, I fail in holding the seal over against the corresponding sensation; like a bad archer, I miss and fall wide of the mark-- and this is called falsehood.

Theaet. Yes; it is rightly so called.

Soc. When, therefore, perception is present to one of the seals or impressions but not to the other, and the mind fits the seal of the absent perception on the one which is present, in any case of this sort the mind is deceived; in a word, if our view is sound, [194b] there can be no error or deception about things which a man does not know and has never perceived, but only in things which are known and perceived; in these alone opinion turns and twists about, and becomes alternately true and false;--true when the seals and impressions of sense meet straight and opposite--false when they go awry and are crooked.

Theaet. And is not that, Socrates, nobly said?

Soc. Nobly! yes; but wait a little and hear the explanation, and then you will say so with more reason; for to think truly is noble and to be deceived is base.

Theaet. Undoubtedly.

Soc. And the origin of truth and error, men say, is as follows:--When the wax in the soul of any one is deep and abundant, and smooth and perfectly tempered, then the impressions which pass through the senses and sink into the heart of the soul, as Homer says in a parable, meaning to indicate the likeness of the soul to wax; these, I say, being pure and clear, and having a [194d] sufficient depth of wax, are also lasting, and minds such as these easily learn and easily retain, and are not liable to confuse the imprints of sensations, but have true thoughts; for, having clear impressions well spaced out, they can quickly 'say what they are',--that is, distribute them into their proper places on the block. And such men are called wise. Do you agree?

Theaet. Entirely. [194e]

Soc. But when the heart of anyone is shaggy--a quality which the all-wise poet commends--or muddy and of impure wax, or very soft, or very hard, then there is a corresponding defect in the mind; the soft are good at learning, but apt to forget, and the hard are the reverse; the shaggy and rugged and gritty, or those who have an admixture of earth or dung in their composition, [195a] have the impressions indistinct, as also the hard, for there is no depth in them; and the soft too are indistinct, for their impressions are easily confused and effaced. Yet greater is the indistinctness when they are all jostled together in a little soul, which has no room. These are the natures which are prone to false opinion; for when they see or hear or think of anything, they are slow in assigning the right objects to the right impressions--in their stupidity they confuse them, and are apt to see and hear and think amiss--and such men are said to be deceived in their knowledge of objects, and ignorant.

Theaet. No man, Socrates, can say anything truer than that. [195b]

Soc. Then now we may admit the existence of false opinion in us?

Theaet. Certainly.

Soc. And of true opinion also?

Theaet. Yes.

Soc. We have at length satisfactorily proven that beyond a doubt there are these two sorts of opinion?

Theaet. Undoubtedly.

Soc. Alas, Theaetetus, what a tiresome creature is a man who is fond of talking!

Theaet. What makes you say so?

Soc. Because I am disheartened at my own stupidity and [195c] tiresome garrulity; for what other term will describe the habit of a man who is always arguing on all sides of a question; whose dullness cannot be convinced, and who will never leave off?

Theaet. But what puts you out of heart?

Soc. I am not only out of heart, but in positive despair; for I do not know what to answer if anyone were to ask me:--O Socrates, have you indeed discovered that false opinion arises neither in the comparison of perceptions with one another nor yet in thought, but in the linking of thought with perception? [195d] Yes, I shall say, with the complacence of one who thinks that he has made a noble discovery.

Theaet. I see no reason why we should be ashamed of our demonstration, Socrates.

Soc. He will say: You mean to argue that the man whom we only think of and do not see, cannot be confused with the horse which we do not see or touch, but only think of and do not perceive? That I believe to be my meaning, I shall reply.

Theaet. Quite right. [195e]

Soc. Well, then, he will say, according to that argument, the number eleven, which is only thought, can never be mistaken for twelve, which is only thought: How would you answer him?

45

Theaet. I should say that a mistake may very likely arise between the eleven or twelve which are seen or handled, but that no similar mistake can arise between the eleven and twelve which are in the mind.

Soc. Well, but do you think that no one ever put before his [196a] own mind five and seven,--I do not mean five or seven men or other such objects, but five or seven in the abstract, which, as we say, are recorded on the waxen block, and in which false opinion is held to be impossible;--did no man ever ask himself how many these numbers make when added together, and answer that they are eleven, while another thinks that they are twelve, or would all agree in thinking and saying that they are twelve? [196b]

Theaet. Certainly not; many would think that they are eleven, and in the higher numbers the chance of error is greater still; for I assume you to be speaking of numbers in general.

Soc. Exactly; and I want you to consider whether this does not imply that the twelve in the waxen block are supposed to be eleven?

Theaet. Yes, that seems to be the case.

Soc. Then do we not come back to the old difficulty? For he who makes such a mistake does think one thing which he knows to be another thing which he knows; but this, as we said, was [196c] impossible, and afforded an irresistible proof of the non-existence of false opinion, because otherwise the same person would inevitably know and not know the same thing at the same time.

Theaet. Most true.

Soc. Then false opinion cannot be explained as a confusion of thought and sense, for in that case we could not have been mistaken about pure conceptions of thought; and thus we are obliged to say, either that false opinion does not exist, or that a man may not know that which he knows;--which alternative do you prefer?

Theaet. It is hard to determine, Socrates. [196d]

Soc. And yet the argument will scarcely admit of both. But, as we are at our wits' end, suppose that we do a shameless thing?

Theaet. What is it?

Soc. Let us attempt to explain what it is like 'to know'.

Theaet. And why should that be shameless?

Soc. You seem not to be aware that the whole of our discussion from the very beginning has been a search after knowledge, of which we are assumed not to know the nature.

Theaet. Nay, but I am well aware.

Soc. And is it not shameless when we do not know what knowledge is, to be explaining the verb 'to know'? The truth is, Theaetetus, that we have long been infected with logical [196e] impurity. Thousands of times have we repeated the words 'we know', and 'do not know', and 'we have or have not science or knowledge', as if we could understand what we are saying to one another, even while we remain ignorant about knowledge; and at this moment we are using the words 'we understand', 'we are ignorant', as though we could still employ them when deprived of knowledge or science.

Theaet. But if you avoid these expressions, Socrates, how will you ever argue at all?

Soc. I could not, being the man I am. The case would be [197a] different if I were a true hero of dialectic: and O that such an one were present!

for he would have told us to avoid the use of these terms; at the same time he would not have spared in you and me the faults which I have noted. But, seeing that we are no great wits, shall I venture to say what knowing is? for I think that the attempt may be worth making.

Theaet. Then by all means venture, and no one shall find fault with you for using the forbidden terms.

Soc. You have heard the common explanation of the verb 'to know'?

Theaet. I think so, but I do not remember it at the moment.

Soc. They explain the word 'to know' as meaning 'to have [197b] knowledge'.

Theaet. True.

Soc. I propose that we make a slight change, and say 'to possess' knowledge.

Theaet. How do the two expressions differ?

Soc. Perhaps there may be no difference; but still I should like you to hear my view, that you may help me to test it.

Theaet. I will, if I can.

Soc. I should distinguish 'having' from 'possessing': for example, a man may buy and keep under his control a garment which he does not wear; and then we should say, not that he has, but that he possesses the garment.

Theaet. It would be the correct expression. [197c]

Soc. Well, may not a man 'possess' and yet not 'have' knowledge in the sense of which I am speaking? As you may suppose a man to have caught wild birds--doves or any other birds--and to be keeping them in an aviary which he has constructed at home; we might say of him in one sense, that he always has them because he possesses them, might we not?

Theaet. Yes.

Soc. And yet, in another sense, he has none of them; but they are in his power, and he has got them under his hand in an enclosure of his own, and can take and have them whenever he likes,--he can catch any which he likes, and let the bird go [197d] again, and he may do so as often as he pleases.

Theaet. True.

Soc. Once more, then, as in what preceded we made a sort of waxen tablet in the mind, so let us now suppose that in the mind of each man there is an aviary of all sorts of birds--some flocking together apart from the rest, others in small groups, others solitary, flying anywhere and everywhere. [197e]

Theaet. Let us imagine such an aviary--and what is to follow?

Soc. We may suppose that the birds are kinds of knowledge, and that when we were children, this receptacle was empty; whenever a man has gotten and detained in the enclosure a kind of knowledge, he may be said to have learned or discovered the thing which is the subject of the knowledge: and this is to know.

Theaet. Granted.

Soc. [198a] And further, when any one wishes to catch any of these knowledges or sciences, and having taken, to hold it, and again to let them go, how will he express himself?--will he describe the 'catching' of them and the original 'possession' in the same words? I will make my meaning clearer by an example:--You admit that there is an art of arithmetic?

Theaet. To be sure.

Soc. Conceive this as an attempt to capture knowledge of every species of the odd and even.

Theaet. I follow.

Soc. Having the use of the art, the arithmetician, if I am not mistaken, has the conceptions of number under his hand, and can [198b] transmit them to another.

Theaet. Yes.

Soc. And when transmitting them he may be said to teach them, and when receiving to learn them, and when having them in possession in the aforesaid aviary he may be said to know them.

Theaet. Exactly.

Soc. Attend to what follows: must not the perfect arithmetician know all numbers, for he has the science of all numbers in his mind?

Theaet. True.

Soc. And he can reckon abstract numbers in his head, or [198c] things about him which are numerable?

Theaet. Of course he can.

Soc. And to reckon is simply to consider how much such and such a number amounts to?

Theaet. Very true.

Soc. And so he appears to be searching into something which he knows, as if he did not know it, for we have already admitted that he knows all numbers;--you have heard these perplexing questions raised?

Theaet. I have.

Soc. May we not pursue the image of the doves, and say that [198d] the chase after knowledge is of two kinds? one kind is prior to possession and for the sake of possession, and the other for the sake of taking and holding in the hands that which is possessed already. And thus, when a man has learned and known something long ago, he may resume and get hold of the knowledge which he has long possessed, but has not at hand in his mind.

Plato: Philebus 21b - 22b

Soc. But if you had neither mind, nor memory, nor knowledge, nor true opinion, you would in the first place be utterly ignorant of whether you were pleased or not, because you would be entirely devoid of intelligence.

Pro. Certainly.

Soc. And similarly, if you had no memory you would not recollect that you had ever been pleased, nor would the slightest [21c] recollection of the pleasure which you feel at any moment remain with you; and if you had no true opinion you would not think that you were pleased when you were; and if you had no power of calculation you would not be able to calculate on future pleasure, and your life would not be the life of a man, but of a mollusc, or any creature of the sea which 'lives' enclosed in a shell. Could this be otherwise?

Pro. No. [21d]

Soc. But is such a life to be chosen?

Pro. I cannot answer you, Socrates; the argument has taken away from me the power of speech.

Soc. We must not weaken;--let us now take the life of mind and examine it in turn.

Pro. And what is this life of mind?

Soc. I want to know whether anyone of us would consent to live, having wisdom and mind and knowledge and memory of all things, but having no sense of pleasure or pain, either more or [21e] less, and wholly unaffected by these and the like feelings?

Pro. Neither life, Socrates, appears eligible to me, nor is likely, as I should imagine, to be chosen by anyone else.

Soc. What would you say, Protarchus, to both of these in one, [22a] or to one that was made out of the union of the two?

Pro. Out of the union, that is, of pleasure with mind and wisdom?

Soc. Yes, that is the life which I mean.

Pro. There can be no difference of opinion; not some but all would surely choose this third rather than either of the other two, and in addition to them.

Soc. But do you see the consequence?

Pro. To be sure I do. The consequence is, that two out of the three lives which have been proposed are neither sufficient nor [22b] eligible for man or for animal.

Soc. Then now there can be no doubt that neither of them has the good, for the one which had would certainly have been sufficient and perfect and eligible for all plants and animals, if they were able to spend their whole lives in the activity selected; and if any of us had chosen any other, he would have chosen contrary to the nature of the truly eligible, and not of his own free will, but either through ignorance or from some unhappy necessity.

Plato: Philebus 33c - 39a

Soc. The other class of pleasures, which as we were saying is purely mental, is entirely derived from memory.

Pro. What do you mean?

Soc. I must first of all analyse memory, or rather perception which is prior to memory, if the subject of our discussion is ever to be properly cleared up.

Pro. How will you proceed? [33d]

Soc. Let us imagine affections of the body which are extinguished before they reach the soul, and leave her unaffected; and again, other affections which vibrate through both soul and body, and impart a shock to both and to each of them.

Pro. Granted.

Soc. And the soul may be truly said to be oblivious of the first but not of the second? [33e]

Pro. Quite true.

Soc. When I say oblivious, do not suppose that I here mean forgetfulness in a literal sense; for forgetfulness is the exit of memory, which in this case has not yet entered; and to speak of the loss of that which is not yet in existence, and never has been, is a contradiction; do you see?

Pro. Yes.

Soc. Then just be so good as to change the terms.

Pro. How shall I change them?

Soc. [34a] Instead of the oblivion of the soul, when you are describing the state in which she is unaffected by the shocks of the body, say unconsciousness or insensibility.

Pro. I see.

Soc. And the union or communion of soul and body in one feeling and motion would be properly called consciousness or sensation?

Pro. Most true.

Soc. Then now we know the meaning of the word sensation?

Pro. Yes.

Soc. Hence memory may, I think, be rightly described as the preservation of sensation? [34b]

Pro. Right.

Soc. But do we not distinguish recollection from memory?

Pro. I think so.

Soc. And when the soul recovers by her own unaided power some feeling which she previously experienced in company with the body, is not this what we call recollecting?

Pro. Certainly.

Soc. And again when she revives by herself alone the lost memory of some sensation or knowledge, the recovery in all such cases is termed recollection? [34c]

Pro. Very true.

Soc. There is a reason why I say all this.

Pro. What is it?

Soc. I want to attain the plainest possible notion of pleasure and desire, as they exist in the mind only, apart from the body; and the previous analysis helps to show the nature of both.

Pro. Then now, Socrates, let us proceed to the next point.

Soc. There are certainly many things to be considered in discussing the generation and whole complexion of pleasure. [34d] Indeed, before any advance can be made we must determine the nature and seat of desire.

Pro. Aye; let us inquire into that, for we shall lose nothing.

Soc. Nay, Protarchus, we shall surely lose the puzzle if we find the answer.

Pro. A fair retort; but let us proceed.

Soc. Did we not place hunger, thirst, and the like, in the class [34e] of desires?

Pro. Certainly.

Soc. And yet they are very different; what common nature have we in view when we call them by a single name?

Pro. By heavens, Socrates, that is a question which is not easily answered; but it must be answered.

Soc. Then let us go back to our examples.

Pro. Where shall we begin?

Soc. Do we mean anything when we say 'a man thirsts'?

Pro. Yes.

Soc. We mean to say that he 'is empty'?

Pro. Of course.

Soc. And is not thirst desire?

Pro. Yes, of drink.

Soc. Would you say of drink, or of replenishment with drink? [35a]

Pro. I should say, of replenishment with drink.

Soc. Then he who is empty desires, as would appear, the opposite of what he experiences; for he is empty and desires to be full?

Pro. Clearly so.

Soc. But how can a man who is empty for the first time, attain either by perception or memory to any apprehension of replenishment, of which he has no present or past experience?

Pro. Impossible. [35b]

Soc. And yet he who desires, surely desires something?

Pro. Of course.

Soc. He does not desire that which he experiences, for he experiences thirst, and thirst is emptiness; but he desires replenishment?

Pro. True.

Soc. Then there must be something in the thirsty man which in some way apprehends replenishment?

Pro. There must.

Soc. And that cannot be the body, for the body is supposed to be emptied?

Pro. Yes.

Soc. The only remaining alternative is that the soul apprehends the replenishment by the help of memory; as is obvious, [35c] for what other way can there be?

Pro. I cannot imagine any other.

Soc. But do you see the consequence?

Pro. What is it?

Soc. That there is no such thing as desire of the body.

Pro. Why so?

Soc. Why, because the argument shows that the endeavour of every animal is to the reverse of his bodily state.

Pro. Yes.

Soc. And the impulse which leads him to the opposite of what he is experiencing proves that he has a memory of the opposite state.

Pro. True. [35d]

Soc. And the argument, having proved that memory is the power by which we are attracted towards the objects of desire, proves also that the impulses and the desires and the moving principle of the whole animal have their origin in the soul.

Pro. Most true.

Soc. The argument will not allow that our body either hungers or thirsts or has any similar experience.

Pro. Quite right.

Soc. Let me make a further observation; the argument appears to me to imply that there is a kind of life which consists in these affections.

Pro. Of what affections, and of what kind of life, are you [35e] speaking?

51

Soc. I am speaking of being emptied and replenished, and of all that relates to the preservation and destruction of living beings, as well as of the pain which is felt in one of these states and of the pleasure which succeeds to it.

Pro. True.

Soc. And what would you say of the intermediate state?

Pro. What do you mean by 'intermediate'?

Soc. I mean when a person is in actual suffering and yet remembers past pleasures which, if they would only return, would relieve him; but as yet he has them not. May we not say of him, that he is in an intermediate state? [36a]

Pro. Certainly.

Soc. Would you say that he was wholly pained or wholly pleased?

Pro. Nay, I should say that he has two pains; in his body there is the actual experience of pain, and in his soul longing and expectation.

Soc. What do you mean, Protarchus, by the two pains? May not a man who is empty have at one time a manifest hope of being filled, and at other times be quite in despair? [36b]

Pro. Very true.

Soc. And has he not the pleasure of memory when he is hoping to be filled, and yet in that he is empty is he not at the same time in pain?

Pro. Certainly.

Soc. Then man and the other animals have at the same time both pleasure and pain?

Pro. I suppose so.

Soc. But when a man is empty and has no hope of being filled, there will be the double experience of pain. You observed [36c] this and inferred that the double experience was the single case possible.

Pro. Quite true, Socrates.

Soc. Shall the inquiry into these states of feeling be made the occasion of raising a question?

Pro. What question?

Soc. Whether we ought to say that the pleasures and pains of which we are speaking are true or false, or some true and some false.

Pro. But how, Socrates, can there be false pleasures and pains?

Soc. And how, Protarchus, can there be true and false fears, or true and false expectations, or true and false opinions? [36d]

Pro. I grant that opinions may be true or false, but not these other things.

Soc. What do you mean? I am afraid that we are raising a very serious inquiry.

Pro. There I agree.

Soc. And yet, my boy, for you are one of Philebus' boys, the point to be considered is whether the inquiry is relevant to the previous argument.

Pro. Surely.

Soc. No tedious and irrelevant discussion can be allowed; what is said should be pertinent.

Pro. Right. [36e]

Soc. I am always wondering at the question which has now been raised. What is your position? Do you deny that some pleasures are false, and others true?

Pro. To be sure I do.

Soc. Would you say that no one ever seemed to rejoice and yet did not rejoice, or seemed to feel pain and yet did not feel pain, sleeping or waking, mad or lunatic?

Pro. So we have all been accustomed to hold, Socrates. [37a]

Soc. But were you right? Shall we inquire into the truth of your opinion?

Pro. I think that we should.

Soc. Let us then put into more precise terms the question which has arisen about pleasure and opinion. Is there such a thing as opinion?

Pro. Yes.

Soc. And such a thing as pleasure?

Pro. Yes.

Soc. And such a thing as an object of opinion?

Pro. True.

Soc. And an object in which that which is pleased takes pleasure?

Pro. Quite correct.

Soc. And whether the opinion be right or wrong, makes no difference; it will still be an opinion?

Pro. Certainly. [37b]

Soc. And he who is pleased, whether he is rightly pleased or not, will always have a real feeling of pleasure?

Pro. Yes; that is also quite true.

Soc. Then, how can opinion be both true and false, and pleasure true only, although pleasure and opinion are both equally real?

Pro. Yes; that is the question.

Soc. You mean that opinion admits of truth and falsehood, and hence becomes not merely opinion, but opinion of a certain [37c] quality; and this is what you think should be examined?

Pro. Yes.

Soc. And further, even if we admit the existence of qualities in other objects, but think pleasure and pain to be simple and devoid of quality, we must agree upon the reasons for this.

Pro. Clearly.

Soc. But there is no difficulty in seeing that pleasure and pain as well as opinion have qualities, for they are great or small, and have various degrees of intensity; as was indeed said long ago by us. [37d]

Pro. Quite true.

Soc. And if badness attaches to any of them, Protarchus, then we should speak of a bad opinion or of a bad pleasure?

Pro. Quite true, Socrates.

Soc. And if rightness attaches to any of them, should we not speak of a right opinion or right pleasure; and in like manner of the reverse of rightness?

Pro. Certainly.

Soc. And if what is opined be erroneous, might we not say that [37e] the opinion, being erroneous, is not right or rightly opined?

Pro. Certainly.

Soc. And if we see a pleasure or pain which errs in respect of its object, shall we call that right or good, or by any honourable name?

Pro. Not if the pleasure is mistaken; how could we?

Soc. And surely pleasure often appears to accompany an opinion which is not true, but false?

Pro. [38a] Certainly it does; and in that case, Socrates, as we were saying, the opinion is false, but no one could call the actual pleasure false.

Soc. How eagerly, Protarchus, do you rush to the defence of pleasure!

Pro. Nay, Socrates, I only repeat what I hear.

Soc. And is there no difference, my friend, between that pleasure which is associated with right opinion and knowledge, and that which is often found in all of us associated with falsehood and ignorance? [38b]

Pro. There must be a very great difference between them.

Soc. Then, now let us proceed to contemplate this difference.

Pro. Lead, and I will follow.

Soc. Well, then, my view is--

Pro. What is it?

Soc. We agree--do we not?--that there is such a thing as false, and also such a thing as true opinion?

Pro. Yes.

Soc. And pleasure and pain, as I was just now saying, are often consequent upon these--upon true and false opinion, I mean.

Pro. Very true.

Soc. And do not opinion and the endeavour to form an opinion always spring from memory and perception? [38c]

Pro. Certainly.

Soc. Might we imagine the process to be something of this nature?

Pro. Of what nature?

Soc. An object may be often seen at a distance not very clearly, and the seer may want to determine what it is which he sees.

Pro. Very likely.

Soc. Soon he begins to interrogate himself.

Pro. In what manner?

Soc. He asks himself--'What is that which appears to be standing by the rock under the tree?' This is the question which he may [38d] be supposed to put to himself when he sees such an appearance.

Pro. True.

Soc. To which he may guess the right answer, saying as if in a whisper to himself--'It is a man.'

Pro. Very good.

Soc. Or again, he may be misled, thinking that it is a figure made by some shepherds, and call it an image.

Pro. Yes.

Soc. And if he has a companion, he repeats his thought to him [38e] in articulate sounds, and what was before an opinion, has now become a proposition.

Pro. Certainly.

Soc. But if he be walking alone when these thoughts occur to him, he may not unfrequently keep them in his mind for a considerable time.

Pro. Very true.

Soc. Well, now, I wonder whether you would agree in my explanation of this phenomenon.

Pro. What is your explanation?

Soc. I think that the soul at such times is like a book.

Pro. How so?

Soc. Memory and perception meet, and they and their attendant [39a] feelings seem to me almost to write down words in the soul. When the inscribing feeling writes truly, then true opinion and true propositions are formed within us in consequence of its work--but when the scribe within us writes falsely, the result is false.

Pro. I quite assent and agree to your statement.

Soc. I must bespeak your favour also for another artist, who is busy at the same time in the chambers of the soul.

Pro. Who is he?

Soc. The painter, who, after the scribe has done his work, draws images in the soul of the things which he has described.

Plato: Timaeus 25e - 26a

I have told you briefly, Socrates, what the aged Critias heard from Solon and related to us. And when you were speaking yesterday about your city and citizens, the tale which I have just been repeating to you came into my mind, and I remarked with astonishment how, by some mysterious coincidence, you agreed in almost every particular with the narrative of Solon; but I did [26a] not like to speak at the moment. For a long time had elapsed, and I had forgotten too much; I thought that I must first of all run over the narrative in my own mind, and then I would speak. And so I readily assented to your request yesterday, considering that in all such cases the chief difficulty is to find a tale suitable to our purpose, and that with such a tale we should be fairly well provided.

ARISTOTLE

384 B.C. - 322 B.C.

From: *The Works of Aristotle Translated into English*. Edited by W. D. Ross. Published by Oxford University Press, 1928-1952.

Son of the court physician of the king of Macedon, Aristotle spent twenty years at Plato's Academy in Athens. He left the Academy on Plato's death and in 342 B.C. became tutor to the future Alexander the Great at the Macedonian court. About 335 B.C. he returned to Athens and opened his own school, the Lyceum. The surviving treatises of Aristotle appear to have been lecture notes or textbooks used in his school. After Alexander's death in 323 B.C. Aristotle took refuge on the island of Chalcis where he died.

Aristotle accepted the Platonic view of knowledge as representing what is permanent and unchanging, but he came to reject the doctrine of forms, that the objects of knowledge are nonsensible and other-worldly, and the associated doctrine that knowledge is recollected from a previous life (e.g., *Analytica Priora*). As he systematically studied the various branches of knowledge he was led towards a scientific empiricism that differed profoundly from Plato. Elements of empiricism and of Platonic idealism both appear in Aristotle's work on memory. The short *De Memoria et Reminiscentia (On Memory and Reminiscences)* gives a strongly empiricist account of the mechanism of learning in terms of frequency of association. This is complemented by the emphasis in other works (e.g., *Analytica Posteriora*) that knowledge is not derived from the senses, since its concepts are universal, but is due to the intellectual function of the soul.

Supplementary readings:

Allan, D. J. (1970). *The Philosophy of Aristotle*. Oxford: Oxford University Press.

Lloyd, G. E. R. (1968). *Aristotle: The Growth and Structure of His Thought*. Cambridge: Cambridge University Press.

ARISTOTLE

Table of Contents

Explanation of contents: Before each work, on the left of the page, is given the volume number (large Roman numerals) of the work in the Ross edition. Excerpts of particular works are referenced by book and chapter (Roman followed by Arabic numerals) or by chapter alone for works not divided into books (Arabic numerals). These are followed by the Becker numbers for the passage, a standard citation system contained in the Ross edition, which refers to the page, column, and line numbers of the Greek text published by the Berlin Academy from 1831 to 1870, edited by Emmanual Becker. For example, the first excerpt, I. Analytica Priora, II.21.66b.20, is from Volume I of the Ross edition, from the work titled Analytica Priora, from Book II, chapter 21, and begins on page 66, column b, line 20 of the Becker edition. Becker numbers that appear in the Ross edition are included here in the text [in brackets]. These numbers appear in most modern translations and allow the reader to find any of the excerpted passages. The table of contents lists the first Becker number contained in the passage referenced. Editor's comments are not included.

II.21.66b.20 - II.21.67a.20

It sometimes happens that just as we are deceived in the arrangement of the terms so error may arise in our thought about [66b.20] them, e.g. if it is possible that the same predicate should belong to more than one subject immediately, but although knowing the one, a man may forget the other and think the opposite true. Suppose that A belongs to B and to C in virtue of their nature, and that B and C belong to all D in the same way. If then a man thinks that A belongs to all B, and B to D, but A to no C, and C to all [25] D, he will both know and not know the same thing in respect of the same thing. Again if a man were to make a mistake about the members of a single series; e.g. suppose A belongs to B, B to C, and C to D, but some one thinks that A belongs to all B, but to no C: he will both know that [30] A belongs to D, and think that it does not. Does he then maintain after this simply that what he knows, he does not think? For he knows in a way that A belongs to C through B, since the part is included in the whole; so that what he knows in a way, this he maintains he does not think at all: but that is impossible.

[35] In the former case, where the middle term does not belong to the same series, it is not possible to think both the premisses with reference to each of the two middle terms: e.g. that A belongs to all B, but to no C, and both B and C belong to all D. For it turns out that the first premiss of the one syllogism is either wholly or partially contrary to the first premiss of the other. For if he thinks that A belongs to everything to which B belongs, and he knows that B belongs to D, then he knows that A belongs [67a.1] to D. Consequently if again he thinks that A belongs to nothing to which C belongs, he thinks that A does not belong to some of that to which B belongs; but if he thinks that A belongs to everything to which B belongs, and again thinks that A does not belong to some of that to which B belongs, these beliefs are wholly or partially [5] contrary. In this way then it is not possible to think; but nothing prevents a man thinking one premiss of each syllogism or both premisses of one of the two syllogisms: e.g. A belongs to all B, and B to D, and again A belongs to no C. An error of this kind is similar to the error into which we fall concerning particulars: e.g. if A belongs to all B, and B to all C, A will belong to all C. If then [10] a man knows that A belongs to everything to which B belongs, he knows that A belongs to C. But nothing prevents his being ignorant that C exists; e.g. let A stand for two right angles, B for triangle, C for a particular diagram of a triangle. A man might think that C did not exist, though he knew that every triangle contains two [15] right angles; consequently he will know and not know the same thing at the same time. For the expression 'to know that every triangle has its angles equal to two right angles' is ambiguous, meaning to have the knowledge either of the universal or of the particulars. Thus then he knows that C contains two right angles with a knowledge of the universal, but not with a knowledge of the particulars; consequently [20] his knowledge will not be contrary to his ignorance. The argument in the *Meno* that learning is recollection may be criticized in a similar way.

[99b.20] We have already said that scientific knowledge through demonstration is impossible unless a man knows the primary immediate premisses. But there are questions which might be raised in respect of the apprehension of these immediate premisses: one might not only ask whether it is of the same kind as the apprehension of the conclusions, but also whether there is or is not scientific knowledge of both; or scientific knowledge of the latter, and of the former a different kind of knowledge; and, further, whether the [25] developed states of knowledge are not innate but at first unnoticed. Now it is strange if we possess them from birth; for it means that we possess apprehensions more accurate than demonstration and fail to notice them. If on the other hand we acquire them and do not previously possess them, how could we apprehend and learn without a basis of preexistent knowledge? For that is impossible, as we used [30] to find in the case of demonstration. So it emerges that neither can we possess them from birth, nor can they come to be in us if we are without knowledge of them to the extent of having no such developed state at all. Therefore we must possess a capacity of some sort, but not such as to rank higher in accuracy than these developed states. And this at least is an obvious characteristic of all animals, for they possess a congenital discriminative capacity which is called [35] sense-perception. But though sense-perception is innate in all animals, in some the sense-impression comes to persist, in others it does not. So animals in which this persistence does not come to be have either no knowledge at all outside the act of perceiving, or no knowledge of objects of which no impression persists; animals in which it does come into being have perception and can continue to retain the sense-impression in the soul: and when such persistence is [100a.1] frequently repeated a further distinction at once arises between those which out of the persistence of such sense-impressions develop a power of systematizing them and those which do not. So out of sense-perception comes to be what we call memory, and out of frequently repeated memories of the same thing develops experience; for a [5] number of memories constitute a single experience. From experience again--i.e. from the universal now stabilized in its entirety within the soul, the one beside the many which is a single identity within them all--originate the skill of the craftsman and the knowledge of the man of science, skill in the sphere of coming to be and science in the sphere of being.

We conclude that these states of knowledge are neither innate in a determinate form, nor developed from other [10] higher states of knowledge, but from sense-perception. It is like a rout in battle stopped by first one man making a stand and then another, until the original formation has been restored. The soul is so constituted as to be capable of this process.

Aristotle: Topica II.4.111b.25 - 30

Moreover, look at the time involved, to see if there be any [111b.25] discrepancy anywhere: e.g. suppose a man to have stated that what is being nourished of necessity grows: for animals are always of necessity being nourished, but they do not always grow. Likewise, also, if he has said that knowing is remembering: for the one is concerned with past time, whereas the other has to do also with the present and the future. For we are said to know things present and future [30] (e.g. that there will be an eclipse), whereas it is impossible to remember anything save what is in the past.

Aristotle: Topica IV.4.125a.5 - 15

You should look, therefore, and see whether he places a term of one [125a.5] kind inside a genus that is not of that kind, e.g. suppose he has said that 'memory' is the 'abiding of knowledge'. For 'abiding' is always found in that which abides, and is used of that, so that the abiding of knowledge also will be found in knowledge. Memory, then, is found in knowledge, seeing that it is the abiding of knowledge. But this is impossible, for memory is always found in the soul. The aforesaid [10] commonplace rule is common to the subject of Accident as well: for it is all the same to say that 'abiding' is the genus of memory, or to allege that it is an accident of it. For if in any way whatever memory be the abiding of knowledge, the same argument in regard to it will apply.

Again, see if he has placed what is a 'state' inside the [15] genus 'activity', or an activity inside the genus 'state', e.g. by defining 'sensation' as 'movement communicated through the body': for sensation is a 'state', whereas movement is an 'activity'. Likewise, also, if he has said that memory is a 'state that is retentive of a conception', for memory is never a state, but rather an activity.

Aristotle: Topica VIII.14.163b.20 - 30

[163b.20] Moreover, get a good stock of definitions: and have those of familiar and primary ideas at your fingers' ends: for it is through these that reasonings are effected. You should try, moreover, to master the heads under which other arguments mostly tend to fall. For just as in geometry it is useful to be practised in the elements, and in arithmetic to have the [25] multiplication table up to ten at one's fingers' ends--and indeed it makes a great difference in one's knowledge of the multiples of other numbers too--likewise also in arguments it is a great advantage to be well up in regard to first principles, and to have a thorough knowledge of premisses at the tip of one's tongue. For just as in a person with a trained memory, a memory of things themselves [30] is immediately caused by the mere mention of their loci, so these habits too will make a man readier in reasoning, because he has his premisses classified before his mind's eye, each under its number. It is better to commit to memory a premiss of general application than an argument: for it is difficult to be even moderately ready with a first principle, or hypothesis.

Aristotle: De Anima III.3.427b.10 - 25

That perceiving and practical thinking are not identical is therefore obvious; for the former is universal in the animal world, the latter is found in only a small division of it. Further, speculative thinking is also distinct from perceiving--I mean that in which we find rightness and [427b.10] wrongness--rightness in prudence, knowledge, true opinion, wrongness in their opposites; for perception of the special objects of sense is always free from error, and is found in all animals, while it is possible to think falsely as well as truly, and thought is found only where there is discourse of reason as well as sensibility. For imagination is different from [15] either perceiving or discursive thinking, though it is not found without sensation, or judgement without it. That this activity is not the same kind of thinking as judgement is obvious. For imagining lies within our own power whenever we wish (e.g. we can call up a picture, as in the practice of mnemonics by the use of mental images), [20] but in forming opinions we are not free: we cannot escape the alternative of falsehood or truth. Further, when we think something to be fearful or threatening, emotion is immediately produced, and so too with what is encouraging; but when we merely imagine we remain as unaffected as persons who are looking at a painting of some dreadful or encouraging scene. Again within the field of judgement [25] itself we find varieties--knowledge, opinion, prudence, and their opposites; of the differences between these I must speak elsewhere.

Aristotle: The Parva Naturalia: De Memoria et Reminiscentia

1.449b.5 - 2.453b.10

Chapter 1

We have, in the next place, to treat of Memory and Remembering, considering its nature, its cause and the part of [449b.5] the soul to which this experience, as well as that of Recollecting, belongs. For the persons who possess a retentive memory are not identical with those who excel in power of recollection; indeed, as a rule, slow people have a good memory, whereas those who are quick-witted and clever are better at recollecting.

We must first form a true conception of the objects of [10] memory, a point on which mistakes are often made. Now to remember the future is not possible, but this is an object of opinion or expectation (and indeed there might be actually a science of expectation, like that of divination, in which some believe); nor is there memory of the present, but only sense-perception. For by the latter we know not the future, nor the past, but the [15] present only. But memory relates to the past. No one would say that he remembers the present, when it is present, e.g. a given white object at the moment when he sees it; nor would one say that he remembers an object of scientific contemplation at the moment when he is actually contemplating it, and has it full before his mind;--of the former he would say only that he perceives it, of the latter only that he knows it. But when one has scientific knowledge, or perception, apart [20] from the actualizations of the faculty concerned, he thus 'remembers' [that the angles of a triangle are together equal to two right angles]; as to the former, that he learned it, or thought it out for himself, as to the latter, that he heard, or saw, it, or had some such sensible experience of it. For whenever one exercises the faculty of remembering, he must say within himself, 'I formerly heard (or otherwise perceived) this' or 'I formerly had this thought'.

Memory is, therefore, neither Perception nor Conception, but a state or affection of one of these, conditioned by lapse of [25] time. As already observed, there is no such thing as memory of the present while present, for the present is object only of perception, and the future, of expectation, but the object of memory is the past. All memory, therefore, implies a time elapsed; consequently only those animals which perceive time remember, and the organ whereby they perceive time is also that whereby they remember.

The subject of 'presentation' has been already considered [30] in our work *de Anima*. Without a presentation intellectual activity is impossible. For there is in such activity an incidental [450a.1] affection identical with one also incidental in geometrical demonstrations. For in the latter case, though we do not for the purpose of the proof make any use of the fact that the quantity in the triangle [for example, which we have drawn] is determinate, we nevertheless draw it determinate in quantity. So likewise when one exerts the intellect [e.g. on the subject of first principles], although the object may not be quantitative, [5] one envisages it as quantitative, though he thinks it in abstraction from quantity; while, on the other hand, if the object of the intellect is essentially of the class of things that are quantitative, but indeterminate, one envisages it as if it had determinate quantity, though subsequently, in thinking it, he abstracts from its determinateness. Why we cannot exercise the intellect on any object absolutely apart from the continuous, or apply it even to non-temporal things unless in [10] connexion with time, is another question. Now, one must cognize magnitude and motion by means of the same faculty by which one cognizes time [i.e. by that which is also the faculty of memory], and the presentation [involved in such cognition] is an affection of the *sensus communis*; whence this follows, viz. that the cognition of these objects [magnitude, motion, time] is effected by the [said *sensus communis*, i.e. the] primary faculty of perception. Accordingly, memory [not merely of sensible, but] even of intellectual objects involves a presentation: hence we may conclude that it belongs to the faculty of intelligence only incidentally, while directly and essentially it belongs to the primary faculty of sense-perception.

Hence not only human beings and the beings which possess [15] opinion or intelligence, but also certain other animals, possess memory. If memory were a function of [pure] intellect, it would not have been as it is an attribute of many of the lower animals, but probably, in that case, no mortal beings would have had memory; since, even as the case stands, it is not an attribute of them all, just because all have not the faculty of perceiving time. Whenever one actually remembers having seen or heard, or learned, something, he includes in this act (as [20] we have already observed) the consciousness of 'formerly'; and the distinction of 'former' and 'latter' is a distinction in time.

Accordingly, if asked, of which among the parts of the soul memory is a function, we reply: manifestly of that part to which 'presentation' appertains;

and all objects capable of being presented [viz. *aistheta*] are immediately and properly objects of memory, while those [viz. *noeta*] which necessarily involve [but *only* involve] presentation are objects of memory [25] incidentally.

One might ask how it is possible that though the affection [the presentation] alone is present, and the [related] fact absent, the latter--that which is not present--is remembered. [This question arises], because it is clear that we must conceive that which is generated through sense-perception in the sentient soul, and in the part of the body which is its seat,--viz. that affection the state whereof we call memory--to be some such thing as a picture. The process of movement [30] [sensory stimulation] involved in the act of perception stamps in, as it were, a sort of impression of the percept, just as [450b.1] persons do who make an impression with a seal. This explains why, in those who are strongly moved owing to passion, or time of life, no mnemonic impression is formed; just as no impression would be formed if the movement of the seal were to impinge on running water; while there are others in whom, owing to the receiving surface being frayed, as [5] happens to [the stucco on] old [chamber] walls, or owing to the hardness of the receiving surface, the requisite impression is not implanted at all. Hence both very young and very old persons are defective in memory; they are in a state of flux, the former because of their growth, the latter, owing to their decay. In like manner, also, both those who are too [10] quick and those who are too slow have bad memories. The former are too soft, the latter too hard [in the texture of their receiving organs], so that in the case of the former the presented image [though imprinted] does not remain in the soul, while on the latter it is not imprinted at all.

But then, if this truly describes what happens in the genesis of memory, [the question stated above arises:] when one remembers, is it this impressed affection that he remembers, or is it the objective thing from which this was derived? If the former, it would follow that we remember nothing which [15] is absent; if the latter, how is it possible that, though perceiving directly only the impression, we remember that absent thing which we do not perceive? Granted that there is in us something like an impression or picture, why should the perception of the mere impression be memory of something else, instead of being related to this impression alone? For when one actually remembers, this impression is what he contemplates, and this is what he perceives. How then does he remember what is not present? One might as well suppose it possible also to see or hear that which is not present. In reply, we suggest that this very thing is quite conceivable, [20] nay, actually occurs in experience. A picture painted on a panel is at once a picture and a likeness: that is, while one and the same, it is both of these, although the 'being' of both is not the same, and one may contemplate it either as a picture, or as a likeness. Just in the same way e have to conceive that the mnemonic presentation within us is something which [25] by itself is merely an object of contemplation, while, in relation to something else, it is also a presentation of that other thing. In so far as it is regarded in itself, it is only an object of contemplation, or a presentation; but when considered as relative to something else, e.g., as its likeness, it is also a mnemonic token. Hence, whenever the residual sensory process implied by it is actualized in consciousness, if the soul perceives this in so far as it is something absolute, it appears to occur as a mere thought or presentation; but if the soul perceives it *qua* related to something else, then,--just as when one contemplates the painting in the picture as being a likeness, and without having [at the moment] seen [30] the actual Koriskos, contemplates it as a likeness of Koriskos, and in that case the experience involved in this contemplation [451a.1] of it [as relative] is different from what one has when he contemplates it simply as a painted figure--[so in the case of memory we have the analogous difference, for], of the objects in the soul, the one [the unrelated object] presents itself simply as a thought, but the other [the related object], just because, as in the painting, it is a likeness, presents itself as a mnemonic token.

We can now understand why it is that sometimes, when we have such processes, based on some former act of perception, occurring in the soul, we do not know whether this really [5] implies our having had perceptions corresponding to them, and we doubt whether the case is or is not one of memory. But occasionally it happens that [while thus doubting] we get a sudden idea and recollect that we heard or saw something formerly. This [occurrence of the 'sudden idea'] happens whenever, from contemplating a mental object as absolute, one changes his point of view, and regards it as relative to something else.

The opposite [sc. to the case of those who at first do not recognize their phantasms as mnemonic] also occurs, as happened in the cases of Antipheron of Oreus and others suffering [10] from mental derangement; for they were accustomed to speak of their mere phantasms as facts of their past experience, and as if remembering them. This takes place whenever one contemplates what is not a likeness as if it were a likeness.

Mnemonic exercises aim at preserving one's memory of something by repeatedly reminding him of it; which implies nothing else [on the learner's part] than the frequent contemplation of something [viz. the 'mnemonic', whatever it may be] as a likeness, and not as out of relation.

[15] As regards the question, therefore, what memory or remembering is, it has now been shown that it is the state of a presentation, related as a likeness to that of which it is a presentation; and as to the question of which of the faculties within us memory is a function, [it has been shown] that it is a function of the primary faculty of sense-perception, i.e. of that faculty whereby we perceive time.

Chapter 2

Next comes the subject of Recollection, in dealing with which we must assume as fundamental the truths elicited [20] above in our introductory discussions. For recollection is not the 'recovery' or 'acquisition' of memory; since at the instant when one at first learns [a fact of science] or experiences [a particular fact of sense], he does not thereby 'recover' a memory, inasmuch as none has preceded, nor does he acquire one *ab initio*. It is only at the instant when the aforesaid state or affection is implanted in the soul that memory exists, and therefore [25] memory is not itself implanted concurrently with the continuous implantation of the [original] sensory experience.

Further: at the very individual and concluding instant when first [the sensory experience or scientific knowledge] has been completely implanted, there is then already established in the person affected the [sensory] affection, or the scientific knowledge (if one ought to apply the term 'scientific knowledge' to the [mnemonic] state or affection; and indeed one may well remember, in the 'incidental' sense, some of the things which are properly objects of scientific knowledge); but to remember, strictly and properly speaking, is an activity which will not be immanent until the [30] original experience has undergone lapse of time. For one remembers now what one saw or otherwise experienced formerly; the moment of the original experience and the moment of the memory of it are never identical.

Again, [even when time has elapsed, and one can be said really to have acquired memory, this is not necessarily recollection, for firstly] it is obviously possible, without any [451b.1] present act of recollection, to remember as a continued consequence of the original perception or other experience; whereas when [after an interval of obliviscence] one recovers some scientific knowledge which he had before, or some perception, or some other experience, the state of which we above declared to be memory, it is then, and then only, that this recovery may amount to a recollection of any of the things aforesaid. But, [though, as observed above, remembering does [5] not necessarily imply recollecting], recollecting always implies remembering, and actualized memory follows [upon the successful act of recollecting].

But secondly, even the assertion that recollection is the reinstatement in consciousness of something which was there before but had disappeared requires qualification. This assertion may be true, but it may also be false; for the same person may twice learn [from some teacher] or twice discover [i.e. excogitate], the same fact. Accordingly, the act of recollecting ought [in its definition] to be distinguished from these acts; i.e. recollecting must imply in those who recollect the presence of some spring over and above that from which they originally learn.

[10] Acts of recollection, as they occur in experience, are due to the fact that one movement has by nature another that succeeds it in regular order.

If this order be necessary, whenever a subject experiences the former of two movements thus connected, it will [invariably] experience the latter; if, however, the order be not necessary, but customary, only in the majority of cases will the subject experience the latter of the two movements. But it is a fact that there are some movements, by a single experience of which persons take the impress of custom more deeply [15] than they do by experiencing others many times; hence upon seeing some things but once we remember them better than others which we may have seen frequently.

Whenever, therefore, we are recollecting, we are experiencing certain [read *tinas* with Freudenthal] of the antecedent movements until finally we experience the one after which customarily comes that which we seek. This explains why we hunt up the series [of *kineseis*], having started in thought either from a present intuition or some other, and from something either similar, or contrary, to what we seek, or else from that which is contiguous with it. Such is the empirical ground [20] of the process of recollection; for the mnemonic movements involved in these starting-points are in some cases identical, in others, again, simultaneous, with those of the idea we seek, while in others they comprise a portion of them, so that the remnant which one experienced after that portion [and which still requires to be excited in memory] is comparatively small.

Thus, then, it is that persons seek to recollect, and thus, too, it is that they recollect even without the effort of seeking to do so, viz. when the movement implied in recollection has [25] supervened on some other which is its condition. For, as a rule, it is when antecedent movements of the classes here described have first been excited, that the particular movement implied in recollection follows. We need not examine a series of which the beginning and end lie far apart, in order to see how [by recollection] we remember; one in which they lie near one another will serve equally well. For it is clear that the method is in each case the same, that is, one hunts up the objective series, without any previous search or previous recollection. For [there is, besides the natural order, viz. the order of the *pragmata*, or events of the primary experience, also a customary order, and] by the effect of custom the mnemonic movements tend to succeed one another in a certain [30] order. Accordingly, therefore, when one wishes to recollect, this is what he will do: he will try to obtain a beginning of movement whose sequel shall be the movement which he desires to reawaken. This explains why attempts at recollection succeed soonest and best when they start from [452a.1] a beginning [of some objective series]. For, in order of succession, the mnemonic movements are to one another as the objective facts [from which they are derived]. Accordingly, things arranged in a fixed order, like the successive demonstrations in geometry, are easy to remember [or recollect], while badly arranged subjects are remembered with difficulty.

Recollecting differs also in this respect from relearning, [5] that one who recollects will be able, somehow, to move, solely by his own effort, to the term next after the starting-point. When one cannot do this of himself, but only by external assistance, he no longer remembers [i.e. he has totally forgotten, and therefore of course cannot recollect]. It often happens that, though a person cannot recollect at the moment, yet by seeking he can do so, and discovers what he seeks. This he succeeds in doing by setting up many movements, until finally he excites one of a kind which will have for its sequel the fact he wishes to recollect. For remembering [10] [which is the *condicio sine qua non* of recollecting] is the existence, potentially, in the mind of a movement capable of stimulating it to the desired movement, and this, as has been said, in such a way that the person should be moved [prompted to recollection] from within himself, i.e. in consequence of movements wholly contained within himself.

But one must get hold of a starting-point. This explains why it is that persons are supposed to recollect sometimes by starting from mnemonic loci. The cause is that they pass swiftly in thought from one point to another, e.g. from milk [15] to white, from white to mist, and thence to moist, from which one remembers Autumn [the 'season of mists'], if this be the season he is trying to recollect.

It seems true in general that the middle point also among all things is a good mnemonic starting-point from which to reach any of them. For if one does not recollect before, he will do so when he has come to this, or, if not, nothing can help him; as, e.g. if one were to have in mind the numerical series [20] denoted by the symbols A, B, C, D, E, F, G, H, I. For, if he does not remember what he wants at E, then at E he remembers I; because from E movement in either direction is possible, to D or to F. But, if it is not for one of these that he is searching, he will remember [what he is searching for] when he has come to C, if he is searching for H or G. But if [it is] not [for H or G that he is searching, but for one of the terms that remain], he will remember by going to A, and so in all cases [in which one starts from a middle point]. '[25] The cause of one's sometimes recollecting and sometimes not, though starting from the same point, is, that from the same starting-point a movement can be made in several directions, as, for instance, from C to G or to D. If, then, the mind has not [when starting from E] moved in an old path [i.e. one in which it moved when first having the objective experience, and that, therefore, in which un-'ethized' *phusis* would have it again move], it tends to move to the more customary; for [the mind having, by chance or otherwise, *missed* moving in the 'old' way] Custom now assumes the role of Nature. Hence the rapidity with which we recollect what we frequently think about. For as regular sequence of events is in accordance with nature, so, too, regular sequence is observed in the actualization of *kineseis* [in consciousness], and here frequency tends to produce [the regularity of] nature. [30] And since in the realm of nature occurrences take place which [452b.1] are even contrary to nature, or fortuitous, the same happens *a fortiori* in the sphere swayed by custom, since in this sphere natural law is not similarly established. Hence it is that [from the same starting-point] the mind receives an impulse to move sometimes in the required direction, and at other times otherwise, [doing the latter] particularly when something else somehow deflects the mind from the right direction and attracts it to itself. This last consideration explains too [5] how it happens that, when we want to remember a name, we remember one somewhat like it, indeed, but blunder in reference to [i.e. in pronouncing] the one we intended.

Thus, then, recollection takes place.

But the point of capital importance is that [for the purpose of recollection] one should cognize, determinately or indeterminately, the time-relation [of that which he wishes to recollect]. There is,--let it be taken as a fact,--something by which one distinguishes a greater and a smaller time; and it is reasonable to think that one does this in a way analogous to that in which one discerns [spatial] magnitudes. For it [10] is not by the mind's reaching out towards them, as some say a visual ray from the eye does [in seeing], that one thinks of large things at a distance in space (for even if they are not there, one may similarly think them); but one does so by a proportionate mental movement. For there are in the mind the like figures and movements [i.e. 'like' to those of objects and events]. Therefore, when one thinks the greater objects, in what will his thinking those differ from his thinking the smaller? [In nothing,] because all the internal though smaller are as it were proportional to the external. Now, as we may assume within a person something proportional [15] to the forms [of distant magnitudes], so, too, we may doubtless assume also something else proportional to their distances. As, therefore, if one has [psychically] the movement in AB, BE, he constructs in thought [i.e. knows objectively] CD, since AC and CD bear equal ratios respectively [to AB and BE], [so he who recollects also proceeds]. Why then does he construct CD rather than FG? Is it not because as AC is to AB, so is H to I? These movements therefore [20] [sc. in AB, BE, and in H:I] he has simultaneously. But if he wishes to construct to thought FG, he has in mind BE in like manner as before [when constructing CD], but now, instead of [the movements of the ratio] H:I, he has in mind [those of the ratio] J : K; for J : K: : FA : BA.

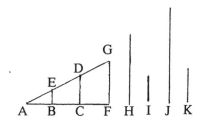

When, therefore, the 'movement' corresponding to the object and that corresponding to its time concur, then one actually remembers. If one supposes [himself to move in these different but concurrent ways] without really doing so, [25] he supposes himself to remember. For one may be mistaken, and think that he remembers when he really does not. But it is not possible, conversely, that when one actually remembers he should not suppose himself to remember, but should remember unconsciously. For remembering, as we have conceived it, essentially implies consciousness of itself. If, however, the movement corresponding to the objective fact takes place without that corresponding to the time, or, if the latter takes place without the former, one does not remember.

[30] The movement answering to the time is of two kinds. Sometimes in remembering a fact one has no determinate [453a.1] time-notion of it, no such notion as that, e.g., he did something or other on the day before yesterday; while in other cases he has a determinate notion of the time. Still, even though one does not remember with actual determination of the time, he genuinely remembers, none the less. Persons are wont to say that they remember [something], but yet do not know when [it occurred, as happens] whenever they do not know determinately the exact length of time implied in the 'when'.

It has been already stated that those who have a good [5] memory are not identical with those who are quick at recollecting. But the act of recollecting differs from that of remembering, not only chronologically, but also in this, that many also of the other animals [as well as man] have memory, but, of all that we are acquainted with, none, we venture to say, except man, shares in the faculty of recollection. The cause of this is that recollection is, as it were, a mode of inference. [10] For he who endeavours to recollect *infers* that he formerly saw, or heard, or had some such experience, and the process [by which he succeeds in recollecting] is, as it were, a sort of investigation. But to investigate in this way belongs naturally to those animals alone which are also endowed with the faculty of deliberation; [which proves what was said above], for deliberation is a form of inference.

That the affection is corporeal, i.e. that recollection is a [15] searching for an 'image' in a corporeal substrate, is proved by the fact that in some persons, when, despite the most strenuous application of thought, they have been unable to recollect, it [viz. the *anamnesis* = the effort at recollection] excites a feeling of discomfort, which, even though they abandon the effort at recollection, persists in them none the less; and especially in persons of melancholic temperament. For these are most powerfully moved by presentations. [20] The reason why the effort of recollection is not under the control of their will is that, as those who throw a stone cannot stop it at their will when thrown, so he who tries to recollect and 'hunts' [after an idea] sets up a process in a material part, [that] in which resides the affection. Those who have moisture around that part which is the centre of sense-perception suffer most discomfort of this kind. For when once the moisture has been set in motion it is not easily [25] brought to rest, until the idea which was sought for has again presented itself, and thus the movement has found a straight course. For a similar reason bursts of anger or fits of terror, when once they have excited such motions, are not at once allayed, even though the angry or terrified persons [by efforts of will] set up counter motions, but the passions continue to move them on, in the same direction as at first, in opposition to such counter motions. The affection resembles also that in the case of words, tunes, or sayings, whenever one of them has become inveterate on the lips. People give them up and [30] resolve to avoid them; yet again and again they find themselves humming the forbidden air, or using the prohibited word.

[453b.1] Those whose upper parts are abnormally large, as is the case with dwarfs, have abnormally weak memory, as compared with their opposites, because of the great weight which they have resting upon the organ of perception, and because their mnemonic movements are, from the very first, not able to keep true to a course, but are dispersed, and because, in the effort [5] at recollection, these movements do not easily find a direct onward path. Infants and very old persons have bad memories, owing to the amount of movement going on within them; for the latter are in process of rapid decay, the former in process of vigorous growth; and we may add that children, until considerably advanced in years, are dwarf-like in their bodily structure. Such then is our theory as regards memory and remembering--their nature, and the particular

71

organ of the soul by which animals remember; also as regards recollection, [10] its formal definition, and the manner and causes of its performance.

Aristotle: The Parva Naturalia: De Somniis 1.458b.20 - 25

So, too, in sleep we sometimes have thoughts other than the mere phantasms immediately before our minds. This would be manifest to any one who should attend and try, immediately on arising from sleep, to remember [his dreaming experiences]. There are cases of persons [458b.20] who have seen such dreams, those, for example, who believe themselves to be mentally arranging a given list of subjects according to the mnemonic rule. They frequently find themselves engaged in something else besides the dream, viz. in setting a phantasm which they envisage into its mnemonic position. Hence it is plain that not every 'phantasm' in sleep is a mere dream-image, and that the further thinking which we [25] perform then is due to an exercise of the faculty of opinion.

Aristotle: The Parva Naturalia: De Somno et Vigilia 2.465a.25

Some persons move in their sleep, and perform many acts like waking. acts, but not without a phantasm or an exercise of sense perceptions; for a dream is in a certain way a sense impression. But of them we have to speak later on. Why it is that persons when aroused to remember their dreams, but do not remember these acts which are like waking acts, has been already explained in the work 'On Problems'.

Aristotle: Historia Animalium I.1.488b.20 - 25

[488b.20] Further, some are crafty and mischievous, as the fox; some are spirited and affectionate and fawning, as the dog; others are easy-tempered and easily domesticated, as the elephant; others are cautious and watchful, as the goose; others are jealous and self-conceited, as the peacock. But of all animals man alone is capable of deliberation.

[25] Many animals have memory, and are capable of instruction; but no other creature except man can recall the past at will.

With regard to the several genera of animals, particulars as to their habits of life and modes of existence will be discussed more fully by and by.

Aristotle: De Motu Animalium 8.701b.35 - 8.702a.5

But to return, the object we pursue or avoid in the field of action is, as has been explained, the original of movement [701b.35], and upon the conception and imagination of this there necessarily follows a change in the temperature of the body. For what is painful we avoid, what is pleasing we pursue. We are, however, unconscious of what happens in the minute parts; still anything painful or pleasing is [702a.1] generally speaking accompanied by a definite change of temperature in the body. One may see this by considering the affections. Blind courage and panic fears, erotic motions, and the rest of the corporeal affections, pleasant and painful, are all accompanied by a change of temperature, some in a particular member, others in the body generally. So, memories and anticipations, using as it were the reflected images of these pleasures and pains, are now more and now less causes of the same changes of temperature.

Aristotle: Physiognomonica 3.808b.10

A Good Memory is signified when the upper parts are disproportionately small, and are delicate and tolerably [808b.10] well covered with flesh.

Aristotle: Metaphysica I.1.980a.25 - I.1.980b.25

All men by nature desire to know. An indication of this is the delight we take in our senses; for even apart from their usefulness they are loved for themselves; and above all others the sense of sight. For not only with a view to action, but even when we are not going to do anything, we prefer [980a.25] sight to almost everything else. The reason is that this, most of all the senses, makes us know and brings to light many differences between things.

By nature animals are born with the faculty of sensation, and from sensation memory is produced in some of them, though not in others. And therefore the former are more [980b.1] intelligent and apt at learning than those which cannot remember; those which are incapable of hearing sounds are intelligent though they cannot be taught, e.g. the bee, and any other race of animals that may be like it; and those which besides memory have this sense of hearing, can be taught.

The animals other than man live by appearances and [25] and memories, and have but little of connected experience; but the human race lives also by art and reasonings. And from memory experience is produced in men; for many memories of the same thing produce finally the capacity for a single experience.

Aristotle: Magna Moralia I.5.1185b.1 - 5

First, then, we ought to speak about the soul in which [1185b.1] it resides, not to say what the soul is (for to speak about that is another matter), but to divide it in outline. Now the soul is, as we say, divided into two parts, the rational and the irrational. In the rational part, then, there resides [5] wisdom, readiness of wit, philosophy, aptitude to learn, memory, and so on; but in the irrational those which are called the virtues--temperance, justice, courage, and such other moral states as are held to be praiseworthy. For it is in respect of these that we are called praiseworthy; but no one is praised for the virtues of the rational part.

Aristotle: Ethica Eudemia VII.14.1248b.1

For the moving principle seems to become stronger when the reasoning power is relaxed. So the blind remember better, their memory being freed from concern with the visible.

Aristotle: De Virtutibus et Vitiis 4.1250a.30 - 35

[30] To prudence belongs right decision, right judgement as to what is good and bad and all in life that is to be chosen and avoided, noble use of all the goods that belong to us, correctness in social intercourse, the grasping of the right moment, the sagacious use of word and deed, the possession [35] of experience of all that is useful. Memory, experience, tact, good judgement, sagacity--each of these either arises from prudence or accompanies it. Or possibly some of them are, as it were, subsidiary causes of prudence (such as experience and memory), while others are, as it were, parts of it, e.g. good judgement and sagacity.

Aristotle: Rhetorica II.1390a.10

They live by memory rather than by hope; for what is left to them of life is but little as compared with the long past; and hope is of the future, memory of the past. This, again, is the cause of their loquacity; they are continually talking of the past, because they enjoy [10] remembering it.

MARCUS TULLIUS CICERO

106 B. C. - 43 B. C.

From: *De Oratore*. Translated by E. W. Sutton. Completed with an introduction by H. Rackham. The Loeb Classical Library, published by William Heinemann, 1942.

Tusculan Disputations. Translated by J. E. King. The Loeb Classical Library, published by William Heinemann, 1927.

Background: Cicero was a statesman, philosopher and orator in the final years of the Roman republic. During periods of enforced retirement from public office he was a prolific writer. He promoted the ideal of the statesman-philosopher who uses knowledge to guide human affairs. The best preparation for this role he saw as a liberal education in which the art of persuasion was developed through the study of philosophy and rhetoric. Memory training was an integral part of rhetoric.

Supplementary readings:

Hunt, H. A. K. (1954). *The Humanism of Cicero*. Melbourne: Melbourne University Press.

Petersson, T. (1963). *Cicero: A Biography*. New York: Biblo & Tannen.

Yates, F. A. (1966). *The Art of Memory*. London: Routledge & Kegan Paul.

CICERO

Table of Contents

Explanation of contents: Both works are divided, in the Loeb editions, into books (large Roman numerals), chapters (small Roman numerals) and sections (Arabic numerals). For example, the first excerpt, "De Oratore" I.iv.16, begins in Book I, chapter iv, section 16. Beginnings and ends of sections are not indicated exactly in the Loeb edition and so the location indicated in the text here is approximate.

But the truth is that this oratory is a greater thing, and has its sources in more arts and branches of study, than people suppose.

[v] For, where the number of students is very great, the supply of masters of the very best, the quality of natural ability outstanding, the variety of issues unlimited, the prizes open to eloquence exceedingly splendid, what else could anyone think to be the cause, unless it be the really incredible vastness and difficulty of the subject? [17] To begin with, a knowledge of very many matters must be grasped, without which oratory is but an empty and ridiculous swirl of verbiage: and the distinctive style has to be formed, not only by the choice of words, but also by the arrangement of the same; and all the mental emotions, with which nature has endowed the human race, are to be intimately understood, because it is in calming or kindling the feelings of the audience that the full power and science of oratory are to be brought into play. To this there should be added a certain humour, flashes of wit, the culture befitting a gentleman, and readiness and terseness alike in repelling and in delivering the attack, the whole being combined with a delicate charm and urbanity. [18] Further, the complete history of the past and a store of precedents must be retained in the memory, nor may a knowledge of statute law and our national law in general be omitted. And why should I go on to describe the speaker's delivery? That needs to be controlled by bodily carriage, gesture, play of features and changing intonation of voice; and how important that is wholly by itself, the actor's trivial art and the stage proclaim; for there, although all are labouring to regulate the expression, the voice, and the movements of the body, everyone knows how few actors there are, or ever have been, whom we could bear to watch! What need to speak of that universal treasure-house the memory? Unless this faculty be placed in charge of the ideas and phrases which have been thought out and well weighed, even though as conceived by the orator they were of the highest excellence, we know that they will all be wasted.

Cicero: De Oratore II.lxxiv.299 - 301

But I am not at the moment talking about some outstanding and exceptional ability but about ordinary average capacity. For instance, we are told that the famous Athenian Themistocles was endowed with wisdom and genius on a scale quite surpassing belief; and it is said that a certain learned and highly accomplished person went to him and offered to impart to him the science of mnemonics, which was then being introduced for the first time; and that when Themistocles asked what precise result that science was capable of achieving, the professor asserted that it would enable him to remember everything; and Themistocles replied that he would be doing him a greater kindness if he taught him to forget what he wanted than if he taught him to remember. [300] Do you observe what mental force and penetration the man possessed, what power and range of intellect? Inasmuch as his answer brings home to us that nothing that had once been introduced into his mind had ever been able to pass out of it, inasmuch as he would rather have been able to forget something that he did not wish to remember than to remember everything that he had once heard or seen. But this reply of Themistocles must not cause us to neglect the training of the memory, and the exceptional intellectual powers of Crassus must not make us ignore the caution and nervousness in pleading a case that I assigned to myself; for neither Themistocles nor Crassus attributed any competence to me, but indicated competence of their own. [301]

Cicero: De Oratore II.lxxxvi.351 - lxxxviii.360

[351] "Oh, as for that," said Antony, "the amount I shall have left to you will be for you to decide; if you want complete candour, what I leave to you is the whole subject, but if you want me to keep up the pretence, it is for you to consider how you may satisfy our friends here. But to return to the subject," he continued, "I am not myself as clever as Themistocles was, so as to prefer the science of forgetting to that of remembering; and I am grateful to the famous Simonides of Ceos, who is said to have first invented the science of mnemonics. [352] There is a story that Simonides was dining at the house of a wealthy nobleman named Scopas at Crannon in Thessaly, and chanted a lyric poem which he had composed in honour of his host, in which he followed the custom of the poets by including for decorative purposes a long passage referring to Castor and Pollux; whereupon Scopas with excessive meanness told him he would pay him half the fee agreed on for the poem, and if he liked he might apply for the balance to his sons of Tyndareus, as they had gone halves in the panegyric. [353] The story runs that a little later a message was brought to Simonides to go outside, as two young men were standing at the door who earnestly requested him to come out; so he rose from his seat and went out, and could not see anybody; but in the interval of his absence the roof of the hall where Scopas was giving the banquet fell in, crushing Scopas himself and his relations underneath the ruins and killing them; and when their friends wanted to bury them but were altogether unable to know them apart as they had been completely crushed, the story goes that Simonides was enabled by his recollection of the place in which each of them had been reclining at table to identify them for separate interment; and that this circumstance suggested to him the discovery of the truth that the best aid to clearness of memory consists in orderl arrangement. [354] He inferred that persons desiring to train this faculty must select localities and form mental images of the facts they wish to remember and store those images in the localities, with the result that the arrangement of the localities will preserve the order of the facts, and the images of the facts will designate the facts themselves, and we shall employ the localities and images respectively as a wax writing tablet and the letters written on it. [lxxxvii.355] But what business is it of mine to specify the value to a speaker and the usefulness and effectiveness of memory? of retaining the information given you when you were briefed and the opinions you yourself have formed? of having all your ideas firmly planted in your mind and all your resources of vocabulary neatly arranged? of giving such close attention to the instructions of your client and to the speech of the opponent you have to answer that they may seem not just to pour what they say into your ears but to imprint it on your mind? Consequently only people with a powerful memory know what they are going to say and for

78

how long they are going to speak and in what style, what points they have already answered and what still remains; and they also can remember from other cases many arguments which they have previously advanced and many which they have heard from other people. [356] And consequently for my own part I confess that the chief source of this endowment, as of all the things I have spoken of before, is nature; but the efficacy of the whole of this science, or perhaps I should say pseudoscience, of rhetoric, is not that it wholly originates and engenders something no part of which is already present in our minds, but that it fosters and strengthens things that have already sprung to birth within us; [357] though nevertheless hardly anybody exists who has so keen a memory that he can retain the order of all the words or sentences without having arranged and noted his facts, nor yet is anybody so dull-witted that habitual practice in this will not give him some assistance. It has been sagaciously discerned by Simonides or else discovered by some other person, that the most complete pictures are formed in our minds of the things that have been conveyed to them and imprinted on them by the senses, but that the keenest of all our senses is the sense of sight, and that consequently perceptions received by the ears or by reflexion can be most easily retained in the mind if they are also conveyed to our minds by the mediation of the eyes, with the result that things not seen and not lying in the field of visual discernment are earmarked by a sort of outline and image and shape so that we keep hold of as it were by an act of sight things that we can scarely embrace by an act of thought. [358] But these forms and bodies, like all the things that come under our view require an abode, inasmuch as a material object without a locality is inconceivable. Consequently (in order that I may not be prolix and tedious on a subject that is well known and familiar) one must employ a large number of localities which must be clear and defined and at moderate intervals apart, and images that are effective and sharply outlined and distinctive, with the capacity of encountering and speedily penetrating the mind; the ability to use these will be supplied by practice, which engenders habit, and by marking off similar words with an inversion and alteration of their cases or a transference from species to genus, and by representing a whole concept by the image of a single word, on the system and method of a consummate painter distinguishing the positions of objects by modifying their shapes.

[lxxxviii.359] But a memory for words, which for us is less essential, is given distinctness by a greater variety of images; for there are many words which serve as joints connecting the limbs of the sentence, and these cannot be formed by any use of simile--of these we have to model images for constant employment; but a memory for things is the special property of the orator--this we can imprint on our minds by a skillful arrangement of the several masks that represent them, so that we may grasp ideas by means of images and their order by means of localities. [360] Nor is it true, as unscientific people assert, that memory is crushed beneath a weight of images and even what might have been retained by nature unassisted is obscured; for I have myself met eminent people with almost superhuman powers of memory, Charmadas at Athens and Metrodorus of Scepsis in Asia, who is said to be still living, each of whom used to say that he wrote down things he wanted to remember in certain 'localities' in his possession by means of images, just as if he were inscribing letters on wax.

It follows that this practice cannot be used to draw out the memory if no memory has been given to us by nature, but it can undoubtedly summon it to come forth if it is in hiding.

Cicero: Tusculan Disputations I.xxiv.56 - xxv.61

In the first place, soul has memory, a memory too without limit of things without number; and this Plato wishes to make the recollection of a previous life. For in the book entitled *Meno* Socrates asks a little lad certain geometrical questions about the measurement of the square. To these questions the boy makes answer as a boy would, yet the questions are so easy that by giving his answers step by step he gets to the same conclusion as he would if he had learnt geometry: this Socrates regards as proof that learning is nothing but recollecting. This subject he develops too with much greater care in the conversation which he held on the very day he departed this life; for he there teaches that anyone, though to all appearance totally ignorant, shows in answer to skillful questioning that he is not at the time learning a lesson but taking knowledge of things afresh by remembrance; indeed in no other way was it possible for us to possess from childhood [57] such a number of important ideas, innate and as it were impressed on our souls and called *ennoiai*, unless the soul, before it had entered the body, had been active in acquiring knowledge. And since there is no true existence in any sensible object, as Plato [58] everywhere argues--for he thinks that nothing that has a beginning and an ending exists, and only that exists which is always constant to its nature: this he calls [in Greek] *idea* and we "idea" -- the soul in the prison-house of the body could not have apprehended ideas; it brought the knowledge with it: consequently our feeling of wonder at the extent of our knowledge is removed. Yet the soul, when suddenly shifted into such an unaccustomed and disordered dwelling-place, does not clearly see ideas, but when it has composed and recovered itself it apprehends them by remembrance. Thus, according to Plato, learning is nothing but recollecting.

But for my part I wonder at memory in a still greater degree. For what is it that enables us to remember, or what character has it, or what is its origin? I am not inquiring into the powers of memory which, it is said, Simonides possessed, Theodectes [59], or the powers of Cineas, whom Pyrrhus sent as ambassador to the Senate, or the powers in recent days of Charmadas, or of Scepsius Metrodorus, who was lately alive, or the powers of our own Hortensius. I am speaking of the average memory of man, and chiefly of those who are engaged in some higher branch of study and art, whose mental capacity it is hard to estimate, so much do they remember.

[xxv.60] What then is the object of what I am saying? I think it must be clear by now what the power so displayed is and whence it comes. Certainly it is not a quality of heart or blood or brain or atoms. Whether it is of breath or fire I know not, and I am not ashamed, as those others were, of admitting my ignorance where I am ignorant: this I do say, if I could make any other assertions on a subject of such difficulty. I should be ready to swear that, whether soul is breath or fire, it is divine. For consider, I pray, can you really think that it is from earth, where our atmosphere is so watery and foggy, that the prodigious power of memory has originated or been formed? If you do not see the right answer to the question, yet you see the problem it involves; if you do not see even that much, yet surely you see its importance. What then? Do we think that there is in the soul a sort of roominess into which the things we remember can be poured as if into a kind of vessel? That would be ridiculous; what can we understand as the bottom or shape of such a soul, or what room at all can it have that is adequate? Or do we think that like wax the soul has marks impressed upon it and that memory consists of the traces of things registered in [61] the mind? What can be the traces of words, of actual objects, what further could be the enormous space adequate to the representation of such a mass of material?

Cicero: Tusculan Disputations I.xxvi.65 - I.xxvii.68

A power able to bring about such a number of important results is to my mind wholly divine. For what is the memory of facts and words? What further is discovery? Assuredly nothing can be comprehended even in God of greater value than this. I do not think the gods delight in ambrosia or nectar or Hebe filling the cups, and I do not listen to Homer who says that Ganymede was carrie off by the gods for his beauty to serve as cup-bearer to Jupiter: there was no just reason why such cruel wrong should be inflicted on Laomedon. Homer imagined these things and attributed human feelings to the gods: I had rather he had attributed divine feelings to us. But what do we understand by divine attributes? Activity, wisdom, discovery, memory. Therefore the soul is, as I say, divine, as Euripides dares to say, God: and in fact, if God is either air or fire, so also is the soul of man: for just as the heavenly nature is free from earth and moisture, so the human soul is without trace of either element. But if there is a kind of fifth nature, first introduced by Aristotle, this is the nature of both gods and souls.

This view we have supported and given the sense of in these precise words in the *Consolatio*: [xxvii.66] "No beginning of souls can be discovered on earth; for there is no trace of blending or combination in souls or any particle that could seem born or fashioned from earth, nothing even that partakes either of moist or airy or fiery. For in these elements there is nothing to possess the power of memory, thought, reflection, nothing capable of retaining the past, or foreseeing the future and grasping the present, and these capacities are nothing but divine: and never will there be found any source from which they can come to men except from God. [67] There is then a peculiar essential character belonging to the soul, distinct from these common and well-known elements. Accordingly, whatever it is that is conscious, that is wise, that is active must be heavenly and divine and for that reason eternal. And indeed God Himself who is comprehended by us, can be comprehended in no other way save as a mind unfettered and free, severed from all perishable matter, conscious of all and moving all and self-endowed with perpetual motion." Of such sort and of the same nature is the human mind.

Where then and what is such a mind?--Where and what is yours? Can you say? Or if I do not possess all the faculties for comprehension I could have wished, will you not give me leave to use even those which I have?--The soul has not the power of itself to see itself, but, like the eye, the soul, though it does not see itself, yet discerns other things. But it does not see, what is a matter of very little moment, its own shape,--and yet possibly it may do that too, but still no matter--assuredly it sees its power, wisdom, memory, rapidity of movement. [68] These things are of real moment, these are divine, these are everlasting. About its outward aspect or place of habitation we need not even enquire.

ANONYMOUS

RHETORICA AD HERENNIUM

c. 86 B.C.

From: *(Cicero) Ad G. Herennium de Ratione Dicendi*. Translated by H. Caplan. The Loeb Classical Library, published by William Heinemann, 1954.

This work, addressed to Gaius Herennius, has sometimes been attributed to Cicero. While we do not know who wrote *Ad Herennium*, we do know a little about the author. The author was a teacher of rhetoric in Rome in the first century B.C. He was inspired by Cicero's interest in rhetoric and the application of mnemonics to rhetoric. This brief work is the most important classical document on the pragmatic aspects of memory. The sources on which it is based have not survived and so it became the main source of information about classical practices for Renaissance scholars who were interested in pragmatic aspects of memory.

Supplementary reading:

Yates, F. A. (1966). *The Art of Memory*. London: Routledge & Kegan Paul.

ANONYMOUS

RHETORICA AD HERENNIUM

Table of Contents

Explanation of contents: "Ad Herennium" is divided by book (large Roman numerals), chapter (small Roman numerals) and section numbers (Arabic numerals) in Caplan's translation. For example I.x.17 refers to Book I, chapter x, section 17.

Anonymous: Ad Herennium

To Gaius Herennius: On the Theory of Public Speaking

I.i.1 - I.ii.2

[1] My private affairs keep me so busy that I can hardly find enough leisure to devote to study, and the little that is vouchsafed to me I have usually preferred to spend on philosophy. Yet your desire, Gaius Herennius, has spurred me to compose a work on the Theory of Public Speaking, lest you should suppose that in a matter which concerns you I either lacked the will or shirked the labour. And I have undertaken this project the more gladly because I knew that you had good grounds in wishing to learn rhetoric, for it is true that copiousness and facility in expression bear abundant fruit, if controlled by proper knowledge and a strict discipline of the mind.

That is why I have omitted to treat those topics which, for the sake of futile self-assertion, Greek writers have adopted. For they, from fear of appearing to know too little, have gone in quest of notions irrelevant to the art, in order that the art might seem more difficult to understand. I, on the other hand, have treated those topics which seemed pertinent to the theory of public speaking. I have not been moved by hope of gain or desire for glory, as the rest have been, in undertaking to write, but have done so in order that, by my painstaking work, I may gratify your wish. To avoid prolixity, I shall now begin my discussion of the subject, as soon as I have given you this one injunction: Theory without continuous practice in speaking is of little avail; from this you may understand that the precepts of theory here offered ought to be applied in practice.

[ii.2] The task of the public speaker is to discuss capably those matters which law and custom have fixed for the uses of citizenship, and to secure as far as possible the agreement of his hearers. There are three kinds of causes which the speaker must treat: Epideictic, Deliberative, and Judicial. The epideictic kind is devoted to the praise or censure of some particular person. The deliberative consists in the discussion of policy and embraces persuasion and dissuasion. The judicial is based on legal controversy, and comprises criminal prosecution or civil suit, and defence.

Now I shall explain what faculties the speaker should possess, and then show the proper means of treating these causes.

Anonymous: Ad Herennium I.ii.3

The speaker, then, should possess the faculties of Invention, Arrangement, Style, Memory and Delivery. Invention is the devising of matter, true or plausible, that would make the case convincing. Arrangement is the ordering and distribution of the matter, making clear the place to which each thing is to be assigned. Style is the adaptation of suitable words and sentences to the matter devised. Memory is the firm retention in the mind of the matter, words, and arrangement. Delivery is the graceful regulation of voice, countenance, and gesture.

Anonymous: Ad Herennium I.x.17

[17] The Division of the cause falls into two parts. When the Statement of Facts has been brought to an end, we ought first to make clear what we and our opponents agree upon, if there is agreement on the points useful to us, and what remains contested, as follows: "Orestes killed his mother; on that I agree with my opponents. But did he have the right to commit the deed, and was he justified in committing it? That is in dispute." Likewise in reply: "They admit that Agamemnon was killed by Clytemnestra; yet despite this they say that I ought not to have avenged my father."

Then, when we have done this, we should use the Distribution. The Distribution has two parts: the Enumeration and the Exposition. We shall be using the Enumeration when we tell by number how many points we are going to discuss. The number ought not to exceed three; for otherwise, besides the danger that we may at some time include in the speech more or fewer points than we enumerated, it instils in the hearer the suspicion of premeditation and artifice, and this robs the speech of conviction. The Exposition consists in setting forth, briefly and completely, the points we intend to discuss.

Anonymous: Ad Herennium II.xxx.47

[xxx.47] Conclusions, among the Greeks called epilogoi, are tripartite, consisting of the Summing Up, Amplification, and Appeal to Pity. We can in four places use a Conclusion: in the Direct Opening, after the Statement of Facts, after the strongest argument, and in the Conclusion of the speech.

The Summing Up gathers together and recalls the points we have made--briefly, that the speech may not be repeated in entirety, but that the memory of it may be refreshed; and we shall reproduce all the points in the order in which they have been presented, so that the hearer, if he has committed them to memory, is brought back to what he remembers. Again, we must take care that the Summary should not be carried back to the Introduction or the Statement of Facts. Otherwise the speech will appear to have been fabricated and devised with elaborate pains so as to demonstrate the speaker's skill, advertise his wit, and display his memory. Therefore the Summary must take its beginning from the Division. Then we must in order and briefly set forth the points treated in the Proof and Refutation.

Anonymous: Ad Herennium III.xvi.28 - III.xxiv.40

[xvi.28] Now let me turn to the treasure-house of the ideas supplied by Invention, to the guardian of all the parts of rhetoric, the Memory.

The question whether memory has some artificial quality, or comes entirely from nature, we shall have another, more favourable, opportunity to discuss. At present I shall accept as proved that in this matter art and method are of great importance, and shall treat the subject accordingly. For my part, I am satisfied that there is an art of memory--the grounds of my belief I shall explain elsewhere. For the present I shall disclose what sort of thing memory is.

There are, then, two kinds of memory: one natural, and the other the product of art. The natural memory is that memory which is imbedded in our minds, born simultaneously with thought. The artificial memory is that memory which is strengthened by a kind of training and system of discipline. But just as in everything else the merit of natural excellence often rivals acquired learning, and art, in its turn, reinforces and develops the natural advantages, so does it happen in this instance. [29] The natural memory, if a person is endowed with an exceptional one, is often like this artificial memory, and this artificial memory, in its turn, retains and develops the natural advantages by a method of discipline. Thus the natural memory must be strengthened by discipline so as to become exceptional, and, on the other hand, this memory provided by discipline requires natural ability. It is neither more nor less true in this instance than in the other arts that science thrives by the aid of innate ability, and nature by the aid of the rules of art. The training here offered will therefore also be useful to those who by nature have a good memory, as you will yourself soon come to understand. But even if these, relying on their natural talent, did not need our help, we should still be justified in wishing to aid the less well-endowed. Now I shall discuss the artificial memory.

The artificial memory includes backgrounds and images. By backgrounds I mean such scenes as are naturally or artificially set off on a small scale, complete and conspicuous, so that we can grasp and embrace them easily by the natural memory--for example, a house, an intercolumnar space, a recess, an arch, or the like. An image is, as it were, a figure, mark, or portrait of the object we wish to remember; for example, if we wish to recall a horse, a lion, or an eagle, we must place its image in a definite background. [30] Now I shall show what kind of backgrounds we should invent and how we should discover the images and set them therein.

[xvii] Those who know the letters of the alphabet can thereby write out what is dictated to them and read aloud what they have written. Likewise, those who have learned mnemonics can set in backgrounds what they have heard, and from these backgrounds deliver it by memory. For the backgrounds are very much like wax tablets or papyrus, the images like the letters, the arrangement and disposition of the images like the script, and the delivery is like the reading. We should therefore, if we desire to memorize a large number of items, equip ourselves with a large number of backgrounds, so that in these we may set a large number of images. I likewise think it obligatory to have these backgrounds in a series, so that we may never by confusion in their order be prevented from following the images--proceeding from any background we wish, whatsoever its place in the series, and whether we go forwards or

backwards--nor from delivering orally what has been committed to the backgrounds. [xviii] For example, if we should see a great number of our acquaintances standing in a certain order, it would not make any difference to us whether we should tell their names beginning with the person standing at the head of the lire or at the foot or in the middle. So with respect to the backgrounds. If these have been arranged in order, the result will be that, reminded by the images, we can repeat orally what we have committed to the backgrounds, proceeding in either direction from any background we please. [31] That is why it also seems best to arrange the backgrounds in a series.

We shall need to study with special care the backgrounds we have adopted so that they may cling lastingly in our memory, for the images, like letters, are effaced when we make no use of them, but the backgrounds, like wax tablets, should abide. And that we may by no chance err in the number of backgrounds, each fifth background should be marked. For example, if in the fifth we should set a golden hand, and in the tenth some acquaintance whose first name is Decimus, it will then be easy to station like marks in each successive fifth background. [xix] Again, it will be more advantageous to obtain backgrounds in a deserted than in a populous region, because the crowding and passing to and fro of people confuse and weaken the impress of the images, while solitude keeps their outlines sharp. Further, backgrounds differing in form and nature must be secured, so that, thus distinguished, they may be clearly visible; for if a person has adopted many intercolumnar spaces, their resemblance to one another will so confuse him that he will no longer know what he has set in each background. And these backgrounds ought to be of moderate size and medium extent, for when excessively large they render the images vague, and when too small often seem incapable of receiving an arrangement of images. [32] Then the backgrounds ought to be neither too bright nor too dim, so that the shadows may not obscure the images nor the lustre make them glitter. I believe that the intervals between backgrounds should be of moderate extent, approximately thirty feet; for, like the external eye, so the inner eye of thought is less powerful when you have moved the object of sight too near or too far away.

Although it is easy for a person with a relatively large experience to equip himself with as many and as suitable backgrounds as he may desire, even a person who believes that he finds no store of backgrounds that are good enough, may succeed in fashioning as many such as he wishes. For the imagination can embrace any region whatsoever and in it at will fashion and construct the setting of some background. Hence, if we are not content with our ready-made supply of backgrounds, we may in our imagination create a region for ourselves and obtain a most serviceable distribution of appropriate backgrounds.

On the subject of backgrounds enough has been said; let me now turn to the theory of images.

[xx.33] Since, then, images must resemble objects, we ought ourselves to choose from all objects likenesses for our use. Hence likenesses are bound to be of two kinds, one of subject-matter, the other of words. Likenesses of matter are formed when we enlist images that present a general view of the matter with which we are dealing; likenesses of words are established when the record of each single noun or appellative is kept by an image.

Often we encompass the record of an entire matter by one notation, a single image. For example, the prosecutor has said that the defendant killed a man by poison, has charged that the motive for the crime was an inheritance, and declared that there are many witnesses and accessories to this act. If in order to facilitate our defence we wish to remember this first point, we shall in our first background form an image of the whole matter. We shall picture the man in question as lying ill in bed, if we know his person. If we do not know him, we shall yet take someone to be our invalid, but not a man of the lowest class, so that he may come to mind at once. And we shall place the defendant at the bedside, holding in his right hand a cup, and in his left tablets, and on the fourth finger a ram's testicles. In this way we can record the man who was poisoned, the inheritance, and the witnesses. [34] In like fashion we shall set the other counts of the charge in backgrounds successively, following their order, and whenever we wish to remember a point, by properly arranging the patterns of the backgrounds and carefully imprinting the images, we shall easily succeed in calling back to mind what we wish.

[xxi] When we wish to represent by images the likenesses of words, we shall be undertaking a greater task and exercising our ingenuity the more.

This we ought to effect in the following way:

Iam domum itionem reges Atridae parant.

"And now their home-coming the kings, the sons of
Atreus, are making ready."

If we wish to remember this verse, in our first background we should put Domitius, raising hands to heaven while he is lashed by the Marcii Reges--that will represent "Iam domum itionem reges" ("And now their home-coming the kings,"); in the second background, Aesopus and Cimber, being dressed as for the roles of Agamemnon and Menelaus in Iphigenia--that will represent "Atridae parant" ("the sons of Atreus, are making ready"). By this method all the words will be represented. But such an arrangement of images succeeds only if we use our notation to stimulate the natural memory, so that we first go over a given verse twice or three times to ourselves and then represent the words by means of images. In this way art will supplement nature. For neither by itself will be strong enough, though we must note that theory and technique are much the more reliable. I should not hesitate to demonstrate this in detail, did I not fear that, once having departed from my plan, I should not so well preserve the clear conciseness of my instruction.

[35] Now, since in normal cases some images are strong and sharp and suitable for awakening recollection, and others so weak and feeble as hardly to

succeed in stimulating memory, we must therefore consider the cause of these differences, so that, by knowing the cause, we may know which images to avoid and which to seek.

[xxii] Now nature herself teaches us what we should do. When we see in everyday life things that are petty, ordinary, and banal, we generally fail to remember them, because the mind is not being stirred by anything novel or marvellous. But if we see or hear something exceptionally base, dishonourable, extraordinary, great, unbelievable, or laughable, that we are likely to remember a long time. Accordingly, things immediate to our eye or ear we commonly forget; incidents of our childhood we often remember best. Nor could this be so for any other reason than that ordinary things easily slip from the memory while the striking and novel stay longer in mind. [36] A sunrise, the sun's course, a sunset, are marvellous to no one because they occur daily. But solar eclipses are a source of wonder because they occur seldom, and indeed are more marvellous than lunar eclipses, because these are more frequent. Thus nature shows that she is not aroused by the common, ordinary event, but is moved by a new or striking occurrence. Let art, then, imitate nature, find what she desires, and follow as she directs. For in invention nature is never last, education never first; rather the beginnings of things arise from natural talent, and the ends are reached by discipline.

[37] We ought, then, to set up images of a kind that can adhere longest in the memory. And we shall do so if we establish likenesses as striking as possible; if we set up images that are not many or vague, but doing something; if we assign to them exceptional beauty or singular ugliness; if we dress some of them with crowns or purple cloaks, for example, so that the likeness may be more distinct to us; or if we somehow disfigure them, as by introducing one stained with blood or soiled with mud or smeared with red paint, so that its form is more striking, or by assigning certain comic effects to our images, for that, too, will ensure our remembering them more readily. The things we easily remember when they are real we likewise remember without difficulty when they are figments, if they have been carefully delineated. But this will be essential--again and again to run over rapidly in the mind all the original backgrounds in order to refresh the images.

[xxiii.38] I know that most of the Greeks who have written on the memory have taken the course of listing images that correspond to a great many words, so that persons who wished to learn these images by heart would have them ready without expending effort on a search for them. I disapprove of their method on several grounds. First, among the innumerable multitude of words it is ridiculous to collect images for a thousand. How meagre is the value these can have, when out of the infinite store of words we shall need to remember now one, and now another? Secondly, why do we wish to rob anybody of his initiative, so that, to save him from making any search himself, we deliver to him everything searched out and ready? Then again, one person is more struck by one likeness, and another more by another. Often in fact when we declare that some one form resembles another, we fail to receive universal assent, because things seem different to different persons. The same is true with respect to images; one that is well-defined to us appears relatively inconspicuous to others. [39] Everybody, therefore, should in equipping himself with images suit his own convenience. Finally, it is the instructor's duty to teach the proper method of search in each case, and for the sake of greater clarity, to add in illustration some one or two examples of its kind, but not all. For instance, when I discuss the search for Introductions, I give a method of search and do not draught a thousand kinds of Introductions. The same procedure I believe should be followed with respect to images.

[xxiv] Now, lest you should perchance regard the memorizing of words either as too difficult or as of too little use, and so rest content with the memorizing of matter, as being easier and more useful, I must advise you why I do not disapprove of memorizing words. I believe that they who wish to do easy things without trouble and toil must previously have been trained in more difficult things. Nor have I included memorization of words to enable us to get verse by rote, but rather as an exercise whereby to strengthen that other kind of memory, the memory of matter, which is of practical use. Thus we may without effort pass from this difficult training to ease in that other memory. [40] In every discipline artistic theory is of little avail without unremitting exercise, but especially in mnemonics theory is almost valueless unless made good by industry, devotion, toil, and care. You can make sure that you have as many backgrounds as possible and that these conform as much as possible to the rules; in placing the images you should exercise every day. While an engrossing preoccupation may often distract us from our other pursuits, from this activity nothing whatever can divert us. Indeed there is never a moment when we do not wish to commit something to memory, and we wish it most of all when our attention is held by business of special importance. So, since a ready memory is a useful thing, you see clearly with what great pains we must strive to acquire so useful a faculty. Once you know its uses you will be able to appreciate this advice. To exhort you further in the matter of memory is not my intention, for I should appear either to have lacked confidence in your zeal or to have discussed the subject less fully than it demands.

I shall next discuss the fifth part of rhetoric. You might rehearse in your mind each of the first four divisions, and--what is especially necessary--fortify your knowledge of them with exercise.

PLINY

23 - 79 A.D.

From: *Natural History* (Vol. II), *Libri III-VII*. Translated by H. Rackham. The Loeb Classical Library, published by William Heinemann, 1952.

Pliny the Elder was born in Transalpine Gaul and died near Pompei while observing the eruption of Vesuvius in 79 A.D. A soldier by profession, he was prefect of a fleet at the time of his death. He was a devoted scholar. His only extant work, the Natural History, is a wide-ranging description of the natural world which pays a lot of attention to unusual objects and events.

Supplementary reading:

Weathered, H. N. (1937). *The Mind of the Ancient World: A Consideration of Pliny's Natural History.* London and New York: Longman's, Green & Co.

Table of Contents

Explanation of contents: The works of Pliny are organized by books (large Roman numerals), and chapters (small Roman numerals). Arabic numerals refer to an independent system of division into sections and are only given in the text at the start of each passage. For example VII.xxiv.88 refers to Book VII, chapter xxiv, section 88. Excerpts are from Volume II of the 10 volumes of the Heinemann edition of "Natural History".

xxiv.88 As to memory, the boon most necessary for life, it is not easy to say who most excelled in it, so many men having gained renown for it. King Cyrus could give their names to all the soldiers in his army, Lucius Scipio knew the names of the whole Roman people, King Pyrrhus's envoy Cineas knew those of the senate and knighthood at Rome the day after his arrival. Mithridates who was king of twenty-two races gave judgements in as many languages, in an assembly addressing each race in turn without an interpreter. A person in Greece named Charmadas recited the contents of any volumes in libraries that anyone asked him to quote, just as if he were reading them. Finally, a memoria technica was constructed, which was invented by the lyric poet Simonides and perfected by Metrodorus of Scepsis, enabling anything heard to be repeated in the identical words. Also no other human faculty is equally fragile: injuries from, and even apprehensions of, diseases and accident may affect in some cases a single field of memory and in others the whole. A man has been known when struck by a stone to forget how to read and write but nothing else. One who fell from a very high roof forgot his mother and his relatives and friends, another when ill forgot his servants also; the orator Messala Corvinus forgot his own name. Similarly tentative and hesitating lapses of memory often occur when the body even when uninjured is in repose; also the gradual approach of sleep curtails the memory and makes the unoccupied mind wonder where it is.

xxv.92 The most outstanding instance of innate mental vigour I take to be the dictator Caesar; and I am not now thinking of valour and resolution, nor of a loftiness embracing all the contents of the firmament of heaven, but of native vigour and quickness winged as it were with fire. We are told that he used to write or read and dictate or listen simultaneously, and to dictate to his secretaries four letters at once on his important affairs--or, if otherwise unoccupied, seven letters at once.

QUINTILLIAN

c. 40 A.D. - c. 96 A.D.

From: *The Institutio Oratoria of Quintillian*. Translated by H. E. Butler. The Loeb Classical Library, published by William Heinemann, 1920.

Quintillian was a prominent teacher of rhetoric in the first century A.D. He established the first public school in Rome, receiving his salary from the state. His *Institutio Oratoria (On the Education of the Orator)* describes classical approaches to rhetoric and education as they existed in practice rather than as they might ideally be. Familiar with Cicero's works and with *Ad Herennium*, Quintillian taught memory techniques to his students; however, he frowned upon the "artificial" techniques as inefficient and distracting. Quintillian's focus is pragmatic. He had little patience with pedantic details and strong views about matters of practical importance.

Supplementary readings:

Gwynn, A. O. (1966). *Roman Education from Cicero to Quintillian*. New York: Teachers College Press.

Kennedy, G. A. (1969). *Quintillian*. New York: Twayne.

QUINTILLIAN

Table of Contents

Explanation of contents: The works of Quintillian are organized by books (large Roman numerals), chapters (small Roman numerals) and sections (Arabic numerals). For example, III.iii.1 refers to Book III, chapter iii, section 1. All excerpts are from Volume 1 of the four volumes in the Loeb edition of the Institutio.

iii. The skilful teacher will make it his first care, as soon as a boy is entrusted to him, to ascertain his ability and character. The surest indication in a child is his power of memory. The characteristics of a good memory are twofold: it must be quick to take in and faithful to retain impressions of what it receives. The indication of next importance is the power of imitation: for this is a sign that the child is teachable: but he must imitate merely what he is taught, and must not, for example, mimic someone's gait or bearing or defects.

Quintillian: Institutio Oratoria III.iii.1 - 10

iii. The art of oratory, as taught by most authorities, and those the best, consists of five parts:--*invention, arrangement, expression, memory,* and *delivery* or *action* (the two latter terms being used synonymously). But all speech expressive of purpose involves also a *subject* and *words.* If such expression is brief [2] and contained within the limits of one sentence, it may demand nothing more, but longer speeches require much more. For not only what we say and how we say it is of importance, but also the circumstances under which we say it. It is here that the need of arrangement comes in. But it will be impossible to say everything demanded by the subject, putting each thing in its proper place, without the aid of memory. It is for this reason that memory [3] forms the fourth department. But a delivery, which is rendered unbecoming either by voice or gesture, spoils everything and almost entirely destroys the effect of what is said. Delivery therefore must be assigned the fifth place.

Those (and Albutius is among them), who maintain [4] that there are only three departments on the ground that memory and delivery (for which I shall give instructions in their proper place) are given us by nature not by art, may be disregarded, although Thrasymachus held the same views as regards delivery. Some have added a sixth department, subjoining [5] *judgment* to *invention,* on the ground that it is necessary first to *invent* and then to *exercise our judgment.* For my own part I do not believe that *invention* can exist apart from *judgment,* since we do not say that a speaker has *invented* inconsistent, two-edged or foolish arguments, but merely that he has failed to avoid them. It is true that Cicero in his Rhetorica includes [6] *judgment* under *invention*; but in my opinion judgment is so inextricably mingled with the first three departments of rhetoric (for without judgment neither *expression* nor *arrangement* are possible), that I think that even delivery owes much to it. I say [7] this with all the greater confidence because Cicero in his *Partitiones oratoriae* arrives at the same five-fold division of which I have just spoken. For after an initial division of oratory into *invention* and *expression,* he assigns *matter* and *arrangement* to *invention, words* and *delivery* to *expression,* and makes *memory* a fifth department common to them all and acting as their guardian. Again in the *Orator* he states that eloquence consists of five things, and in view of the fact that this is a later work we may accept this as his more settled opinion. Others, who seem to me to [8] have been no less desirous than those mentioned above to introduce some novelty, have added order, although they had already mentioned arrangement, as though *arrangement* was anything else than the marshalling of arguments in the best possible order. Dion taught that oratory consisted only of *invention* and *arrangement*, but added that each of these departments was twofold in nature, being concerned with words and things, so that *expression* comes under *invention*, and *delivery* under *arrangement*, while *memory* must be added as a fifth department. The followers of Theodorus divide *invention* into two parts, the one concerned with *matter* and the other with *expression*, and then add the three remaining departments. [9] Hermagoras places *judgment, division, order* and everything relating to *expression* under the heading of *economy*, a Greek word meaning the management of domestic affairs which is applied metaphorically to oratory and has no Latin equivalent.

A further question arises at this point, since [10] some make *memory* follow *invention* in the list of departments, while others make it follow *arrangement*. Personally I prefer to place it fourth. For we ought not merely to retain in our minds the fruits of our *invention*, in order that we may be able to arrange them, or to remember our *arrangement* in order that we may express it, but we must also commit to *memory* the words which we propose to use, since memory embraces everything that goes to the composition of a speech.

Quintillian: Institutio Oratoria XI.ii.1 - 51

ii. Some regard memory as being no more than one of nature's gifts: and this view is no doubt true to a great extent: but, like everything else, memory may be improved by cultivation. And all the labour of which I have so far spoken will be in vain unless all the other departments be co-ordinated by the animating principle of memory. For our whole education depends upon memory, and we shall receive instruction all in vain if all we hear slips from us, while it is the power of memory alone that brings before us all the store of precedents, laws, rulings, sayings and facts which the orator must possess in abundance and which he must always hold ready for immediate use. Indeed it is not without good reason that memory has been called the treasure-house of eloquence. But [2] pleaders need not only to be able to retain a number of facts in their minds, but also to be quick to take them in; it is not enough to learn what you have written by dint of repeated reading: it is just as necessary to follow the order both of matter and words when you have merely thought out what you are going to say, while you must also remember what has been said by your opponents, and must not be content merely with refuting their arguments in the order in which they were advanced, but must be in a position to deal with each in its appropriate place. Nay, even extempore eloquence, in my [3] opinion, depends on no mental activity so much as memory. For while we are saying one thing, we must be considering something else that we are going to say: consequently, since the mind is always looking ahead, it is continually in search of something which is more remote: on the other hand, whatever it discovers, it deposits by some mysterious process in the safe-keeping of memory, which acts as a transmitting agent and hands on to the delivery what it has received from the imagination. I do [4] not conceive, however, that I need dwell upon the question of the precise function of memory, although many hold the view that

97

certain impressions are made upon the mind, analogous to those which a signet-ring makes on wax. Nor, again, shall I be so credulous, in view of the fact that the retentiveness or slowness of the memory depends upon our physical condition, as to venture to allot a special art to memory. My inclination is rather to marvel [5] at its powers of reproducing and presenting a number of remote facts after so long an interval, and, what is more, of so doing not merely when we seek for such facts, but even at times of its own accord, and not only in our waking moments, but even when we are sunk in sleep. And my wonder is [6] increased by the fact that even beasts, which seem to be devoid of reason, yet remember and recognise things, and will return to their old home, however far they have been taken from it. Again, is it not an extraordinary inconsistency that we forget recent and remember distant events, that we cannot recall what happened yesterday and yet retain a vivid impression of the acts of our childhood? And what, again, shall [7] we say of the fact that the things we search for frequently refuse to present themselves and then occur to us by chance, or that memory does not always remain with us, but will even sometimes return to us after it has been lost? But we should never have realised the fullness of its power nor its supernatural capacities, but for the fact that it is memory which has brought oratory to its present position of glory. For it provides the orator not [8] merely with the order of his thoughts, but even of his words, nor is its power limited to stringing merely a few words together; its capacity for endurance is inexhaustible, and even in the longest pleadings the patience of the audience flags long before the memory of the speaker. This fact may [9] even be advanced as an argument that there must be some art of memory and that the natural gift can be helped by reason, since training enables us to do things which we cannot do before we have had any training or practice. On the other hand, I find that Plato asserts that the use of written characters is a hindrance to memory, on the ground, that is, that once we have committed a thing to writing, we cease to guard it in our memory and lose it out of sheer carelessness. And there can be no doubt that [10] concentration of mind is of the utmost importance in this connexion; it is, in fact, like the eyesight, which turns to, and not away from, the objects which it contemplates. Thus it results that after writing for several days with a view to acquiring by heart what we have written, we find that our mental effort has of itself imprinted it on our memory.

The first person to discover an art of memory is [11] said to have been Simonides, of whom the following well-known story is told. He had written an ode of the kind usually composed in honour of victorious athletes, to celebrate the achievement of one who had gained the crown for boxing. Part of the sum for which he had contracted was refused him on the ground that, following the common practice of poets, he had introduced a digression in praise of Castor and Pollux, and he was told that, in view of what he had done, he had best ask for the rest of the sum due from those whose deeds he had extolled. And according to the story they paid their debt. For when a great banquet was given [12] in honour of the boxer's success, Simonides was summoned forth from the feast, to which he had been invited, by a message to the effect that two youths who had ridden to the door urgently desired his presence. He found no trace of them, but what followed proved to him that the gods had shown their gratitude. For he had scarcely crossed the [13] threshold on his way out, when the banqueting hall fell in upon the heads of the guests and wrought such havoc among them that the relatives of the dead who came to seek the bodies for burial were unable to distinguish not merely the faces but even the limbs of the dead. Then it is said, Simonides, who remembered the order in which the guests had been sitting, succeeded in restoring to each man his own dead. There is, however, great disagreement [14] among our authorities as to whether this ode was written in honour of Glaucus of Carystus, Leocrates, Agatharcus or Scopas, and whether the house was at Pharsalus, as Simonides himself seems to indicate in a certain passage, and as is recorded by Apollodorus, Eratosthenes, Euphorion and Eurypylus of Larissa, or at Crannon, as is stated by Apollas Callimachus, who is followed by Cicero, to whom the wide circulation of this story is due. It is [15] agreed that Scopas, a Thessalian noble, perished at this banquet, and it is also said that his sister's son perished with him, while it is thought that a number of descendants of an elder Scopas met their death at the same time. For my own part, however, I [16] regard the portion of the story which concerns Castor and Pollux as being purely fictitious, since the poet himself has nowhere mentioned the occurrence; and he would scarcely have kept silence on an affair which was so much to his credit.

This achievement of Simonides appears to have [17] given rise to the observation that it is an assistance to the memory if localities are sharply impressed upon the mind, a view the truth of which everyone may realise by practical experiment. For when we return to a place after considerable absence, we not merely recognise the place itself, but remember things that we did there, and recall the persons whom we met and even the unuttered thoughts which passed through our minds when we were there before. Thus, as in most cases, art originates in experiment. Some place is chosen of the [18] largest possible extent and characterised by the utmost possible variety, such as a spacious house divided into a number of rooms. Everything of note therein is carefully committed to the memory, in order that the thought may be enabled to run through all the details without let or hindrance. And undoubtedly the first task is to secure that there shall be no delay in finding any single detail, since an idea which is to lead by association to some other idea requires to be fixed in the mind with more than ordinary certitude. The next step [19] is to distinguish something which has been written down or merely thought of by some particular symbol which will serve to jog the memory; this symbol may have reference to the subject as a whole, it may, for example, be drawn from navigation, warfare, etc., or it may, on the other hand, be found in some particular word. (For even in cases of forgetfulness one single word will serve to restore the memory.) However, let us suppose that the symbol is drawn from navigation, as, for instance, an anchor; or from warfare, as, for example, some weapon. These symbols are then arranged as follows. [20] The first thought is placed, as it were, in the forecourt; the second, let us say, in the living-room; the remainder are placed in due order all round the *impluvium* and entrusted not merely to bedrooms and parlours, but even to the care of statues and the like. This done, as soon as the memory of the facts requires to be revived, all these places are visited in turn and the various deposits are demanded from their custodians, as the sight of each recalls the respective details. Consequently, however large the number of these which it is required to remember, all are linked one to the other like dancers hand in hand, and there can be no mistake since they join what precedes to what follows, no trouble being required except the preliminary labour of committing the various points to memory. What [21] I have spoken of as being done in a house, can equally well be done in connexion with public buildings, a long journey, the ramparts of a city, or even pictures. Or we may even imagine such places to ourselves. We require, therefore, places, real or imaginary, and images or symbols, which we must, of course, invent for ourselves. By images I mean the words by which we distinguish the things which we have to learn by heart; in fact, as Cicero says, we use "places like wax tablets and symbols in lieu of letters." It will be best to [22] give his words *verbatim*: "We must for this purpose employ a number of remarkable places, clearly envisaged and separated by short intervals: the images which we use must be active, sharply-cut and distinctive, such as may occur to the mind and strike it with rapidity." This makes me wonder all the more, how Metrodorus should have found three hundred and sixty different localities in the twelve signs of the Zodiac through which the sun passes. It was doubtless due to the vanity and boastfulness of a man who was inclined to vaunt his memory as being the result of art rather than of natural gifts.

I am far from denying that those devices may be [23] useful for certain purposes, as, for example, if we have to reproduce a number of names in the order in which we heard them. For those who use such aids place the things which have to be remembered in localities which they have previously fixed in the memory; they put a table, for instance, in the forecourt, a platform in the hall and so on with the rest, and then, when they retrace their steps, they find the objects where they had placed them. Such [24] a practice may perhaps have been of use to those who, after an auction, have succeeded in stating what object they had sold to each buyer, their statements being checked by the books of the moneytakers; a feat which it is alleged was performed by Hortensius. It will, however, be of less service in learning the various parts of a set speech. For thoughts do not call up the same images as material things, and a symbol requires to be specially invented for them, although even here a particular place may serve to remind us, as, for example, of some conversation that may have been held there. But how can such a method grasp a whole series of connected words? I pass by the fact that there are [25] certain things which it is impossible to represent by symbols, as, for example, conjunctions. We may, it is true, like shorthand writers, have definite symbols for everything, and may select an infinite number of places to recall all the words contained in the five books of the second pleading against Verres, and we may even remember them all as if they were deposits placed in safe-keeping. But will not the flow of our speech inevitably be impeded by the double task imposed upon our memory? For how [26] can our words be expected to flow in connected speech, if we have to look back at separate symbols for each individual word? Therefore the experts mentioned by Cicero as having trained their memory by methods of this kind, namely Charmadas, and Metrodorus of Scepsis, to whom I have just referred, may keep their systems for their own use. My precepts on the subject shall be of a simpler kind.

If a speech of some length has to be committed [27] to memory, it will be well to learn it piecemeal, since there is nothing so bad for the memory as being overburdened. But the sections into which we divide it for this purpose should not be very short: otherwise they will be too many in number, and will break up and distract the memory. I am not, however, prepared to recommend any definite length; it will depend on the natural limits of the passage concerned, unless, indeed, it be so long as itself to require subdivision. But some limits must be fixed to enable us, [28] by dint of frequent and continuous practice, to connect the words in their proper order, which is a task of no small difficulty, and subsequently to unite the various sections into a whole when we go over them in order. If certain portions prove especially difficult to remember, it will be found advantageous to indicate them by certain marks, the remembrance of which will refresh and stimulate the memory. For there can [29] be but few whose memory is so barren that they will fail to recognise the symbols with which they have marked different passages. But if anyone is slow to recognise his own signs, he should employ the following additional remedy, which, though drawn from the mnemonic system discussed above, is not without its uses: he will adapt his symbols to the nature of the thoughts which tend to slip from his memory, using an anchor, as I suggested above, if he has to speak of a ship, or a spear, if he has to speak of a battle. For symbols are highly efficacious, and one idea [30] suggests another: for example, if we change a ring from one finger to another or tie a thread round it, it will serve to remind us of our reason for so doing. Specially effective are those devices which lead the memory from one thing to another similar thing which we have got to remember; for example, in the case of names, if we desire to remember the name Fabius, we should think of the famous Cunctator, whom we are certain not to forget, or of some friend bearing the same name. This is specially easy with names [31] such as Aper, Ursus, Naso, or Crispus, since in these cases we can fix their origin in our memory. Origin again may assist us to a better remembrance of derivative names, such as Cicero, Verrius, or Aurelius. However, I will say no more on this point.

There is one thing which will be of assistance to [32] everyone, namely, to learn a passage by heart from the same tablets on which he has committed it to writing. For he will have certain tracks to guide him in his purusit of memory, and the mind's eye will be fixed not merely on the pages on which the words were written, but on individual lines, and at times he will speak as though he were reading aloud. Further, if the writing should be interrupted by some erasure, addition or alteration, there are certain symbols available, the sight of which will prevent us from wandering from the track. This device bears [33] some resemblance to the mnemonic system which I mentioned above, but if my experience is worth anything, is at once more expeditious and more effective. The question has been raised as to whether we should learn by heart in silence; it would be best to do so, save for the fact that under such circumstances the mind is apt to become indolent, with the result that other thoughts break in. For this reason the mind should be kept alert by the sound of the voice, so that the memory may derive assistance from the double effort of speaking and listening. But our voice should be subdued, rising scarcely above a murmur. On the other hand, if we [34] attempt to learn by heart from another reading aloud, we shall find that there is both loss and gain; on the one hand, the process of learning will be slower, because the perception of the eye is quicker than that of the ear, while, on the other hand, when we have heard a passage once or twice, we shall be in a position to test our memory and match it against the voice of the reader. It is, indeed, important for other reasons to test ourselves thus from time to time, since continuous reading has this drawback, that it passes over the passages which we find hard to remember at the same speed as those which we find less difficulty in retaining. By testing ourselves to see [35] whether we remember a passage, we develop greater concentration without waste of time over the repetition of passages which we already know by heart. Thus, only those passages which tend to slip from the memory are repeated with a view to fixing them in the mind by frequent rehearsal, although as a rule the mere fact that they once slipped our memory makes us ultimately remember them with special accuracy. Both learning by heart and writing have this feature in common: namely, that good health, sound digestion, and freedom from other preoccupations of mind contribute largely to the success of both. But for the purpose of getting a real grasp [36] of what we have written under the various heads, division and artistic structure will be found of great value, while, with the exception of practice, which is the most powerful aid of all, they are practically the only means of ensuring an accurate remembrance of what we have merely thought out. For correct division will be an absolute safeguard against error in the order of our speech, since there are certain points [37] not merely in the distribution of the various questions in our speech, but also in their development (provided we speak as we ought), which naturally come first, second, and third, and so on, while the connexion will be so perfect that nothing can be omitted or inserted without the fact of the omission or insertion being obvious. We are told that Scaevola, [38] after a game of draughts in which he made the first move and was defeated, went over the whole game again in his mind on his way into the country, and on recalling the move which had cost him the game, returned to tell the man with whom he had been playing, and the latter acknowledged that he was right. Is order, then, I ask you, to be accounted of less importance in a speech, in which it depends entirely on ourselves, whereas in a game our opponent has an equal share in its development? Again, if [39] our structure be what it should, the artistic sequence will serve to guide the memory. For just as it is easier to learn verse than prose, so it is easier to learn prose when it is artistically constructed than when it has no such organisation. If these points receive attention, it will be possible to repeat *verbatim* even such passages as gave the impression of being delivered extempore. My own memory is of a very ordinary kind, but I found that I could do this with success on occasions when the interruption of a declamation by persons who had a claim to such a courtesy forced me to repeat part of what I had said. There are persons still living, who were then present to witness if I lie.

However, if anyone asks me what is the one [40] supreme method of memory, I shall reply, practice and industry. The most important thing is to learn much by heart and to think much, and, if possible, to do this daily, since there is nothing that is more increased by practice or impaired by neglect than memory. Therefore boys should, as I have already [41] urged, learn as much as possible by heart at the earliest stage, while all who, whatever their age, desire to cultivate the power of memory, should endeavour to swallow the initial tedium of reading and re-reading what they have written or read, a process which we may compare to chewing the cud. This task will be rendered less tiresome if we begin by confining ourselves to learning only a little at a time, in amounts not sufficient to create disgust: we may then proceed to increase the amount by a line a day, an addition which will not sensibly increase the labour of learning, until at last the amount we can attack will know no limits. We should begin with poetry and then go on to oratory, while finally we may attempt passages still freer in rhythm and less akin to ordinary speech, such, for example, as passages from legal writers. For passages intended [42] as an exercise should be somewhat difficult in character if they are to make it easy to achieve the end for which the exercise is designed; just as athletes train the muscles of their hands by carrying weights of lead, although in the actual contests their hands will be empty and free. Further, I must not omit the fact, the truth of which our daily practice will teach us, that in the case of the slower type of mind the memory of recent events is far from being exact. It is [43] a curious fact, of which the reason is not obvious, that the interval of a single night will greatly increase the strength of the memory, whether this be due to the fact that it has rested from the labour, the fatigue of which constituted the obstacle to success, or whether it be that the power of recollection, which is the most important element of memory, undergoes a process of ripening and maturing during the time which intervenes. Whatever the cause, things which could not be recalled on the spot are easily co-ordinated the next day, and time itself, which is generally accounted one of the causes of forgetfulness, actually serves to strengthen the memory. On the other hand, the abnormally rapid [44] memory fails as a rule to last and takes its leave as though, its immediate task accomplished, it had no further duties to perform. And indeed there is nothing surprising in the fact that things which have been implanted in the memory for some time should have a greater tendency to stay there.

The difference between the powers of one mind and another, to which I have just referred, gives rise to the question whether those who are intending to speak should learn their speeches verbatim or whether it is sufficient to get a good grasp of the essence and the order of what they have got to say. To this problem no answer is possible that will be of universal application. Give me a reliable memory [45] and plenty of time, and I should prefer not to permit a single syllable to escape me: otherwise writing would be superfluous. It is specially important to train the young to such precision, and the memory should be continually practised to this end, that we may never learn to become indulgent to its failure. For this reason I regard it as a mistake to permit the student to be prompted or to consult his manuscript, since such practices merely encourage carelessness, and no one will ever realise that he has not got his theme by heart, if he has no fear of forgetting it. It is this which causes interruptions in the flow of [46] speech and makes the orator's language halting and jerky, while he seems as though he were learning what he says by heart and loses all the grace that a well-written speech can give, simply by the fact that he makes it obvious that he has written it. On the other hand, a good memory will give us credit for quickness of wit as well, by creating the impression that our words have not been prepared in the seclusion of the study, but are due to the inspiration of the moment, an impression which is of the utmost assistance both to the orator and to his cause. For [47] the judge admires those words more and fears them less which he does not suspect of having been specially prepared beforehand to outwit him. Further, we must make it one of our chief aims in pleading to deliver passages which have been constructed with the utmost care, in such manner as to make it appear that they are but casually strung together, and to suggest that we are thinking out and hesitating over words which we have, as a matter of fact, carefully prepared in advance.

It should now be clear to all what is the best [48] course to adopt for the cultivation of memory. If, however, our memory be naturally somewhat dull or time presses, it will be useless to tie ourselves down rigidly to every word, since if we forget any one of them, the result may be awkward hesitation or even a tongue-tied silence. It is, therefore, far safer to secure a good grasp of the facts themselves and to leave ourselves free to speak as we will. For the loss of even a single word that we [49] have chosen is always a matter for regret, and it is hard to supply a substitute when we are searching for the word that we had written. But even this is no remedy for a weak memory, except for those who have acquired the art of speaking extempore. But if both memory and this gift be lacking, I should advise the would-be orator to abandon the toil of pleading altogether and, if he has any literary capacity, to betake himself by preference to writing. But such a misfortune will be of but rare occurrence.

For the rest there are many historical examples [50] of the power to which memory may be developed by natural aptitude and application. Themistocles is said to have spoken excellently in Persian after a year's study; Mithridates is recorded to have known twenty-two languages, that being the number of the different nations included in his empire; Crassus, surnamed the Rich, when commanding in Asia had such a complete mastery of five different Greek dialects, that he would give judgement in the dialect employed by the plaintiff in putting forward his suit; Cyrus is believed to have known the name of every soldier in his army, while Theodectes is [51] actually said to have been able to repeat any number of verses after only a single hearing. I remember that it used to be alleged that there were persons still living who could do the same, though I never had the good fortune to be present at such a performance. Still, we shall do well to have faith in such miracles, if only that he who believes may also hope to achieve the like.

PLOTINUS

205 - 270 A.D.

From: *Plotinus: The Enneads*. Translated by Stephen MacKenna. Third edition revised by B. S. Page, published by Faber and Faber Limited, 1962.

Plotinus is believed to have been born in Egypt in 205 A.D. In 232 he began study in Alexandria which he terminated in 243 to join an expedition of the Emperor Gordian to the East. Gordian was murdered during the expedition, forcing Plotinus to escape to Antioch. From 244 until his death he taught philosophy and wrote about his philosophical system in the Enneads. Plotinus regarded himself as a follower of Plato, but the influences of several other scholars, including Aristotle, are apparent in his work.

Supplementary readings:

Pisterius, P. V. (1952). *Plotinus and Neo-Platonism: An Introductory Study.* Cambridge: Bowes & Bowes.

Graeser, A. (1972). *Plotinus and the Stoics.* Leiden: Brill Press.

Table of Contents

Explanation of contents: The Enneads is divided into books (large Roman numerals), tractates (first Arabic numeral), and sections (second Arabic numeral). Thus IV.6.1 refers to Book IV, tractate 6, section 1.

IV.6.1 - IV.6.3

1.   Perceptions are no imprints, we have said, are not to be thought of as seal-impressions on soul or mind: accepting this statement, there is one theory of memory which must be definitely rejected.

Memory is not to be explained as the retaining of information in virtue of the lingering of an impression which in fact was never made; the two things stand or fall together; either an impression is made upon the mind and lingers when there is remembrance, or, denying the impression, we cannot hold that memory is its lingering. Since we reject equally the impression and the retention we are obliged to seek for another explanation of perception and memory, one excluding the notions that the sensible object striking upon soul or mind makes a mark upon it, and that the retention of this mark is memory.

If we study what occurs in the case of the most vivid form of perception, we can transfer our results to the other cases, and so solve our problem.

In any perception we attain by sight, the object is grasped there where it lies in the direct line of vision; it is there that we attack it; there, then, the perception is formed; the mind looks outward; this is ample proof that it has taken and takes no inner imprint, and does not see in virtue of some mark made upon it like that of the ring on the wax; it need not look outward at all if, even as it looked, it already held the image of the object, seeing by virtue of an impression made upon itself. It includes with the object the interval, for it tells at what distance the vision takes place: how could it see as outlying an impression within itself, separated by no interval from itself? Then, the point of magnitude: how could the mind, on this hypothesis, define the external size of the object or perceive that it has any--the magnitude of the sky, for instance, whose stamped imprint would be too vast for it to contain? And, most convincing of all, if to see is to accept imprints of the objects of our vision, we can never see these objects themselves; we see only vestiges they leave within us, shadows: the things themselves would be very different from our vision of them. And, for a conclusive consideration, we cannot see if the living object is in contact with the eye; we must look from a certain distance; this must be more applicable to the mind; supposing the mind to be stamped with an imprint of the object, it could not grasp as an object of vision what is stamped upon itself. For vision demands a duality, of seen and seeing: the seeing agent must be distinct and act upon an impression outside it, not upon one occupying the same point with it: sight can deal only with an object not inset but outlying.

2.   But if perception does not go by impression, what is the process?

The mind affirms something not contained within it: this is precisely the characteristic of a power--not to accept impression but, within its allotted sphere, to act.

Besides, the very condition of the mind being able to exercise discrimination upon what it is to see and hear is not, of course, that these objects be equally impressions made upon it; on the contrary, there must be no impressions, nothing to which the mind is passive; there can be only acts of that in which the objects become known.

Our tendency is to think of any of the faculties as unable to know its appropriate object by its own uncompelled act; to us it seems to submit to its environment rather than simply to perceive it, though in reality it is the master, not the victim.

As with sight, so with hearing. It is the air which takes the impression, a kind of articulated stroke which may be compared to letters traced upon it by the object causing the sound; but it belongs to the faculty, and the soul-essence, to read the imprints thus appearing before it, as they reach the point at which they become matter of its knowledge.

In taste and smell also we distinguish between the impressions received and the sensations and judgements; these last are mental acts, and belong to an order apart from the experiences upon which they are exercised.

The knowing of the things belonging to the Intellectual is not in any such degree attended by impact or impression: they come forward, on the contrary, as from within, unlike the sense-objects known as from without: they have more emphatically the character of Acts; they are Acts in the stricter sense, for their origin is in the Soul, and every concept of this Intellectual order is the Soul about its Act.

Whether, in this self-vision, the Soul is a duality and views itself as from the outside--while seeing the Intellectual-Principle as a unity, and itself with the Intellectual-Principle as a unity--this question is investigated elsewhere.

3.   With this prologue we come to our discussion of Memory.

That the Soul, or mind, having taken no imprint, yet achieves perception of what it in no way contains need not surprise us; or rather, surprising though it is, we cannot refuse to believe in this remarkable power.

The Soul is the Reason-Principle of the universe, ultimate among the Intellectual Beings--its own essential Nature is one of the Beings of the Intellectual Realm--but it is the primal Reason-Principle of the entire realm of sense.

Thus it has dealings with both orders--benefited and quickened by the one, but by the other beguiled, falling before resemblances, and so led downwards as under spell. Poised midway, it is aware of both spheres.

Of the Intellectual it is said to have intuition by memory upon approach, for it knows them by a certain natural identity with them; its knowledge is not attained by besetting them, so to speak, but by in a definite degree possessing them; they are its natural vision; they are itself in a more radiant mode, and it rises from its duller pitch to that greater brilliance in a sort of awakening, a progress from its latency to its Act.

To the sense-order it stands in a similar nearness and to such things it gives a radiance out of its own store and, as it were, elaborates them to visibility: the power is always ripe and, so to say, in travail towards them, so that, whenever it puts out its strength in the direction of what has once been present in it, it sees that object as present still; and the more intent its effort the more durable is the presence. This is why, it is agreed, children are better at remembering; the things presented to them are not constantly withdrawn but remain in sight; in their case the attention is still limited and not scattered: those whose faculty and mental activity are busied upon a multitude of subjects pass quickly over all, lingering on none.

Now, if memory were a matter of seal-impressions retained, the multiplicity of objects would have no weakening effect on the memory. Further, on the same hypothesis, we would have no need of thinking back to revive remembrance; nor would we be subject to forgetting and recalling; all would lie engraved within.

The very fact that we train ourselves to remember shows that what we get by the process is a strengthening of the mind: just so, exercises for feet and hands enable us to do easily acts which are in no sense contained or laid up in those members, but to which they may be fitted by persevering effort.

How else can it be explained that we forget a thing heard once or twice but remember what is often repeated, and that we recall a long time afterwards what at first hearing we failed to hold?

It is no answer to say that the parts present themselves sooner than the entire imprint--why should they too be forgotten?--(there is no question of parts, for) the last hearing, or our effort to remember, brings the thing back to us in a flash.

All these considerations testify to an evocation of that faculty of the Soul, or mind, in which remembrance is vested: the mind is strengthened, either generally or to this particular purpose.

Observe these facts: memory follows upon attention; those who have memorized much, by dint of their training in the use of leading indications (suggestive words and the like), reach the point of being easily able to retain without such aid: must we not conclude that the basis of memory is the soul-power brought to full strength?

The lingering imprints of the other explanation would tell of weakness rather than power; for to take imprint easily is to be yielding. An impression is something received passively; the strongest memory, then, would go with the least active nature. But what happens is the very reverse: in no pursuit do technical exercises tend to make a man less the master of his acts and states. It is as with sense-perception; the advantage is not to the weak, the weak eye for example, but to that which has the fullest power towards its exercise. In the old, it is significant, the senses are dulled and so is the memory.

Sensation and memory, then, are not passivity but power.

And, once it is admitted that sensations are not impressions, the memory of a sensation cannot consist in the retention of an impression that was never made.

Yes: but if it is an active power of the mind, a fitness towards its particular purpose, why does it not come at once--and not with delay--to the recollection of its unchanging objects?

Simply because the power needs to be poised and prepared: in this it is only like all the others, which have to be readied for the task to which their power reaches, some operating very swiftly, others only after a certain self-concentration.

Quick memory does not in general go with quick wit: the two do not fall under the same mental faculty; runner and boxer are not often united in one person; the dominant Idea differs from man to man.

Yet there could be nothing to prevent men of superior faculty from reading impressions on the mind; why should one thus gifted be incapable of what would be no more than a passive taking and holding?

In general Soul is faculty (and not receptivity), as is evident from its lack of extension (its immateriality).

And--one general reflection--it is not extraordinary that everything concerning soul should proceed in quite other ways than appears to people who either have never inquired, or have hastily adopted delusive analogies from the phenomena of sense, and persist in thinking of perception and remembrance in terms of characters inscribed on plates or tablets; the impossibilities that beset this theory escape those that make the Soul incorporeal equally with those to whom it is corporeal.

AUGUSTINE

354 - 430

From: *Augustine: Confessions and Enchiridion*. Translated and edited by A. C. Outler. Library of the Christian Classics, Vol. VII. Published by the Westminster Press, 1955.

Augustine: Later Works. Translated and selected by J. Burnaby. Library of the Christian Classics, Vol. VIII. Published by the Westminster Press, 1955.

Born in North Africa in the closing years of the Roman Empire, Augustine was a key figure in the transition to the medieval period. He combined the tradition of the early church with the Platonist religious philosophy of the Graeco-Roman world to produce an original statement which provided the central themes of Christianity for the next thousand years. His search for truth and wisdom, recounted in the *Confessions*, began at 18 and led him, through the study of neoPlatonism, to Christianity. During this period he travelled to Rome and to Milan as a teacher of rhetoric. Augustine followed the Platonists in including in his concept of *memoria*, not only the knowledge of the sensible world that we call "memory", but also *a priori* knowledge of forms or abstract concepts. After his baptism at the age of 32, he returned to North Africa where he served for many years as bishop of Hippo. At the time of his death, Vandal forces were closing in on the city.

Supplementary reading:

Bourke, V. J. (1964). *Augustine's View of Reality*.   Villanova, Pennsylvania: Villanova University Press.

AUGUSTINE

Table of Contents

Confessions

The Trinity

Explanation of contents: The "Confessions" is divided into books (first Roman numeral), which are in turn divided into short chapters (second Roman numeral). Paragraphs are also numbered from the beginning of each book (in Arabic numerals); these were included but are not given in the table of contents. "The Trinity" is one of Augustine's later works. It is divided into books (first Roman numeral). Paragraphs are numbered from the beginning of each book (Arabic numerals). In Burnaby's edition a second system for numbering paragraphs is also used but is omitted here.

VIII. [12] I will soar, then, beyond this power of my nature also, still rising by degrees toward him who made me. And I enter the fields and spacious halls of memory, where are stored as treasures the countless images that have been brought into them from all manner of things by the senses. There, in the memory, is likewise stored what we cogitate, either by enlarging or reducing our perceptions, or by altering one way or another those things which the senses have made contact with; and everything else that has been entrusted to it and stored up in it, which oblivion has not yet swallowed up and buried.

When I go into this storehouse, I ask that what I want should be brought forth. Some things appear immediately, but others require to be searched for longer, and then dragged out, as it were, from some hidden recess. Other things hurry forth in crowds, on the other hand, and while something else is sought and inquired for, they leap into view as if to say, "Is it not we, perhaps?" These I brush away with the hand of my heart from the face of my memory, until finally the thing I want makes its appearance out of its secret cell. Some things suggest themselves without effort, and in continuous order, just as they are called for--the things that come first give place to those that follow, and in so doing are treasured up again to be forthcoming when I want them. All of this happens when I repeat a thing from memory.

[13] All these things, each of which came into memory in its own particular way, are stored up separately and under the general categories of understanding. For example, light and all colors and forms of bodies came in through the eyes; sounds of all kinds by the ears; all smells by the passages of the nostrils; all flavors by the gate of the mouth; by the sensation of the whole body, there is brought in what is hard or soft, hot or cold, smooth or rough, heavy or light, whether external or internal to the body. The vast cave of memory, with its numerous and mysterious recesses, receives all these things and stores them up, to be recalled and brought forth when required. Each experience enters by its own door, and is stored up in the memory. And yet the things themselves do not enter it, but only the images of the things perceived are there for thought to remember. And who can tell how these images are formed, even if it is evident which of the senses brought which perception in and stored it up? For even when I am in darkness and silence I can bring out colors in my memory if I wish, and discern between black and white and the other shades as I wish; and at the same time, sounds do not break in and disturb what is drawn in by my eyes, and which I am considering, because the sounds which are also there are stored up, as it were, apart. And these too I can summon if I please and they are immediately present in memory. And though my tongue is at rest and my throat silent, yet I can sing as I will; and those images of color, which are as truly present as before, do not interpose themselves or interrupt while another treasure which had flowed in through the ears is being thought about. Similarly all the other things that were brought in and heaped up by all the other senses, I can recall at my pleasure. And I distinguish the scent of lilies from that of violets while actually smelling nothing; and I prefer honey to mead, a smooth thing to a

rough, even though I am neither tasting nor handling them, but only remembering them.

[14] All this I do within myself, in that huge hall of my memory. For in it, heaven, earth, and sea are present to me, and whatever I can cogitate about them--except what I have forgotten. There also I meet myself and recall myself--what, when, or where I did a thing, and how I felt when I did it. There are all the things that I remember, either having experienced them myself or been told about them by others. Out of the same storehouse, with these past impressions, I can construct now this, now that, image of things that I either have experienced or have believed on the basis of experience--and from these I can further construct future actions, events, and hopes; and I can meditate on all these things as if they were present. "I will do this or that"--I say to myself in that vast recess of my mind, with its full store of so many and such great images--"and this or that will follow upon it." "O that this or that could happen!" "God prevent this or that." I speak to myself in this way; and when I speak, the images of what I am speaking about are present out of the same store of memory; and if the images were absent I could say nothing at all about them.

[15] Great is this power of memory, exceedingly great, O my God--a large and boundless inner hall! Who has plumbed the depths of it? Yet it is a power of my mind, and it belongs to my nature. But I do not myself grasp all that I am. Thus the mind is far too narrow to contain itself. But where can that part of it be which it does not contain? Is it outside and not in itself? How can it be, then, that the mind cannot grasp itself? A great marvel rises in me; astonishment seizes me. Men go forth to marvel at the heights of mountains and the huge waves of the sea, the broad flow of the rivers, the vastness of the ocean, the orbits of the stars, and yet they neglect to marvel at themselves. Nor do they wonder how it is that, when I spoke of all these things, I was not looking at them with my eyes--and yet I could not have spoken about them had it not been that I was actually seeing within, in my memory, those mountains and waves and rivers and stars which I have seen, and that ocean which I believe in--and with the same vast spaces between them as when I saw them outside me. But when I saw them outside me, I did not take them into me by seeing them; and the things themselves are not inside me, but only their images. And yet I knew through which physical sense each experience had made an impression on me.

IX. [16] And yet this is not all that the unlimited capacity of my memory stores up. In memory, there are also all that one has learned of the liberal sciences, and has not forgotten--removed still further, so to say, into an inner place which is not a place. Of these things it is not the images that are retained, but the things themselves. For what literature and logic are, and what I know about how many different kinds of questions there are--all these are stored in my memory as they are, so that I have not taken in the image and left the thing outside. It is not as though a sound had sounded and passed away like a voice heard by the ear which leaves a trace by which it can be called into memory again, as if it were still sounding in mind while it did so no longer outside. Nor

113

is it the same as an odor which, even after it has passed and vanished into the wind, affects the sense of smell--which then conveys into the memory the image of the smell which is what we recall and re-create; or like food which, once in the belly, surely now has no taste and yet does have a kind of taste in the memory; or like anything that is felt by the body through the sense of touch, which still remains as an image in the memory after the external object is removed. For these things themselves are not put into the memory. Only the images of them are gathered with a marvelous quickness and stored, as it were, in the most wonderful filing system, and are thence produced in a marvelous way by the act of remembering.

X. [17] But now when I hear that there are three kinds of questions-- "Whether a thing is? What it is? Of what kind it is?"--I do indeed retain the images of the sounds of which these words are composed and I know that those sounds pass through the air with a noise and now no longer exist. But the things themselves which were signified by those sounds I never could reach by any sense of the body nor see them at all except by my mind. And what I have stored in my memory was not their signs, but the things signified.

How they got into me, let them tell who can. For I examine all the gates of my flesh, but I cannot find the door by which any of them entered. For the eyes say, "If they were colored, we reported that." The ears say, "If they gave any sound, we gave notice of that." The nostrils say, "If they smell, they passed in by us." The sense of taste says, "If they have no flavor, don't ask me about them." The sense of touch says, "If it had no bodily mass, I did not touch it, and if I never touched it, I gave no report about it."

Whence and how did these things enter into my memory? I do not know. For when I first learned them it was not that I believed them on the credit of another man's mind, but I recognized them in my own; and I saw them as true, took them into my mind and laid them up, so to say, where I could get at them again whenever I willed. There they were, then, even before I learned them, but they were not in my memory. Where were they, then? How does it come about that when they were spoken of, I could acknowledge them and say, "So it is, it is true," unless they were already in the memory, though far back and hidden, as it were, in the more secret caves, so that unless they had been drawn out by the teaching of another person, I should perhaps never have been able to think of them at all?

XI. [18] Thus we find that learning those things whose images we do not take in by our senses, but which we intuit within ourselves without images and as they actually are, is nothing else except the gathering together of those same things which the memory already contains--but in an indiscriminate and confused manner--and putting them together by careful observation as they are at hand in the memory; so that whereas they formerly lay hidden, scattered, or neglected, they now come easily to present themselves to the mind which is now familiar with them. And how many things of this sort my memory has stored up, which have already been discovered and, as I said, laid up for ready reference. These are the things we may be said to have learned and to know. Yet, if I cease to recall them even for short intervals of time, they are again so submerged--and slide back, as it were, into the further reaches of the memory-- that they must be drawn out again as if new from the same place (for there is nowhere else for them to have gone) and must be collected [*cogenda*] so that they can become known. In other words, they must be gathered up [*colligenda*] from their dispersion. This is where we get the word *cogitate* [*cogitare*]. For *cogo* [collect] and *cogito* [to go on collecting] have the same relation to each other as *ago* [do] and *agito* [do frequently], and *facio* [make] and *factito* [make frequently]. But the mind has properly laid claim to this word [cogitate] so that not everything that is gathered together anywhere, but only what is collected and gathered together in the mind, is properly said to be "cogitated."

XII. [19] The memory also contains the principles and the unnumbered laws of numbers and dimensions. None of these has been impressed on the memory by a physical sense, because they have neither color nor sound, nor taste, nor sense of touch. I have heard the sound of the words by which these things are signified when they are discussed: but the sounds are one thing, the things another. For the sounds are one thing in Greek, another in Latin; but the things themselves are neither Greek nor Latin nor any other language. I have seen the lines of the craftsmen, the finest of which are like a spider's web, but mathematical lines are different. They are not the images of such things as the eye of my body has showed me. The man who knows them does so without any cogitation of physical objects whatever, but intuits them within himself. I have perceived with all the senses of my body the numbers we use in counting; but the numbers by which we count are far different from these. They are not the images of these; they simply are. Let the man who does not see these things mock me for saying them; and I will pity him while he laughs at me.

XIII. [20] All these things I hold in my memory, and I remember how I learned them. I also remember many things that I have heard quite falsely urged against them, which, even if they are false, yet it is not false that I have remembered them. And I also remember that I have distinguished between the truths and the false objections, and now I see that it is one thing to distinguish these things and another to remember that I did distinguish them when I have cogitated on them. I remember, then, both that I have often understood these things and also that I am now storing away in my memory what I distinguish and comprehend of them so that later on I may remember just as I understand them now. Therefore, I remember that I remembered, so that if afterward I call to mind that I once was able to remember these things it will be through the power of memory that I recall it.

XIV. [21] This same memory also contains the feelings of my mind; not in the manner in which the mind itself experienced them, but very differently according to a power peculiar to memory. For without being joyous now, I can remember that I once was joyous, and without being sad, I can recall my past sadness. I can remember past fears without fear, and former desires without desire. Again, the contrary happens. Sometimes when I am joyous I remember my past sadness, and when sad, remember past joy.

This is not to be marveled at as far as the body is concerned; for the mind is one thing and the body another. If, therefore, when I am happy, I recall some past bodily pain, it is not so strange. But even as this memory is experienced, it is identical with the mind--as when we tell someone to remember something we say, "See that you bear this in mind"; and when we forget a thing, we say, "It did not enter my mind" or "It slipped my mind." Thus we call memory itself mind.

Since this is so, how does it happen that when I am joyful I can still remember past sorrow? Thus the mind has joy, and the memory has sorrow; and the mind is joyful from the joy that is in it, yet the memory is not sad from the sadness that is in it. Is it possible that the memory does not belong to the mind? Who will say so? The memory doubtless is, so to say, the belly of the mind: and joy and sadness are like sweet and bitter food, which when they are committed to the memory are, so to say, passed into the belly where they can be stored but no longer tasted. It is ridiculous to consider this an analogy; yet they are not utterly unlike.

[22] But look, it is from my memory that I produce it when I say that there are four basic emotions of the mind: desire, joy, fear, sadness. Whatever kind of analysis I may be able to make of these, by dividing each into its particular species, and by defining it, I still find what to say in my memory and it is from my memory that I draw it out. Yet I am not moved by any of these emotions when I call them to mind by remembering them. Moreover, before I recalled them and thought about them, they were there in the memory; and this is how they could be brought forth in remembrance. Perhaps, therefore, just as food is brought up out of the belly by rumination, so also these things are drawn up out of the memory recall. But why, then, does not the man who is thinking about the emotions, and is thus recalling them, feel in the mouth of his reflection the sweetness of joy or the bitterness of sadness? Is the comparison unlike in this because it is not complete at every point? For who would willingly speak on these subjects, if as often as we used the term sadness or fear, we should thereby be compelled to be sad or fearful? And yet we could never speak of them if we did not find them in our memories, not merely as the sounds of the names, as their images are impressed on it by the physical senses, but also the notions of the things themselves--which we did not receive by any gate of the flesh, but which the mind itself recognizes by the experience of its own passions, and has entrusted to the memory; or else which the memory itself has retained without their being entrusted to it.

XV. [23] Now whether all this is by means of images or not, who can rightly affirm? For I name a stone, I name the sun, and those things themselves are not present to my senses, but their images are present in my memory. I name some pain of the body, yet it is not present when there is no pain; yet if there were not some such image of it in my memory, I could not even speak of it, nor should I be able to distinguish it from pleasure. I name bodily health when I am sound in body, and the thing itself is indeed present in me. At the same time, unless there were some image of it in my memory, I could not possibly call to mind what the sound of this name signified. Nor would sick people know what was meant when health was named, unless the same image were preserved by the power of memory, even though the thing itself is absent from the body. I can name the numbers we use in counting, and it is not their images but themselves that are in my memory. I name the image of the sun, and this too is in my memory. For I do not recall the image of that image, but that image itself, for the image itself is present when I remember it. I name memory and I know what I name. But where do I know it, except in the memory itself? Is it also present to itself by its image, and not by itself?

XVI. [24] When I name forgetfulness, and understand what I mean by the name, how could I understand it if I did not remember it? And if I refer not to the sound of the name, but to the thing which the term signifies, how could I know what that sound signified if I had forgotten what the name means? When, therefore, I remember memory, then memory is present to itself by itself, but when I remember forgetfulness then both memory and forgetfulness are present together--the memory by which I remember the forgetfulness which I remember. But what is forgetfulness except the privation of memory? How, then, is that present to my memory which, when it controls my mind, I cannot remember? But if what we remember we store up in our memory; and if, unless we remembered forgetfulness, we could never know the thing signified by the term when we heard it--then, forgetfulness is contained in the memory. It is present so that we do not forget it, but since it is present, we do forget.

From this it is to be inferred that when we remember forgetfulness, it is not present to the memory through itself, but through its image; because if forgetfulness were present through itself, it would not lead us to remember, but only to forget. Now who will someday work this out? Who can understand how it is?

[25] Truly, O Lord, I toil with this and labor in myself. I have become a troublesome field that requires hard labor and heavy sweat. For we are not now searching out the tracts of heaven, or measuring the distances of the stars or inquiring about the weight of the earth. It is I myself--I, the mind--who remember. This is not much to marvel at, if what I myself am is not far from me. And what is nearer to me than myself? For see, I am not able to comprehend the force of my own memory, though I could not even call my own name without it. But what shall I say, when it is clear to me that I remember forgetfulness? Should I affirm that what I remember is not in my memory? Or should I say that forgetfulness is in my memory to the end that I should not forget? Both of these views are most absurd. But what third view is there? How can I say that the image of forgetfulness is retained by my memory, and not forgetfulness itself, when I remember it? How can I say this, since for the image of anything to be imprinted on the memory the thing itself must necessarily have been present first by which the image could have been imprinted? Thus I remember Carthage; thus, also, I remember all the other places where I have been. And I remember the faces of men whom I have seen and things reported by the other senses. I remember the health or sickness of the body. And when these objects were present, my memory received images from them so that they

remain present in order for me to see them and reflect upon them in my mind, if I choose to remember them in their absence. If, therefore, forgetfulness is retained in the memory through its image and not through itself, then this means that it itself was once present, so that its image might have been imprinted. But when it was present, how did it write its image on the memory, since forgetfulness, by its presence, blots out even what it finds already written there? And yet in some way or other, even though it is incomprehensible and inexplicable, I am still quite certain that I also remember forgetfulness, by which we remember that something is blotted out.

XVII. [26] Great is the power of memory. It is a true marvel, O my God, a profound and infinite multiplicity! And this is the mind, and this I myself am. What, then, am I, O my God? Of what nature am I? A life various, and manifold, and exceedingly vast. Behold in the numberless halls and caves, in the innumerable fields and dens and caverns of my memory, full without measure of numberless kinds of things--present there either through images as all bodies are; or present in the things themselves as are our thoughts; or by some notion or observation as our emotions are, which the memory retains even though the mind feels them no longer, as long as whatever is in the memory is also in the mind--through all these I run and fly to and fro. I penetrate into them on this side and that as far as I can and yet there is nowhere any end.

So great is the power of memory, so great the power of life in man whose life is mortal! What, then, shall I do, O thou my true life, my God? I will pass even beyond this power of mine that is called memory--I will pass beyond it, that I may come to thee, O lovely Light. And what art thou saying to me? See, I soar by my mind toward thee, who remainest above me. I will also pass beyond this power of mine that is called memory, desiring to reach thee where thou canst be reached, and wishing to cleave to thee where it is possible to cleave to thee. For even beasts and birds possess memory, or else they could never find their lairs and nests again, nor display many other things they know and do by habit. Indeed, they could not even form their habits except by their memories. I will therefore pass even beyond memory that I may reach Him who has differentiated me from the four-footed beasts and the fowls of the air by making me a wiser creature. Thus I will pass beyond memory; but where shall I find thee, who art the true Good and the steadfast Sweetness? But where shall I find thee? If I find thee without memory, then I shall have no memory of thee; and how could I find thee at all, if I do not remember thee?

XVIII. [27] For the woman who lost her small coin and searched for it with a light would never have found it unless she had remembered it. For when it was found, how could she have known whether it was the same coin, if she had not remembered it? I remember having lost and found many things, and I have learned this from that experience: that when I was searching for any of them and was asked: "Is this it? Is that it?" I answered, "No," until finally what I was seeking was shown to me. But if I had not remembered it--whatever it was-- even though it was shown to me, I still would not have found it because I could not have recognized it. And this is the way it always is when we search for and find anything that is lost. Still, if anything is accidentally lost from sight--not from memory, as a visible body might be--its image is retained within, and the thing is searched for until it is restored to sight. And when the thing is found, it is recognized by the image of it which is within. And we do not say that we have found what we have lost unless we can recognize it, and we cannot recognize it unless we remember it. But all the while the thing lost to the sight was retained in the memory.

XIX. [28] But what happens when the memory itself loses something, as when we forget anything and try to recall it? Where, finally, do we search, but in the memory itself? And there, if by chance one thing is offered for another, we refuse it until we meet with what we are looking
for; and when we do, we recognize that this is it. But we could not do this unless we recognized it, nor could we have recognized it unless we remembered it. Yet we had indeed forgotten it.

Perhaps the whole of it had not slipped out of our memory; but a part was retained by which the other lost part was sought for, because the memory realized that it was not operating as smoothly as usual and was being held up by the crippling of its habitual working; hence, it demanded the restoration of what was lacking.

For example, if we see or think of some man we know, and, having forgotten his name, try to recall it--if some other thing presents itself, we cannot tie it into the effort to remember, because it was not habitually thought of in association with him. It is consequently rejected, until something comes into the mind on which our knowledge can rightly rest as the familiar and sought-for object. And where does this name come back from, save from the memory itself? For even when we recognize it by another's reminding us of it, still it is from the memory that this comes, for we do not believe it as something new; but when we recall it, we admit that what was said was correct. But if the name had been entirely blotted out of the mind, we should not be able to recollect it even when reminded of it. For we have not entirely forgotten anything if we can remember that we have forgotten it. For a lost notion, one that we have entirely forgotten, we cannot even search for.

XX. [29] How, then, do I seek thee, O Lord? For when I seek thee, my God, I seek a happy life. I will seek thee that my soul may live. For my body lives by my soul, and my soul lives by thee. How, then, do I seek a happy life, since happiness is not mine till I can rightly say: "It is enough. This is it." How do I seek it? Is it by remembering, as though I had forgotten it and still knew that I had forgotten it? Do I seek it in longing to learn of it as though it were something unknown, which either I had never known or had so completely forgotten as not even to remember that I had forgotten it? Is not the happy life the thing that all desire, and is there anyone who does not desire it at all? But where would they have gotten the knowledge of it, that they should so desire it? Where have they seen it that they should so love it? It is somehow true that we have it, but how I do not know.

There is, indeed, a sense in which when anyone has his desire he is happy. And then there are some who are happy in hope. These are happy in an inferior degree to those that are actually happy; yet they are better off than those who are happy neither in actuality nor in hope. But even these, if they had not known happiness in some degree, would not then desire to be happy. And yet it is most certain that they do so desire. How they come to know happiness, I cannot tell, but they have it by some kind of knowledge unknown to me, for I am very much in doubt as to whether it is in the memory. For if it is in there, then we have been happy once on a time--either each of us individually or all of us in that man who first sinned and in whom also we all died and from whom we are all born in misery. How this is, I do not now ask; but I do ask whether the happy life is in the memory. For if we did not know it, we should not love it. We hear the name of it, and we all acknowledge that we desire the thing, for we are not delighted with the name only. For when a Greek hears it spoken in Latin, he does not feel delighted, for he does not know what has been spoken. But we are as delighted as he would be in turn if he heard it in Greek, because the thing itself is neither Greek nor Latin, this happiness which Greeks and Latins and men of all the other tongues long so earnestly to obtain. It is, then, known to all; and if all could with one voice be asked whether they wished to be happy, there is no doubt they would all answer that they would. And this would not be possible unless the thing itself, which we name "happiness," were held in the memory.

XXI. [30] But is it the same kind of memory as one who having seen Carthage remembers it? No, for the happy life is not visible to the eye, since it is not a physical object. Is it the sort of memory we have for numbers? No, for the man who has these in his understanding does not keep striving to attain more. Now we know something about the happy life and therefore we love it, but still we wish to go on striving for it that we may be happy. Is the memory of happiness, then, something like the memory of eloquence? No, for although some, when they hear the term eloquence, call the thing to mind, even if they are not themselves eloquent--and further, there are many people who would like to be eloquent, from which it follows that they must know something about it--nevertheless, these people have noticed through their senses that others are eloquent and have been delighted to observe this and long to be this way themselves. But they would not be delighted if it were not some interior knowledge; and they would not desire to be delighted unless they had been delighted. But as for a happy life, there is no physical perception by which we experience it in others.

Do we remember happiness, then, as we remember joy? It may be so, for I remember my joy even when I am sad, just as I remember a happy life when I am miserable. And I have never, through physical perception, either seen, heard, smelled, tasted, or touched my joy. But I have experienced it in my mind when I rejoiced; and the knowledge of it clung to my memory so that I can call it to mind, sometimes with disdain and at other times with longing, depending on the different kinds of things I now remember that I rejoiced in. For I have been bathed with a certain joy even by unclean things, which I now detest and execrate as I call them to mind. At other times, I call to mind with longing good and honest things, which are not any longer near at hand, and I am therefore saddened when I recall my former joy.

Book X: The Realization of Self-Knowledge: Memory, Understanding, Will

[17] And now, setting aside for the moment the other activities which the mind is sure of its possessing, let us take for particular consideration these three: memory, understanding, will. On these three points we are accustomed to examine the capacities of children, to find what talents they display. The more tenacious and ready is a boy's memory, the more acute his understanding, the more eager his will to learn, so much the more praiseworthy do we count his disposition. When, however, it is a question of the learning of any individual, we enquire, not how much strength and readiness of memory or sharpness of understanding he possesses, but what he remembers and what he understands. And seeing that a person is judged praiseworthy not only according to his learning but also according to his goodness, we take note not only of what he remembers and understands but of what he wills: not simply of the eagerness of his will, but first of what he wills and then of how much he wills it. For a person who loves intensely only merits praise when what he loves is what ought to be loved intensely. In the three fields of disposition, learning, and practice or use, the test of the first depends upon the individual's capacity in respect of memory, understanding and will; the test of the second, upon the content of his memory and understanding, and the point to which an eager will has brought him. But the third, use, belongs entirely to the will as it deals with the content of memory and understanding, whether as means relative to a particular end, or as an end in which it may rest satisfied. To use, is to take a thing up into the disposal of the will; whereas to enjoy is to use with a satisfaction that is not anticipated but actual. Thus all enjoyment is a kind of use, since it takes up something into the disposal of the will for final delectation; but not all use is enjoyment, if what is taken up into the disposal of the will has been sought after not for its own sake but as a means to something else.

[18] Now this triad of memory, understanding, and will are not three lives, but one; nor three minds, but one. It follows that they are not three substances, but one substance. Memory, regarded as life, mind, or substance, is an absolute term: regarded as memory, it is relative. The same may be said of understanding and of will; for both terms can be used relatively. But life, mind, essence, are always things existing absolutely in themselves. Therefore the three activities named are one, inasmuch as they constitute one life, one mind, one essence; and whatever else can be predicated of each singly in itself, is predicated of them all together in the singular and not in the plural. But they are three inasmuch as they are related to one another; and if they were not equal, not only each to each but each to all, they could not cover or take in one another as they do. For in fact they are covered, not only each by each but all by each. I remember that I possess memory and understanding and will: I understand that I understand and will and remember: I will my own willing and remembering and understanding. [*Note that Augustine is using "remember" not in the sense of actually recollecting, but in that of being able to recall.*] And I

remember at the same time the whole of my memory and understanding and will. Whatever I do not remember as part of my memory, is not in my memory; and nothing can be more fully in my memory than the memory itself. Therefore I remember the whole of it. Again, whatever I understand, I know that I understand, and I know that I will whatever I will; but whatever I know, I remember. Therefore I remember the whole of my understanding and the whole of my will. Similarly, when I understand these three, I understand all three in whole. For there is nothing open to understanding that I do not understand except that of which I am ignorant; and that of which I am ignorant I neither remember nor will. It follows that anything open to understanding that I do not understand, I neither remember nor will, whereas anything open to understanding that I remember and will, I understand. Finally, when I use the whole content of my understanding and memory, my will covers the whole of my understanding and the whole of my memory. Therefore, since all are covered by one another singly and as wholes, the whole of each is equal to the whole of each, and the whole of each to the whole of all together. And these three constitute one thing, one life, one mind, one essence.

[19] We might now attempt to raise our thoughts, with such power of concentration as is at our disposal, towards that supreme and most exalted essence of which the human mind is an image--inadequate indeed, but still truly an image. Yet it may be better to illustrate more clearly the presence in the soul of these same three functions, by means of our bodily sense perceptions of external objects, in which there is impressed upon us in the process of time a knowledge of material things. We found the nature of the mind, in its memory, understanding and willing of itself, to be such that it must be apprehended as always knowing and always willing itself; and therefore also as always at the same time remembering itself, understanding and loving itself, although it does not always keep the thought of itself clearly separated from things which are not identical with it. This makes it difficult to distinguish in it the memory of self and the understanding of self. When they are closely conjoined, neither preceding the other in time, it may look as though they were not two, but one and the same thing under different names. Even love may cease to be felt as such, if not disclosed by the sense of want, as when its object is continually present. All this may become clear to the slower thinker, in the course of an examination of those temporal processes which add to the content of the mind or otherwise affect it: when it remembers what it did not remember before, when it sees what it did not see before, and when it loves what it did not love before. This examination, however, demands to be taken in hand in the next Book.

Augustine: The Trinity XI.1

Book XI: The Image in the Outward Man

We are to look for a likeness of the inward man in the outward; and the particular sense we shall examine is that of sight.

[1] We can distinguish (i) the external object of vision (ii) the perception of it in the sense-organ (iii) the mental attention which fixes the eye on the object.

(a) Sense and attention belong to the perceiving subject and are independent of the object. The form printed on the sense-organ is product of the object only, of which this form is a likeness or image, distinct from the object itself. Its existence in the sense-organ is proved, e.g., by our experience of the "after-image" of a luminous object on closing the eye, and the duplicated image of an unfocused vision. The three elements are thus diverse in substance; but the third (the voluntary act of attention) brings the two former into close union, and is capable, when its emotional tone is intense, even of producing changes in the body of the percipient. (b) When a remembered perception is recalled to mind, we can observe a corresponding "trinity of imagination," this time entirely within the mind, composed of memory, inward vision, and the will which directs attention upon the object in the memory. The resulting mental image may even be mistaken for the "real" thing, especially under the influence of strong desire or fear.

Augustine: The Trinity XIV.13 - 14

Book XIV: The Perfection of the Image in the Contemplation of God

[13] In the knowledge of all those temporal matters, to which we have here referred, certain of the things knowable precede the knowing of them by an interval of time: such are the sensible properties which were already in the outward objects before they were perceived, and all the facts of historical knowledge. Certain others originate simultaneously with being known: if for example an object of sight which had no previous existence should arise before our eyes, it cannot precede our knowing of it; or if a sound is caused in the presence of a hearer, the sound and the hearing of it begin and cease simultaneously. But whether their origin is precedent or simultaneous, it is the "knowables" that beget the knowledge and not vice versa. And when the knowledge has been effected, and the things known take their place in the memory and are recalled to view in the act of recollection, it is obvious that the retention in the memory is temporally prior both to the recollecting vision and to the union of the two by will. It is not so however with the mind itself. It cannot be adventitious to itself, as though to a self already in being there should come from elsewhere an identical self previously non-existent, or as though, instead of coming from elsewhere, there should be born in the existing self an identical self which did not exist before, in the way that faith arises from non-existence in the existing mind. Nor does the mind, after coming to know itself, see itself by recollection as established in its own memory, as though it had not been there before becoming the object of its own knowledge. Assuredly, from the moment of its beginning to be, the mind has never ceased to know itself, to understand itself, and to love itself, as we have already demonstrated. Therefore, in its act of turning upon itself in thought, a trinity is presented in which it is possible to recognize a "word"--formed from the act of thinking, and united to its original by will. Here, then, is where we may recognize the image for which we are seeking.

[14] It may be objected that the faculty by which the mind, which is ever present to itself, is said to "remember" itself, cannot properly be called memory. For memory is of things past, not of things present. Some writers upon the virtues, including Cicero, have analysed prudence into the three elements of memory, understanding and foresight, assigning memory to what is past, understanding to what is present, and foresight to what is future.

Augustine: The Trinity XV.13

Book XV: Review and Re-valuation: Image and Original

[13] No man can comprehend the wisdom by which God knows all things, a wisdom wherein that which we call past does not pass, and that which we call future is not awaited as though not yet available, but both past and future are all together present with what is present: a wisdom wherein there is no thinking on particular things severally, or movement of thought from one thing to another, but the whole universe is presented simultaneously in one single view. No man, I say, can comprehend such a wisdom, which is both foresight and knowledge; inasmuch as even our own wisdom passes our comprehension. We can perceive, in various ways, what is present to our senses or our understanding: what is absent but was once present, we know by memory if we have not forgotten it. We conjecture, not the past from the future, but the future from the past, though we cannot have certain knowledge of it. To some of our thoughts we look forward with a degree of clearness and assurance as about to occur in the immediate future; but when we do so with the maximum of security, we do it by an act of memory, which is evidently concerned not with what is going to happen but with what is past. This is open to experience in the case of speeches or songs which we render from memory in a certain order: did we not foresee in thought what comes next, we could not speak it. But what enables us to foresee is not pre-vision but memory. Until the whole speech or song is ended, there is nothing in its recitation that was not foreseen and looked forward to. Yet in the process our singing and speaking is not ascribed to pre-vision but to memory; and we remark, in those who display exceptional powers of such extended recitation, a strength not of foresight but of memory.

MARTIANUS CAPELLA

410 - 439

From: *Martianus Capella and the Seven Liberal Arts*, Vol. II, *The Marriage of Philology and Mercury*. Translated by W. H. Stahle and R. Johnson, with E. L. Burge. Published by Columbia University Press, 1977.

Capella's *Marriage of Philology and Mercury* is an allegorical encyclopedia of the seven liberal arts (grammar, rhetoric, dialectic [the trivium], and arithmetic, geometry, astronomy, and music [the quadrium]. Widely used by medieval writers, Capella's work is a composite of the handbooks available to him in Carthage (North Africa) during the twilight years of the Roman Empire. The text begins with an account of the marriage of Philology and Mercury, part of which is reprinted here, as it represents, in allegorical form, Capella's view of the relation of memory to other cognitive functions. Also included is an excerpt on rhetoric in the didactic portion of the text which presents Capella's views on how to improve memory performance.

Supplementary reading:

Stahle, W. H., Johnson, R., & Burge, E. L. (1977). *Martianus Capella and the Seven Liberal Arts*, Vol. I. New York: Columbia University Press.

Table of Contents

The Marriage of Mercury and Philology

Explanation of contents: The paragraphs of Stahle and Johnson's translation are numbered continuously from the beginning of "The Marriage" and these numbers are reproduced here [in brackets].

[7] He [Mercury] went then to ask for Psyche, the daughter of Entelechia and Sol, because she was extremely beautiful and the gods had taken great care over her education. On the day of her birth the gods, being invited to a celebration, had brought her many gifts. Jupiter, in fact, had placed on her head a diadem which he had taken from his favored daughter Eternity; Juno had added a band for her hair, made from a gleaming vein of pure gold. Even the Tritonian [Athena] loosed from her tunic the flame-red veil and breastband and, herself a virgin holy and wise, draped the virgin in the very mantle from her own bosom. The Delian also, carrying his laurel branch, showed her with that wand of foresight and prophecy the birds, the bolts of lightning, the motions of heaven itself and the stars. Urania with gentle kindness gave her a gleaming mirror which Wisdom had hung in Rania's rooms amongst her gifts--a mirror in which Psyche could recognize herself and learn her origins. The craftsman of Lemnos kindled for her ever-burning flamelets; she would not then be oppressed by gloomy shadows and blind night. Aphrodite had given to all her senses every kind of pleasure; she had spread ointment on Psyche, garlanded her with flowers, taught her to appreciate and enjoy perfume and to delight in the sweetness of honey; she had implanted in her also a desire for gold and jewelry, a taste for wearing rich ornament. When she rested, Aphrodite brought her rattles and bells with which one lulls a baby to sleep; and then, to make sure that she was never without amusement and delectation, Aphrodite assigned Pleasure to stimulate desire in her by intimate titillation. The Cyllenian himself gave her a vehicle with swift wheels in which she could travel at an astonishing speed, although Memory bound it and weighted it down with golden chains. So the Arcadian [Mercury], his earlier hopes frustrated, sought in marriage Psyche, wealthy as she was in the gifts of heaven and richly adorned by the gods. But Virtue, almost in tears and clinging fast to the Cyllenian, confessed that Psyche had been snatched from her company into the hands of Cupid the flying archer, and was being held captive by him in shackles of adamant.

Martianus Capella: Rhetoric 538 - 539

[538] Next to be considered are the precepts of memorization. Although it is accepted that memory is a natural faculty, there is no doubt that it can be assisted by training. This training comprises some brief rules but a lot of practice, the goal of which is that words and ideas should be grasped not only surely but also quickly. We must remember not only what we have found to say but also what our opponent has discussed in his treatment of the case. Simonides, who was both poet and philosopher, is said to have discovered the rules of this subject; for when a banquet hall suddenly collapsed, and the next of kin could not identify those buried, he supplied the seating order and names from memory. From this experience he learned that it is order which makes possible the rules of memory. This order must be exercised on distinct topics, to which be attributed material forms and representations of ideas; for example, you might remember a wedding by the bride veiled in saffron or a homicide by a sword and arm--images, as it were, put down in, and given back by, the appropriate section of our memory. For just as what is written is contained in

wax and letters, so what is committed to memory is written into areas as if in wax and on the written page; but the memory of things is contained in images as if in letters.

[539] But, as I have said, much practice and effort are required for memorization, in which has been discovered the practice of writing for ourselves what we want to remember easily; and if what we must learn is rather long it stays in the mind more readily if it is divided into sections; then it will be of advantage to make symbols individually at those points which we particularly want to remember, they should not be read out loud, but rather memorized under our breath; and it is clear that memory is better aroused at night than during the day, since the silence of night is a great help and our concentration is not distracted by our senses. Memory is applied to things and to words, but words do not always have to be memorized; unless there is time for this, it will be enough for anyone to hold the matter itself in the mind, especially if nothing comes naturally from the memory.

THOMAS AQUINAS

1224 - 1274

From: *Truth*. Vol. 2, Questions X-XX. Translated by J. V. McGlynn. Published by Henry Regnery, 1953.

Summa Theologiae. Translated and edited by T. Gilby, K. Foster, and L. Bright. Published by Blackfriars, in conjunction with McGraw-Hill and Eyre & Spottis-woode, 1964.

Commentary on the Metaphysics of Aristotle. Translated by J. P. Rowan. Published by Henry Regnery, 1961.

Thomas Aquinas, a theologian and philosopher, was the youngest son of a noble Italian family. Educated in Naples, Paris and Cologne, he taught principally at the University of Paris, creating a coherent position that combined Aristotelianism with elements of neoPlatonism, Augustine, and Boethius. Following Aristotle, Aquinas distinguished biological functions shared with all living things from sensory and locomotor functions, shared with animals, and from cognitive functions, unique to humans. The sensory functions he divided into interior and exterior functions. The exterior included the five senses; the interior, perception of objects, memory for images (imagination), and association of these images with past time (sense memory). Aquinas made a clear distinction between the process of abstracting general concepts and the process of recognizing particular instances. Corresponding to this division, he distinguished intellectual memory for general concepts and abstract ideas from sense memory for particular events.

Supplementary readings:

Bourke, V. J. (1965). *Aquinas' Search for Wisdom*. Milwaukee: Bruce Publishing Co.

Meyer, H. (1957). *The Philosophy of St. Thomas Aquinas*. Englewood Cliffs, NJ: Prentice-Hall.

THOMAS AQUINAS

Table of Contents

Truth

Explanation of contents: "Truth" is divided into questions (first numeral), which are subdivided into articles (second numeral). For example, 10.2 refers to question 10, article 2. Points and subpoints of the argument are also numbered in the text but are not used in the table of contents. The "Summa" is divided into three parts, of which the second is subdivided into two. These are conventionally referred to as: 1a, 1a2ae, 2a2ae, 3a. Each part is subdivided into questions (second numeral) which are in turn divided into articles (third numeral). For example, 1a.77.8 refers to Part 1a, question 77, article 8. In many places the points and subpoints of the argument are also numbered in the text. These last occur irregularly and are not listed in the table of contents. Reference to the "Commentary" is made by means of the numbers that appear at the top of each page of the Rowan translation and by paragraph numbers which appear in the text of this translation. The numbers at the top of each page refer to the Spiazzi divisions of Aristotle's text and to the Cathala divisions of Aquinas' commentary. For example, I.L.1:C1-35:10-13 refers to the page headed I.L.1:C1-35 in the Rowan translation, paragraphs 10-13.

Question 10. Article 2. Secondly, We Ask: Is There Memory in the Mind?

Difficulties: It seems that there is not, for

1.   According to Augustine, that which we share with brute animals does not belong to the mind. But memory is common to us and to brute animals, as is also clear from Augustine. Therefore, memory is not in the mind.

2.   The Philosopher [Aristotle] says that memory does not belong to the intellective but to the primary sensitive faculty. Therefore, since mind is the same as understanding, as is clear from what has been said above, memory does not seem to be part of the mind.

3.   Understanding and all that belong to understanding abstract from space and time. Memory, however, does not so abstract, for it deals with a definite time, the past. For memory concerns things past, as Cicero says. Therefore, memory does not pertain to mind or understanding.

4.   Since in memory we retain things that are not being actually apprehended, it follows that, wherever there is memory, there must be a difference between apprehension and retention. But it is in sense only, and not in understanding, that we find this difference. The two can differ in sense because sense makes use of a bodily organ. But not everything that is retained in the body is apprehended. But understanding does not make use of a bodily organ, and so retains things only according to the mode of understanding. So, these things have to be actually understood. Therefore, memory is not part of understanding or mind.

5.   The soul does not remember until it has retained something. But before it receives from the senses, which are the source of all our knowledge, any species which it can retain, it already has the character of image [of the Trinity]. Since memory is part of that image, it does not seem possible for memory to be in the mind.

6.   In so far as mind has the character of image of God, it is directed toward God. But memory is not directed toward God, since it deals with things that belong to time. But God is entirely beyond time. Therefore, memory is not in the mind.

7.   If memory were part of the mind, the intelligible species would be maintained in the mind as they are in the angelic mind. But the angels can understand by turning their attention to the species which they have within them. Therefore, the human mind should be able to understand by turning its attention to the species it retains, without referring to phantasms. But this is obviously false. For, no matter to what degree one has scientific knowledge as a habit, if the organ of the power of imagination or memory is injured, this knowledge cannot be made actual. This would not result if the mind could actually

understand without referring to powers which use organs. So, memory is not part of the mind.

To the Contrary:

1'. The Philosopher [Aristotle] says that the intellective soul, not the whole soul, is the place of the species. But it belongs to place to preserve what is kept in it. Therefore, since the preservation of the species belongs to memory, memory seems to be part of understanding.

2'. That which has a uniform relation to all time is not concerned with any particular time. But memory, even in its proper acceptation, has a uniform relation to all time, as Augustine says and proves with the words of Virgil, who used the names memory and forgetfulness in their proper sense. Therefore, memory is not concerned with any particular time, but with all time. So it belongs to understanding.

3'. Strictly speaking, memory refers to things past. But understanding deals not only with what is present, but also with what is past. For the understanding judges about any time, understanding man to have existed, to exist in the future, and to exist now, as is clear from *The Soul*. Therefore, memory, properly speaking, can belong to understanding.

4'. As memory concerns what is past, so foresight concerns what is in the future, according to Cicero. But foresight, properly speaking, belongs to the intellectual part. For the same reason memory does too.

Reply:

According to the common usage, memory means a knowledge of things past. But to know the past as past belongs to that which has the power of knowing the now as now. Sense is this power. For understanding does not know the singular as singular, but according to some common character, as it is man or white or even particular, but not in so far as it is this man or this particular thing. In a similar way, understanding does not know a present and a past thing as this present and this past thing.

Since memory, taken strictly, looks to what is past with reference to the present, it is clear that memory, properly speaking, does not belong to the intellectual part, but only to the sensitive, as the Philosopher [Aristotle] shows. But, since intellect not only understands the intelligible thing, but also understands that it understands such an intelligible thing, the term memory can be broadened to include the knowledge by which one knows the object previously known in so far as he knows he knew it earlier, although he does not know the object as in the past in the manner earlier explained. In this way all knowledge not received for the first time can be called memory.

This can take place in two ways, either when there is continuous study based on acquired knowledge without interruption, or when the study is interrupted. The latter has more of the character of past, and so it more properly participates in the nature of memory. We have an example of this when we say that we remember a thing which previously we knew habitually but not actually. Thus, memory belongs to the intellective part of our soul. It is in this sense that Augustine seems to understand memory, when he makes it part of the image of the Trinity. For he intends to assign to memory everything in the mind which is stored there habitually without passing into act.

There are various explanations of the manner in which this can take place. Avicenna holds that the fact that the soul has habitual knowledge of anything which it does not actually consider does not come from this, that certain species are retained in the intellectual part. Rather, he understands that it is impossible for the species not actually considered to be kept anywhere except in the sensitive part, either in the imagination, which is the storehouse of forms received by the senses, or in the memory, for particular apprehensions not received from the senses. The species stays in the understanding only when it is actually being considered. But, after the consideration, it ceases to be there. Thus, when one wants actually to consider something again, it is necessary for new intelligible species to flow from the agent intelligence into the possible intellect.

However, it does not follow, according to Avicenna, that the new consideration of what was known previously necessarily entails learning or discovering all over again, for one retains a certain aptitude through which he turns more easily to the agent intellect to receive the species flowing from it than he did before. In us, this aptitude is the habit of scientific knowledge. According to this opinion, memory is not part of the mind because it preserves certain species, but because it has an aptitude for receiving them anew.

But this does not seem to be a reasonable explanation. In the first place, since the possible intellect has a more stable nature than sense, it must receive its species more securely. Thus, the species can be better preserved in it than in the sensitive part. In the second place, the agent intelligence is equally disposed to communicate species suitable for all the sciences. As a consequence, if some species were not conserved in the possible intellect, but there were in it only the aptitude of turning to the agent intellect, man would have an equal aptitude for any intelligible thing. Therefore, from the fact that a man had learned one science he would not know it better than other sciences. Besides, this seems openly opposed to the opinion of the Philosopher [Aristotle], who commends the ancients for holding that the intellective part of the soul is the place of the species.

Therefore, others say that the intelligible species remain in the possible intellect after actual consideration, and that the ordered arrangement of these is the habit of knowledge. In this classification the power by which our minds retain these intelligible species after actual consideration will be called memory. This comes closer to the proper meaning of memory.

Answers to Difficulties:

1. The memory which we have in common with brute animals is that in which particular intentions are preserved. This is not in the mind; only the memory in which intelligible species are kept is there.

2. The Philosopher [Aristotle] is speaking of the memory which deals with the past as related to a particular present in so far as particular. This is not in the mind.

3. The answer to the third difficulty is clear from what has just been said.

4. Actual apprehension and retention differ in the possible intellect, not because the species are there somehow in a bodily manner, but only in an intelligible way. However, it does not follow that one understands according to that species all the time, but only when the possible intellect becomes that species perfectly in act. Sometimes it has the act of this species incompletely, that is, in some way between pure potency and pure act. This is habitual knowledge. The reduction from this to complete act takes place through the will, which, according to Anselm, is the mover of all the powers.

5. Mind has the character of image [of the Trinity] especially in so far as it is directed to God and to itself. It is present to itself and God is present to it before any species are received from sensible things. Furthermore, mind is not said to have the power of memory because it actually preserves something, but because it has the power to preserve something.

6. The answer to the sixth difficulty is clear from what has been said.

7. No power can know anything without turning to its object, as sight knows nothing unless it turns to color. Now, since phantasms are related to the possible intellect in the way that sensible things are related to sense, as the Philosopher [Aristotle] points out, no matter to what extent an intelligible species is present to the understanding, understanding does not actually consider anything according to that species without referring to a phantasm. Therefore, just as our understanding in its present state needs phantasms actually to consider anything before it acquires a habit, so it needs them, too, after it has acquired a habit. The situation is different with angels, for phantasms are not the object of their understanding.

Answers to Contrary Difficulties:

1'. The authority cited can prove only that memory is in the mind in the way we have mentioned, not that it is there properly.

2'. We must understand Augustine's statement to mean that memory can deal with present objects. However, it can never be called memory unless something past is considered, at least past with reference to cognition itself. It is in this way that we say someone, who is present to himself, forgets or remembers himself because he retains or does not retain the past knowledge about himself.

3'. In so far as understanding knows temporal differences through common characters, it can thus make judgments according to any difference of time.

4'. Foresight is in the understanding only according to general considerations about the future. It is applied to particular things through the mediation of particular reason which must act as the medium between general reason, which is the source of movement, and the movement which follows in particular things, as is clear from what the Philosopher [Aristotle] says.

Article 3. In the Third Article We Ask: Is Memory Distinguished from Understanding as One Power from Another?

Difficulties:

It seems that it is not, for

1. Different acts belong to different powers. But the possible intellect and memory, as part of the mind, are said to have the same act, to preserve the species. For Augustine assigns this function to memory and the Philosopher [Aristotle] assigns it to the possible intellect. Therefore, memory is not distinguished from understanding as one power from another.

2. To receive something without paying attention to any difference of time belongs properly to understanding, which abstracts from the here and now. But memory pays no attention to difference of time, for, according to Augustine, memory deals indifferently with things present, past, and future. Therefore, memory is not distinguished from understanding.

3. According to Augustine, intelligence can be taken in two ways. According to the first, we are said to understand that which we actually think. According to the second, we are said to understand that which we do not actually consider. But intelligence, in the meaning of understanding only that which we actually think, is understanding in act. This is not a power, but the activity of a power; hence, it is not distinguished from memory as a power from a power. But, in so far as we understand those things which we do not actually consider, understanding is not in any way distinguished from memory, but belongs to it. This is clear from Augustine: "If we look to the inner memory of the mind by which it remembers itself, to the inner understanding by which it understands itself, and to the inner will by which it loves itself, where these three are always together, whether they are thought about or not, we will see that the image of the Trinity belongs only to the memory." Therefore, understanding is in no way distinguished from memory as a power from a power.

4. Someone may say that intelligence is a power through which the soul is able actually to think, and so, also, that the intelligence through which we are

said to understand only when we are thinking is distinguished from memory as one power from another.--On the contrary, it belongs to the same power to have a habit and to use that habit. But to understand when not thinking is to understand habitually, whereas to understand when thinking is to use the habit. Therefore, to understand when not thinking and to understand when thinking belong to the same power. And so, for this reason, understanding does not differ from memory as one power from another.

5. In the intellective part of the soul there are only the cognoscitive and motive, or affective, powers. But the will is the affective or motive; understanding, the cognoscitive. Therefore, memory is not a different power from understanding.

To the Contrary:

1'. Augustine says that "the soul partakes of the image of God in this, that it can use reason and understanding to know and see." But the soul can see through its powers. Therefore, the image in the soul is considered according to its powers. But the image in the soul is considered according to the presence of memory, understanding, and will in the soul. Therefore, these three are three distinct powers.

2'. If these are not three powers, there must be one of them which is act or activity. But act is not always in the soul, for one does not always actually understand or will. Therefore, these three will not always be in the soul, and consequently the soul will not always be in the image of God, contrary to Augustine.

3'. There is a certain equality among these three which portrays the equality of the divine Persons. But there is no equality among act, habit, and power, because power embraces more than habit and habit more than act. For many habits belong to one power, and many acts can come from one habit. Therefore, one of these cannot be habit and another act.

Reply:

We must say that the image of the Trinity in the soul can be predicated in two ways: one in which there is perfect imitation of the Trinity, the other in which the imitation is imperfect.

For the mind perfectly imitates the Trinity in this, that it actually remembers, actually understands, and actually wills. This is so because in the uncreated Trinity the middle Person is the Word. Now, there can be a word only with actual cognition. Hence, it is according to this kind of perfect imitation that Augustine puts the image in memory, understanding, and will. In it, memory refers to habitual knowledge, understanding to actual cognition which proceeds from habitual knowledge of memory, and will to the actual movement of the will which proceeds from thought. This appears expressly from what he says in *The Trinity*: "Since the word cannot be there," in the mind, "without thought; for

137

everything which we speak we think with that internal word which belongs to the language of no people, the image is found especially in those three: memory, intelligence, and will. Intelligence I now call that by which we understand when thinking; I call that will which joins this offspring [thought] with its parent [intelligence]."

We have the image in which there is imperfect imitation when we designate it according to habits and powers. It is thus that Augustine bases the image of the Trinity in the soul upon mind, knowledge, and love. Here, mind means the power; knowledge and love, the habits existing in it. In place of knowledge he could have said habitual intelligence, for both can be taken in the sense of habit. This is clear from *The Trinity*, where he says: "Can we correctly say that the musician knows music, but he does not now understand it because he is not now thinking about it, or that he now understands geometry because he is now thinking about it? This opinion is obviously absurd." So, in this sense, knowledge and love, taken as habitual, belong only to memory, as is clear from the authoritative citation from Augustine in the objections.

But, since acts have radical existence in powers, as effects in their causes, even perfect imitation according to memory, understanding in act, and will in act can in the first instance be found in the powers through which the soul can remember, actually understand and will, as the citation from Augustine shows. Thus, the image will be based upon the powers, though not in the sense that in the mind memory could be some power besides the understanding. This is clear from what follows.

Diversity of objects is the source of differentiation of powers only when the diversity comes from those things which of themselves belong to the objects, in so far as they are objects of such powers. Thus, hot and cold in something colored do not, as such, differentiate the power of sight. For the same power of sight can see what is colored, whether hot or cold, sweet or bitter. Now, although mind or understanding can in a certain way know what is past, still, since it relates indifferently to knowledge of present, past, and future, the difference of past and present is accidental to what is intelligible, in so far as it is intelligible. For this reason, although memory can be in the mind in a certain way, it cannot be there as a power distinct of itself from other powers in the way in which philosophers speak of the distinction of powers. In this way, memory can be found only in the sensitive part, which is referred to the present as present. For this reason, a higher power than that of sense is needed if it is to relate to the past.

Nevertheless, although memory is not a power distinct from intelligence, taken as a power, the Trinity is still in the soul if we consider those powers in so far as the one power of understanding has an orientation to different things, namely, habitually to keep the knowledge of something, and actually to consider it. It is in this way that Augustine distinguishes lower from higher reason, according to an orientation to different things.

Answers to Difficulties:

1. Although memory as belonging to the mind is not a power distinct from the possible intellect, there is a distinction between memory and possible intellect according to orientation to different things, as we have said.

2. The same answer can be given to the four following difficulties.

Answers to Contrary Difficulties:

1'. In the passage cited, Augustine is not talking about the image which is in the soul according to perfect imitation. This is present when the soul actually imitates the Trinity by understanding it.

2'. In the soul there is always an image of the Trinity in some way, but not always according to perfect imitation.

3'. Between power, act, and habit there can be equality inasmuch as they are referred to one object. Thus, the image of the Trinity is in the soul inasmuch as it is directed to God. Still, even in the ordinary way of speaking about power, habit, and act, there is an equality among them. However, this equality does not follow the distinctive character of the nature, because activity, habit, and power have the act of existence in different ways. But it does follow the relation to act according to which we consider the quantity of these three. It is not necessary to consider only one act numerically, or one habit, but habit and act in general.

Aquinas: Truth 10.7

Article 7. In the Seventh Article We Ask: Is the Image of the Trinity in the Mind as It Knows Material Things or Only as It Knows Eternal Things?

To the Contrary:

1'. Augustine says: "The trinity which is found in a lower science should not be called or be thought to be the image of God, although it does belong to the inner man." But a lower science is that according to which the mind considers temporal things, and is thus distinguished from wisdom, which refers to eternal things. Therefore, the image of the Trinity is not to be found in the mind according to its knowledge of temporal things.

2'. The parts of the image, considered according to their order, should correspond to the three persons. But the order of the persons does not appear in the mind as it knows temporal things. For, in knowing temporal things, understanding does not proceed from memory, as the Word from the Father, but memory rather proceeds from understanding, for we remember those things which we have previously understood. Therefore, the image is not in the mind as it knows things of time.

3'. Augustine, having given that division of the mind (into contemplation of things eternal and activity concerning temporal things), says: "Not only the Trinity, but also the image of God, exists only in that part which is concerned with contemplation of eternal things. Even if we could find a trinity in that which is derived from activity about things of time, we still would not find the image of God there." Thus, we conclude as before.

4'. The image of the Trinity always exists in the soul, but knowledge of temporal things does not, since it is acquired. Therefore, the image of the Trinity is not in the soul as it knows temporal things.

Reply:

Likeness brings the character of image to completion. However, for the character of image not every likeness is sufficient, but the fullest likeness, through which something is represented according to its specific nature. For this reason, in bodies we look for the image more in their shapes, which are the proper marks of species, than in colors and other accidents. There is a likeness of the uncreated Trinity in our soul according to any knowledge which it has of itself, not only of the mind, but also of sense, as Augustine clearly shows. But we find the image of God only in that knowledge according to which there arises in the mind the fuller likeness of God.

Therefore, if we distinguish the knowledge of the mind according to objects, we find in our mind a threefold knowledge. There is the knowledge by which the mind knows God, by which it knows itself, and by which it knows temporal things. In the knowledge by which the mind knows temporal things there is no expressed likeness of the uncreated Trinity, either according to adaptation or according to analogy. It is not according to the first, because material things are more unlike God than is the mind itself. Thus, the mind does not become fully conformed to God for being informed by knowledge of these material things. Nor yet is it according to analogy, for a temporal thing, which begets knowledge, or even actual understanding of itself in the soul, is not of the same substance as the mind, but something extraneous to its nature. Thus, the consubstantiality of the uncreated Trinity cannot be represented through it.

But in the knowledge by which our mind knows itself there is a representation of the uncreated Trinity according to analogy. It lies in this, that the mind, knowing itself in this way, begets a word expressing itself, and love proceeds from both of these, just as the Father, uttering Himself, has begotten the Word from eternity, and the Holy Spirit proceeds from both. But in that cognition by which the mind knows God the mind itself becomes conformed to God, just as every knower, as such, is assimilated to that which is known.

But there is a greater likeness through conformity, as of sight to color, than through analogy, as of sight to understanding, which is related to its objects in a way similar to that of sight. Consequently, the likeness of the Trinity is clearer in mind, as knowing God, than as knowing itself. Therefore, properly speaking, the image of the Trinity is in the mind primarily and mainly, in so far as the mind knows God, and it is there in a certain manner and secondarily, in so far as the mind knows itself, especially when it considers itself in so far as it is the image of God. As a result, its consideration does not stop with itself, but goes on to God. There is no image in the consideration of temporal things, but a kind of likeness of the Trinity, which can partake more of the character of vestige. Such is the likeness which Augustine attributes to the sensitive powers.

Answers to Difficulties:

1. There is indeed a trinity in the mind, as it applies itself to activity concerned with temporal things. But this trinity is not called the image of the uncreated Trinity, as is clear from what Augustine adds to that passage.

2. The equality of the divine persons is better represented in the knowledge of eternal than of temporal things. For we should not look for equality between object and power, but between one power and another. Moreover, although there is greater inequality between our mind and God than between our mind and a temporal thing, yet between the memory which our mind has of God and actual understanding and love of God there is greater equality than between the memory it has of temporal things and the understanding and love of them. For God is knowable and lovable of Himself and is understood and loved by the mind of each to the degree in which He is present to the mind. His presence in the mind is memory of Him in the mind; thus, intelligence is proportioned to the memory of Him, and will or love is proportioned to this intelligence.
    However, physical things as such are not intelligible or lovable and so there is not this equality in the mind with reference to them. Neither is there the same order of origin, since these are present to our memory because we have understood them, and so memory arises from understanding rather than conversely. The opposite of this takes place in the created mind with reference to God from whose presence the mind participates in intellectual light so that it can understand.

3. Although the knowledge which we have of physical things is prior in time to that which we have of God, the latter is prior in dignity. And the fact that we know physical reality better than we know God offers no difficulty, because the least knowledge which can be had about God surpasses all knowledge about creatures. The nobility of knowledge depends on the nobility of the thing known, as is clear from *The Soul* [*De Anima*]. For this reason, the Philosopher [Aristotle] puts the little knowledge which we have of heavenly things before all the knowledge which we have about things here below.

Aquinas: Summa Theologiae 1a.12.9

Part 1a. Question 12. Article 9. Is It by Means of Any Likeness That the Mind Knows God?

THE NINTH POINT. 1. It seems that what is seen in God is seen through a likeness. For knowledge comes about through the assimilation of the knower to the known; the mind in its realization becomes the realized intelligibility of the thing to be known, and the sight in its realization becomes the realized visibility of the thing to be seen: this happens because the knowing power is formed by a likeness of the thing known, as the pupil of the eye is formed by the likeness of colour. If therefore the minds of those who see God in his essence are to understand other creatures they must be formed by the likenesses of these creatures.

2. We remember what we have previously seen, but St. Paul who, according to Augustine, saw the essence of God when he was rapt in his ecstasy, still remembered many things after he had ceased to see it; for he said, *I have heard secret words which it is not given to man to speak.* Some likeness, therefore, of the things he remembered must have remained in his mind and so these likenesses must have been there when he was actually seeing God.

ON THE OTHER HAND it is with one view that we see the mirror and what is in it; but everything we see in God is seen as in a sort of intelligible mirror. Hence since God himself is not seen through any likeness but by his essence, neither are the things seen in him seen by any likeness.

REPLY: The things seen in the essence of God by those who see it are not seen through any likeness but through the essence of God itself in their minds. Each thing is known in so far as its likeness is in the knower. This can happen in two ways: since things which are like to the same thing are like to each other the power of knowing can be conformed to the thing known either by being formed directly by the likeness of the known thing, and then the thing is known in itself, or else by being formed by the likeness of something which is itself like to the known thing, and then the thing is known in a likeness. It is one thing to know a man himself and another to know him from his picture. Thus to know things through their own likenesses in the mind is to know them in themselves, or in their own natures; but to know them through their likenesses pre-existing in God is to see them in God.

Aquinas: Summa Theologiae 1a.77.8

Part 1a. Question 77. Article 8. Whether All the Powers Remain in the Soul When Separated from the Body.

4. Again, memory is a power of the sense-soul, as Aristotle proves. But memory remains in the disembodied soul, for the rich glutton whose soul is in hell was told, *Remember that during your life good things came your way.* Thus memory remains in the disembodied soul, and so too do the other sense powers.

Part 1a. Question 78. Article 4. Whether the Interior Senses Are Suitably Distinguished.

3. Again, Aristotle maintains that imagination and memory are receptivenesses at the primitive level of sensation. But a receptiveness is not divided against its subject. Hence memory and imagination should not be set down as powers distinct from sense.

4. Again, the intellect depends on sensation less than any power of the sense part of the soul does. Yet the intellect knows nothing except by receiving sense-impressions, so that, according to the Posterior Analytics, if anyone lacks one of the senses he lacks a field of knowledge. There is much less reason, then, for postulating a power in the sensitive part which perceives things the senses do not perceive--what we mean by instinct.

5. Moreover, the activity of the cogitative sense, which brings together and fuses and separates, and the act of remembering, which uses a sort of syllogism in its search, are just as far from an instinctive act and from the sense memory as estimative activity of instinct is from an act of imagination. Either, then, cogitation and reminiscence require powers distinct from instinct and memory, or else instinct and memory should not be considered to be powers distinct from imagination.

Consider, though, that the life of a higher animal demands that it grasp a thing not only when present but when absent as well. Otherwise, since its movement and activity depend on its knowledge, it would not move after anything absent. The contrary is clearest in higher animals that move systematically, for it is something absent they have grasped that moves them. Thus the animal has not only, through its sense-soul, to receive the forms of sense objects when they are actually affecting it, but has also to retain and conserve them. Receiving and conserving, however, must be traced to different principles in the physical order, for moist things receive easily and retain badly, dry things the reverse. Hence since the sense power is an activity of a physical organ there has to be one power to receive sense forms and another to conserve them.

Consider further that if the only things that moved an animal were things pleasurable and repugnant to the senses, there would be no need to suppose any power in it except the perception of sense forms in which it would either take pleasure or displeasure. But an animal has to seek and shun things not only because they suit or do not suit its senses but also because they are in other ways fitting and useful or harmful. Thus a lamb, when it sees a wolf approach, flees, not because it does not like the colour or shape, but because it is its natural enemy. And likewise a bird collects straw, not because it pleases its senses, but because it needs it for building its nest. So the animal has to perceive things which no external sense perceives. And there has to be a distinct source of this perception since the perception of sense forms comes from their impact on the senses, but not the perception of the intentions in question here.

So for the reception of sense forms there is the particular sense and the 'common' sense (the distinction between them is treated below). Their retention and conservation require fantasy or imagination, which are the same thing; fantasy or imagination is, as it were, a treasure-store of forms received through the senses. Instinct grasps intentions which are not objects of simple sensation. And the power of memory conserves these; it is a treasure-store of intentions of this kind. A sign of this is that the reason for remembering in animals is an intention of this kind, the fact that something is harmful or serviceable, and the fact of pastness, which is what memory bears on, falls into this category.

Consider now that so far as sense forms are concerned there is no difference between men and other animals; they are affected in the same way by external sense objects. But when it comes to the intentions just discussed there is a difference, for other animals perceive such intentions solely by natural instinct, whereas man perceives them by a process of comparison. And so what we call natural instinct in other animals in man we call cogitation, which comes upon intentions of the kind in question through a process of comparison. Which is why it is also called the particular reason, to which medical scientists assign a fixed part of the body, the middle of the head; for it compares individual intentions the way the reasoning intellect compares universal intentions. As to memory, man not only has it the way other animals do, in terms of sudden recollection of things past, but also in the form of reminiscence, a quasi-syllogistic search among memories of things past in their individuality.

Avicenna did indeed maintain a fifth power, somewhere between instinct and imagination, a power which composes and divides imagined forms, as when from the image of gold and the image of mountain we compose the single form of a golden mountain which we have never seen. But this activity is not found in animals other than man, in whom the power of imagination suffices to account for it. It was to this power that Averroes attributed this activity in a book he did *On Sense and Sensibles*. And so there is no need to maintain more than four powers of the sensitive part of the soul, namely the common sense and imagination, instinct and memory.

Hence: 1. No internal sense is described as common the way a predicate is, as a general classification, but it is common in the sense of being the root and source of the external senses.

2. Each particular sense judges its proper object, discerning it from other things that come under the same sense, for instance discerning white from black or green. But neither sight nor taste can discern the difference between white and sweet, because to discern a difference between two things you have to know both. Hence it must belong to a common sense to discriminate; all sense perceptions are referred to it as to a common terminus. It also perceives sense-perceptions, as when someone is aware that he is seeing. This could

not take place through any particular sense, which knows only the sensible form by which it is affected. Sight arises from the physical impression and this leads to another impression in the common sense, which perceives the act of sight.

3. Just as one power arises from the soul through another as intermediary, as said above, so the soul is a subject for one power through another as intermediary. This is the way imagination and memory are described as receptive at the level of primitive sensation.

4. Granted that the activity of the understanding has its origin in sensation, nevertheless the understanding knows many things in whatever is perceived by the senses which sense itself cannot perceive. The same is true, in a less exalted fashion, of instinct.

5. Cogitation and memory reach so high in man through their similarity to and connection with abstract reason, by a kind of overflow, not through anything belonging to the sense-soul as such. So they are not new powers but the same powers, more perfect than they are in other animals.

6. Augustine calls a vision spiritual when it involves a bodily likeness in the absence of a body. This is obviously true of any form of interior knowledge.

Aquinas: Summa Theologiae 1a.79.6 - 1a.79.7

Part 1a. Question 79. Article 6. Whether Memory Is in the Intellectual Part of the Soul.

THE SIXTH POINT: 1. There are reasons for thinking that memory is not in the intellectual part of the soul. For Augustine says that the things which belong to the higher part of the soul are those that are not common to men and beasts. But memory is common to men and beasts, for he says in the same context that beasts can sense physical things through the body's senses, and commit them to memory. Hence memory does not belong to the soul's intellectual part.

2. Besides, memory is of past things. But past means a fixed point of time. So memory knows something in terms of a fixed time, which is to say it is a here-and-now knowledge. Now such knowledge is the province of sense, not intellect. So memory is in the sensitive area of the soul only, not the intellectual.

3. Besides, memory preserves thoughts not actually being thought about. But this cannot happen in the understanding. For the understanding passes into act by being informed through the object of thought; and the actuality of the thing understood is the understanding itself in act; and so the understanding actually understands anything it has as an object of thought. So memory is not in the intellectual area.

ON THE OTHER HAND Augustine says that *memory, understanding and will are the one mind.*

REPLY: Since the very notion of memory is the conservation of thoughts not actually being attended to, the first thing to consider is whether thoughts can be conserved in the understanding in this way. Avicenna argued that it was impossible. In the field of sense, he said, this could happen in the case of some powers, in that they act through bodily organs in which forms can be conserved without being attended to. But in the understanding, which does not have a physical organ, nothing exists except as an object of thought, so that likeness of which is in the understanding must be actually understood. So according to him, then, the moment anyone ceases thinking about something the thought of it ceases to exist in the intellect, and if he desires to think about it again he must turn to the abstractive intellect, which for him was a separate substance, so that thoughts might flow from it into his receptive understanding. And the practice and custom of turning to the abstractive intellect led the recipient intellect, he held, to enjoy a certain facility in so turning, and this is what he meant by the habit of a field of knowledge. On this view nothing is preserved at the intellectual level except what is present to the attention. It is impossible, on this argument, to admit an intellectual memory.

But this opinion does not agree with Aristotle. For he says that when the recipient intellect *is identified with each thing as knowing it, then it is said to be in act,* and that *this happens when it can act through itself. And even then it is with potentiality, though not the same way as before learning or discovering.* For the recipient intellect is said to become things when it receives them as knowledge-forms. And from the fact that it holds these it has the power to think about them when it will, though it does not follow that it is always actually doing so. For it is still with potentiality, though not in the way it was before understanding, but rather as anyone with habitual knowledge is potential to giving it his actual attention.

Avicenna's position also conflicts with the logic of things. What a thing accepts it accepts in its own way. Now the understanding is more stable and unchanging than any physical thing. So if the body's matter holds the forms it receives while it does something through them, but also retains them after ceasing to act through them, much more can the understanding unchangingly and lastingly take knowledge-forms into itself, whether it gets them from the things of sense or from a higher intelligence. Thus, if memory is taken to mean a power to keep thoughts in mind, then we have to speak of memory as being in the field of intellect.

If, however, we take the very notion of memory to be that it knows a past thing precisely as past, then it is not intellective, but a sense-memory only, which attends to particulars. Because pastness fixes a thing in time it belongs to the realm of the particular.

Hence: 1. The memory which retains thoughts is not common to us and the beasts. For thoughts are not retained in the sense part of the soul, but rather in the body-soul unity, since sense memory is an organic act. But the understanding of itself is retentive of knowledge-forms apart from any physical organ. Thus Aristotle notes that the soul is where thoughts are, not the whole soul, but the understanding.

2. Pastness can be considered either in relation to the thing known or in relation to the act of knowledge. The two are combined in the case of sense knowledge, which grasps something because it is affected by a present sense-object. So an animal remembers, simultaneously, that formerly it sensed something, and that it sensed a past something. But in the intellectual area pastness is irrelevant to a thing when that thing is taken precisely as an object of understanding. Mind understands man as man, and from this point of view it is incidental whether man exists in the past or the present or the future.

When it comes to an act, however, pastness can be found even in the understanding, just as it is in sensation, for any intellectual act of ours is a particular act at a particular time, so that a man is said to think now or yesterday or tomorrow. This is not incompatible with the nature of intellect, for such acts of understanding, though particular, are also non-material, as the intellect is: this we have explained. And so just as the understanding understands itself even though it is one particular faculty of understanding, in the same way it understands its own act of understanding, an individual act which is either past, present or future. So the concept of memory as memory of past things has its application in the intellectual order in that the understanding knows that it has previously understood something, but not in the sense that it grasps the past in its here-and-now character.

3. Sometimes a knowledge-form is potentially in the intellect, which then is said to be in a state of potentiality. But sometimes the act of thought is completed and then we have actual understanding. And sometimes the mind is half-way between potentiality and act, and this is understanding in a state of habit; in this way the understanding has concepts even when it is not actually attending to them.

Part 1a. Question 79. Article 7. Whether Intellectual Memory Is a Power Distinct from Understanding.

SEVENTH POINT: 1. There are reasons for thinking that intellectual memory is a power distinct from understanding. For in the mind Augustine puts memory, intelligence and will. Now memory is obviously a different power from will. So it likewise differs from intellect.

2. Besides, the reason for distinguishing powers is the same for the area of intellect as it is for that of sense. But as we have said, sense memory differs from other senses. So memory of the intellectual order differs from intellect.

3. According to Augustine memory, intelligence and will are equal among themselves, and one originates from another. This would not be the case were memory the same power as intellect. So it is not the same power.

ON THE OTHER HAND it is essential to memory to be a treasure-store or place of conservation for thoughts. Yet this Aristotle assigns to the understanding, as we have seen. So in the intellectual part memory is not a power distinct from understanding.

REPLY: We saw that the soul's powers are distinguished in terms of their different formal objects, so that to think of what a power means is to think about what it is for the sake of, its object. And we also saw that if a power is of its very nature ordered towards an object under one specific aspect, then we do not distinguish between diverse powers in order to deal with the differences of particular details within that common field. For instance the power of sight, which has colour for its formal object, is not sub-distinguished to deal with white and black. Now the understanding deals with being in general as its object, since the recipient intellect is that by which to become all things. Hence different things do not require different recipient understandings.

But the abstractive and recipient intellects differ as powers because, in relation to the same object, a causative power, which makes it an actual object for thought, has to be different from a receptive power which is moved by the object thus actualized. And thus the causative power is related to its object as being in actuality is to being in potentiality. Whereas the recipient power conversely is related to its object as a being in potentiality to a being in actuality.

So the only possible difference in the intellective part is that between the powers of abstracting and receiving, which makes it clear that memory is not a power distinct from understanding. Keeping as well as receiving is of the nature of a recipient power.

Hence: 1. Though we read in the *Sentences* 1, 3, that memory, intelligence and will are three powers, this is not the mind of Augustine, who is explicit that *taking memory, intelligence and will as always present to the soul whether attended to or not, they seem to come back to memory only. But by intelligence I now mean what we understand by while actually thinking; and by will that love or attraction such as unites child and parents.* Plainly Augustine does not regard these three as three powers; he takes memory to express the soul's ability to retain things in the manner known as habit; he uses the word 'intelligence' for the act of understanding, and 'will' for the act of the will.

2. Past and present may well give rise to a difference among the sense powers, but not among the intellectual powers. We have already explained this.

3. Understanding originates from memory in the way that an act proceeds from a habit. In this sense, then, they are equal, but not in the way that one power is equal to another.

Part 1a. Question 87. Article 4. Does the Intellect Understand Acts of the Will?

3. The affective movements of the soul are in the intellect neither by likenesses only, like bodies, nor by presence as in a subject, like the arts, but as derivatives in their origin, which contains their notion. And so Augustine says the affective movements of the soul exist in the memory by way of certain notions.

Part 1a2ae. Question 32. Article 3. Are Hopes and Memories Causes of Pleasure?

Now real union is greater than union through knowledge, and actual union greater than potential: hence, the greatest pleasure is that which comes through the senses and requires the actual presence of a sense-object. The next greatest pleasure is that of hope, in which the union with the pleasurable object is not merely a matter of knowledge of it, but also involves the ability or the prospect of possessing it. The next greatest pleasure is that of memory, in which there is union by knowledge only.

Hence: 1. Hope and memory have as their objects things which are, literally speaking, not present; still, they are present after a fashion, viz. by coming within one's knowledge, or lying within one's (at least imagined) capacity.

2. A thing may very well produce opposite effects from different points of view. Thus with hope: in so far as it proffers here and now the prospect of enjoying something in the future, it gives one pleasure, in so far as it implies that one is at present without it, it makes one sad.

3. Love and desire do indeed cause pleasure. For everything that one loves gives one some pleasure, since love is a kind of union, a sense of natural affinity, with the object loved. Equally, everything that one desires is pleasurable, since desire is above all desire for pleasure. However hope implies a real prospect of attaining the pleasurable object, which is not the case with either love or desire. Hope is therefore said to be more a cause of pleasure than are love, or desire; and more than memory, whose object now lies in the past.

Part 1a2ae. Question 32. Article 4. Is Sorrow a Cause of Pleasure?

THE FOURTH POINT: 1. It would seem that sorrow is not a cause of pleasure. For a thing does not cause its own contrary; but sorrow is the contrary of pleasure. It is not therefore a cause of pleasure.

2. Contraries produce contrary effects. But remembering pleasurable things causes pleasure. Therefore remembering sad things causes pain, not pleasure.

Aquinas: Summa Theologiae 1a2ae.33.2

Part 1a2ae. Question 33. Article 2. Does Pleasure Create a Thirst or Desire for More?

REPLY: There are two ways of considering pleasure: first, as actually existing; second, as existing in memory.

So much for pleasure being actually enjoyed at the present moment. Finally, there is remembered pleasure. This is, of its nature, calculated to evoke a thirst or desire for itself, for it takes a person back to that state of mind in which he found pleasure in the object now past. But if his outlook has radically changed, such memory does not cause pleasure, but distaste: this can be the case, for instance, with the memory of a meal to one who is feeling full.

Aquinas: Summa Theologiae 1a2ae.35.3

Part 1a2ae. Question 35. Article 3. Is Sorrow (or Pain) the Contrary of Pleasure?

2. Pain itself can give pleasure indirectly: by the surprise that goes with it, as in the theatre; or by bringing back the memory of something we have loved, and making us once more conscious of our love of it, even as we grieve over its absence. Since therefore love itself is pleasurable, there is pleasure in the sorrow and all those other things that go with love, because in them we feel that love. This is why the sorrows depicted on the stage give us pleasure; they make us feel the love we have conceived for the character represented.

Aquinas: Summa Theologiae 1a2ae.38.1

Part 1a2ae. Question 38. Article 1. Does All Pleasure Assuage Pain or Sorrow?

Hence: 1. It is true that not every species of pleasure is the contrary of every species of sorrow; but every pleasure and every sorrow fall into contrary genera, as we have seen. As far as the feelings of the person involved are concerned, then, any sorrow may be assuaged by any pleasure.

2. Pleasure does not cause the wicked man sorrow at the time he is enjoying it, but at some later time, when he regrets the evil that once gave him that pleasure. This sorrow will find relief in pleasures which are its contrary.

3. When two forces tend to produce contrary movements, each impedes the other; the one that eventually prevails is the one of greater strength and duration. Now when a man is sorrowing over the things he once enjoyed with a friend who is now dead or absent, there are two forces working on him tending to produce contrary movements. The thought of his friend's death or absence inclines him towards sorrow; present good inclines him towards pleasure; and each of these diminishes the other. However, the sight of things present is of greater strength than remembrance of things past; love of self outlasts love of another; and so eventually pleasure drives out sorrow. Thus a little later in the paragraph quoted, Augustine says that sorrow for his friend at last *gave way to the old forms of pleasure.*

Aquinas: Summa Theologiae 1a2ae.50.4

Part 1a2ae. Question 50. Article 4. Are There Any Dispositions of the Intellect?

There can, however, be dispositions of the interior cognitive sense-faculties: these are the dispositions which make a man good at remembering or guessing or imagining. Aristotle says that habit helps greatly in remembering. This is because these faculties too are brought to act at the command of reason. But the exterior cognitive sense-faculties, such as sight and hearing, are not capable of receiving dispositions, but are by nature constituted to perform a particular activity. In this they are like the members of the body, which have no dispositions, although there are dispositions of the faculties which command their movement.

Aquinas: Summa Theologiae 1a2ae.51.3

Part 1a2ae. Question 51. Article 3. Can a Disposition Be Caused by a Single Action?

The inferior cognitive faculties are not in the same case. It is necessary for the same action to be repeated many times before anything is firmly printed on the memory. That is why Aristotle says that constant thought makes memory stronger.

Aquinas: Summa Theologiae 2a2ae.47.16

Part 2a2ae. Question 47. Article 16. Can Prudence Be Forgotten and So Lost?

2. Besides, Aristotle remarks that a virtue is produced or destroyed by causes in the same class working in opposite directions. Now to produce prudence experience is necessary, and this is formed of many memories, as remarked at the beginning of the *Metaphysics*. Since forgetting is the opposite of remembering, it would seem that prudence can be lost thereby.

151

3. Again, prudence is not without the knowledge of general meanings. And this can be lost through oblivion. Therefore prudence as well.

ON THE OTHER HAND Aristotle holds that art can be forgotten, but not prudence.

REPLY: Forgetting refers only to knowing, and so by forgetting a person can entirely lose an art, and likewise a science, for these lie in the mind. Prudence, however, does not consist in knowing alone, but also in loving, because, as we have said, its chief act is to command, which is to apply the knowledge one possesses to desiring and acting. It follows that prudence is not directly done away with by oblivion, rather is it spoiled by passion; Aristotle speaks of pleasurable things and disagreeable things subverting the judgment of prudence. Wherefore it is written, *Beauty has deceived you and lust has perverted your heart. And again, Take no gifts, for they blind even the prudent.*

Nevertheless forgetfulness can block prudence from issuing into an effective command which depends upon some knowledge which can be lost by forgetting.

Hence: 1. Scientific knowledge is in the reason alone, and accordingly should be judged differently, as we have explained.

2. Prudential experience comes not only from memory, but also from the practice of making good and effective decisions.

3. Prudence, as we have stated, does not consist mainly in knowing general moral truths, but in applying them to our deeds. Accordingly the forgetting of these truths does not destroy the chief act of prudence, though as we have said, it blocks it.

First, as to knowing itself: if it be of the past we have memory, if of the present, whether necessary or contingent, we have insight or intelligence. Second, as to getting to know: if that comes from learning from others we have docility, if of our own discovery, we have acumen, which is accuracy of aim: an element here is ingenuity, which, according to Aristotle, is swift to hit the point.

Aquinas: Summa Theologiae 2a2ae.49.1

Part 2a2ae. Question 49. Article 1. Does Remembering Come into Prudence?

THE FIRST POINT: 1. Apparently not. For according to Aristotle, memory is in the sensitive part of the soul, whereas prudence is in the rational part. Therefore memory is not part of prudence.

2. Besides, prudence is acquired and perfected by practice. Memory, however, is in us by nature, and consequently is not a component of prudence.

3. Then also, memory is of things past, while prudence looks to things to be done in the future, these being the concern of counsel, as noted in the *Ethics*. Remembering, then, is not an element of prudence.

ON THE OTHER HAND Cicero counts memory among the parts of prudence.

REPLY: Prudence, as we have pointed out, is engaged with contingent human doings. Here a person cannot be guided only by norms which are simply and of necessity true, he must also appreciate what happens in the majority of cases. Aristotle remarks that like should be concluded from like; accordingly principles should be proportionate to the conclusions we draw. Now to know what is true in the majority of cases we must be empirical; Aristotle says that intellectual virtue is produced and developed by time and experience. Experience is stocked with memories, as noted in the *Metaphysics*; consequently recalling many facts is required for prudence. Accordingly memory is rightly counted an element in prudence.

Hence: 1. Because prudence, as we have said, applies the knowledge of general principles to the particular incidents with which the senses are occupied, many functions of sensory psychology enter into prudence, and remembering is among them.

2. The aptitude for prudence is from nature, yet its perfection is from practice or from grace. And so Cicero observes that memory is not developed by nature alone, but owes much to art and diligence. We may mention four aids to cultivating a good memory.

First, one who wishes to remember should pick certain images that, while fitting his ideas, are somewhat out of the ordinary, for what is unusual rouses wonder, and so the mind dwells on it the more intently: this is why we better remember the things we saw in childhood. Lighting on such likenesses and images is necessary, because simple and spiritual ideas slip somewhat easily out of mind unless they are tied, as it were, to bodily images; human knowledge has more mastery over objects of sense. Accordingly the memory is located in the sensitive part of the soul.

Second, a person who wishes to hold things in his memory should arrange them in order for his consideration so that he may readily pass from one to another. Aristotle observes that mnemonic loci help us to recollect by causing us to come swiftly from one to another.

Third, a person should put his care and concern into the things he wants to memorize, because the more deeply stamped they are on the mind the less likely are they to disappear. And so Cicero remarks that taking trouble keeps the shapes of images intact.

Fourth, we should frequently ponder over the things we want to remember. Aristotle says that such meditations keep memories alive, because, as he also says, custom is like second nature. Hence the things we often think about are quickly recalled by a sort of instinctive process.

153

Part 3a. Question 85. Article 4. Is the Will the Seat of Penitence?

3. Memory is a faculty which apprehends the past. Now, repentance is an act not of a cognitive but of an appetitive power, presupposing a cognitive act of a faculty which apprehends. Hence penitence is not in the memory, but does presuppose it.

Aquinas: Commentary on the *Metaphysics* of Aristotle

I.L.1:C1-35:10-16

10. *Now in some animals (3).*

Here he [Aristotle] indicates the different kinds and three levels of knowing found among brute animals. For there are certain animals which have sensation, although they do not have memory which comes from sensation. For memory accompanies imagination, which is a movement caused by the senses in their act of sensing, as we find in Book II of *The Soul.* But in some animals imagination does not accompany sensation, and therefore memory cannot exist in them. This is found verified in imperfect animals which are incapable of local motion, such as shellfish. For since sensory cognition enables animals to make provision for the necessities of life and to perform their characteristic operations, then those animals which move towards something at a distance by means of local motion must have memory. For if the anticipated goal by which they are induced to move did not remain in them through memory, they could not continue to move toward the intended goal which they pursue. But in the case of immobile animals the reception of a present sensible quality is sufficient for them to perform their characteristic operations, since they do not move toward anything at a distance. Hence these animals have an indefinite movement as a result of confused [or indeterminate] imagination alone, as he points out in Book III of *The Soul.*

11. Again, from the fact that some animals have memory and some do not, it follows that some are prudent and some not. For, since prudence makes provision for the future from memory of the past (and this is the reason why Tully in his *Rhetoric*, Book II, makes memory, understanding and foresight parts of prudence), prudence cannot be had by those animals which lack memory. Now those animals which have memory can have some prudence, although prudence has one meaning in the case of brute animals and another in the case of man. Men are prudent inasmuch as they deliberate rationally about what they ought to do. Hence it is said in Book VI of the *Ethics*, that prudence is a rationally regulated plan of things to be done. But the judgment about things to be done which is not a result of any rational deliberation but of some natural instinct is called prudence in other animals. Hence in other animals prudence

is a natural estimate about the pursuit of what is fitting and the avoidance of what is harmful, as a lamb follows its mother and runs away from a wolf.

12. But among those animals which have memory some have hearing and some do not. And all those which cannot hear (as the bee or any other similar type of animal that may exist), even though they have prudence, are still incapable of being taught, i.e., in the sense that they can be habituated to the doing or avoiding of something through someone else's instruction, because such instruction is received chiefly by means of hearing. Hence in *The Senses and Their Objects* it is stated that hearing is the sense by which we receive instruction. Furthermore, the statement that bees do not have hearing is not opposed in any way to the observation that they are frightened by certain sounds. For just as a very loud sound kills an animal and splits wood, as is evident in the case of thunder, not because of the sound but because of the violent motion of the air in which the sound is present, in a similar fashion those animals which lack hearing can be frightened by the sounding air even though they have no perception of sound. However, those animals which have both memory and hearing can be both prudent and teachable.

13. It is evident, then, that there are three levels of knowing in animals. The first level is that had by animals which have neither hearing nor memory, and which are therefore neither capable of being taught nor of being prudent. The second level is that of animals which have memory but are unable to hear, and which are therefore prudent but incapable of being taught. The third level is that of animals which have both of these faculties, and which are therefore prudent and capable of being taught. Moreover, there cannot be a fourth level, so that there would be an animal which had hearing but lacked memory. For those senses which perceive their sensible objects by means of an external medium--and hearing is one of these--are found only in animals which have locomotion and which cannot do without memory, as has been pointed out (3:C 10).

14. *Thus other animals (4).*

Here he [Aristotle] explains the levels of human knowing; and in regard to this he does two things. First (4:C 14), he explains how human knowing surpasses the knowing of the abovementioned animals. Second (5:C 17), he shows how human knowing is divided into different levels ("Now in men").

Accordingly, in the first part (4) he says that the life of animals is ruled by imagination and memory: by imagination in the case of imperfect animals, and by memory in the case of perfect animals. For even though the latter also have imagination, still each thing is said to be ruled by that [power] which holds the highest place within it. Now in this discussion life does not mean the being of a living thing, as it is understood in Book II of *The Soul*, when he says that "for living things to live is to be"; for the life of an animal in this sense is not a result of memory or imagination but is prior to both of these. But life is taken to mean vital activity, just as we are also accustomed to speak of association as the life of men. But by the fact that he establishes the truth about the cognition of animals with reference to the management of life, we are given to understand that knowing belongs to these animals, not for the sake of knowing, but because of the need for action.

15. Now, as is stated below (6:C 18), in men the next thing above memory is experience, which some animals have only to a small degree. For an experience arises from the association of many singular [intentions] received in memory. And this kind of association is proper to man, and pertains to the cogitative power (also called particular reason), which associates particular intentions just as universal reason associates universal ones. Now since animals are accustomed to pursue or avoid certain things as a result of many sensations and memory, for this reason they seem to share something of experience, even though it be slight. But above experience, which belongs to particular reason, men have as their chief power a universal reason by means of which they live.

16. And just as experience is related to particular reason [in men], and customary activity to memory in animals, in a similar way art is related to universal reason. Therefore, just as the life of animals is ruled in a perfect way by memory together with activity that has become habitual through training, or in any other way whatsoever, in a similar way man is ruled perfectly by reason perfected by art. Some men, however, are ruled by reason without art; but this rule is imperfect.

156

LEONARDO DA VINCI

1452 - 1519

From: *The Literary Works of Leonardo da Vinci*. Compiled and edited by Jean Paul Richter. Published by Phaidon Press, 1981 (first published in translation in 1883), two volumes.

Artist, scientist, and inventor, Leonardo da Vinci spent the first 30 years of his life in Florence and returned there frequently thereafter. Leonardo produced no cohesive body of written work, but left a collection of notebooks which were scattered after his death. These contain notes on many topics, as well as plans for machines and gadgets. Leonardo accepted the Neoplatonist position that the elements of natural bodies are geometric forms. This, combined with a reliance on observation rather than the authority of books, allowed him to formulate many principles of statics and dynamics. His Treatise on painting presents painting as the first among the arts in which the world is presented to the senses in a form that reveals its mathematical nature and thus its beauty.

Supplementary reading:

Almedingen, M. E. (1969). *Leonardo da Vinci: A Portrait*. London: Bodley Head.

LEONARDO DA VINCI

Table of Contents

Explanation of contents: Richter's compilation of the literary works of Leonardo da Vinci is in two volumes (large Roman numerals). Each volume contains passages numbered consecutively by Richter to reflect the logical order with reference to subjects (arabic numberal). Thus, I.496 refers to passage 496 which appears in Volume I of Richter's compilation.

496. I myself have proved it to be of no small use, when in bed in the dark, to recall in fancy the outlines of forms previously studied, or other noteworthy things conceived by subtle speculation; and this is certainly an admirable exercise, and useful for impressing things on the memory.

502. Any master who should venture to boast that he could remember all the forms and effects of nature would certainly appear to me to be graced with extreme ignorance, inasmuch as these effects are infinite and our memory is not extensive enough to retain them. Hence, O painter! beware lest the lust of gain should supplant in you the dignity of art; for the acquisition of glory is a much greater thing than the glory of riches. Hence, for these and other reasons which might be given, first strive in drawing to represent your intention to the eye by expressive forms, and the idea originally formed in your imagination; then go on taking off and putting on, until you have satisfied yourself. Then have living men, draped or nude, as you may have purposed in your work, and take care that in dimensions and size, as determined by perspective, nothing is left in the work which is not in harmony with reason and the effects in nature. And this will be the way to win honour in your art.

531. When you want to know a thing you have studied in your memory proceed in this way: When you have drawn the same thing so many times that you think you know it by heart, test it by drawing it without the model; but have the model traced on flat thin glass and lay this on the drawing you have made without the model, and note carefully where the tracing does not coincide with your drawing; and where you find you have gone wrong, bear in mind not to repeat the same mistakes and return to the model, and draw the part in which you were wrong again and again till you have it well in your mind. If you have no flat glass for tracing on, take some very thin kid-skin parchment, well oiled and dried. And when you have used it for one drawing you can wash it clean with a sponge and make a second.

572. If you want to acquire facility for bearing in mind the expression of a face, first make yourself familiar with a variety of [forms of] several heads, eyes, noses, mouths, chins and throats, and necks and shoulders: And to put a case: Noses are of 10 types: straight, bulbous, concave, prominent above or below the middle, aquiline, regular, flat, round or pointed. These hold good as to profile. In full face they are of 11 types; these are equal, thick in the middle, thin in the middle, with the tip thick and the root narrow, or narrow at the tip and wide at the root; with the nostrils wide or narrow, high or low, and the openings wide or hidden by the point; and you will find an equal variety in the other details; which things you must draw from nature and fix them in your mind. Or

else, when you have to draw a face by heart, carry with you a little book in which you have noted such features; and when you have cast a glance at the face of the person you wish to draw, you can observe, in private, which nose or mouth is most like, and there make a little mark to recognize it again at home. Of grotesque faces I need say nothing, because they are kept in mind without difficulty.

Leonardo da Vinci: Literary Works II.836

836. The Common Sense is that which judges of things offered to it by the other senses. The ancient speculators have concluded that that part of man which constitutes his judgement is caused by a central organ to which the other five senses refer everything by means of sensation; and to this centre they have given the name Common Sense. And they say that this Sense is situated in the centre of the head between Sensation and Memory. And this name of Common Sense is given to it solely because it is the common judge of all the other five senses, i.e. Seeing, Hearing, Touch, Taste, and Smell. This Common Sense is acted upon by means of Sensation, which is placed as a medium between it and the senses. Sensation is acted upon by means of the images of things presented to it by the external instruments, that is to say, the senses which are the medium between external things and Sensation. In the same way the senses are acted upon by objects. Surrounding things transmit their images to the senses and the senses transfer them to the Sensation. Sensation sends them to the Common Sense, and by it they are stamped upon the memory and are there more or less retained according to the importance or potency of the given thing. That sense is most rapid in its function which is nearest to the sensitive medium, and the eye is the highest, and the chief of the others. Of this then only we will speak, and the others we will leave in order not to make our matter too long. Experience tells us that the eye apprehends ten different natures of things, that is: light and darkness, one being the cause of the perception of the nine others, and the other its absence, colour and substance, form and place, distance and nearness, motion and stillness.

Leonardo da Vinci: Literary Works II.1170 - 1171

1170. Wrongly do men lament the flight of time, accusing it of being too swift, and not perceiving that it is sufficient as it passes; but good memory, with which nature has endowed us, causes everything long past to seem present.

1171. Acquire learning in youth which restores the damage of old age; and if you understand that old age has wisdom for its food, you will so conduct yourself in youth that your old age will not lack sustenance.

Leonardo da Vinci: Literary Works II.1176

1176. Just as eating against one's will is injurious to health, so study without a liking for it spoils the memory, and it retains nothing it takes in.

MONTAIGNE

1533 - 1592

From: *Essays*. Translated by J. M. Cohen. Published by Penguin Books, 1958.

Background: Michel Eyquem de Montaigne, French sceptical philosopher, was born of a wealthy merchant family near Bordeaux. His most important philosophical work, the *Essays*, is a series of elegant discussions that provided a statement of scepticism and set out the issues for seventeenth century philosophy. The *Essays* also provide an engaging self-portrait, including the self-deprecating description of memory failures reproduced below. Montaigne held that both sensory experience and reason are limited as paths to knowledge and that the human condition is therefore necessarily one of uncertainty. His position influenced both Descartes and Bacon who attempted to answer the sceptical arguments that Montaigne raised. Montaigne held that we acquire truth only by the grace of God. Reason cannot lead us to faith, but faith, tempered by tolerance, is a rational choice.

Supplementary readings:

Frame, D. M. (1965). *Montaigne: A Biography*. New York: Harcourt, Brace, & World.

Norton, G. P. (1975). *Montaigne and the Introspective World*. The Hague: Mouton.

Table of Contents

Explanation of contents: A single passage from the Essays is included here. Paragraph numbers have been added to the text by the editors [in brackets].

[1] The memory is an instrument of wonderful utility, and without it the judgement can hardly perform its duties; I am almost completely without it. Anything that is put before me must be presented piecemeal. For it is beyond my powers to reply to a proposition with several heads. I cannot take a message if I have not put it down in my notebook; and when I have an important speech to make that is of any length, I am reduced to the mean and miserable necessity of learning by heart, word for word, what I am going to say. Otherwise, I should have neither power nor assurance, but should always be afraid that my memory was going to play me a trick. But this method is just as difficult for me. It takes me three hours to learn three lines; and then, if I have composed it myself, the freedom and authority with which I change the order, or alter a word, and my constant variations of matter, make it more difficult to keep in mind. Now, the more I distrust my memory, the more confused it becomes; it serves me best by accident, I have to woo it unconcernedly. For if I press it, it becomes bewildered; and once it has begun to waver, the more I sound it the more perplexed and embarrassed it grows; it serves me at its own hours, not at mine.

[2] This same defect that I find in my memory, I find also in several other places. I avoid commands, obligations, and constraint. What I do easily and naturally, I can no longer do if I command myself to do it by an express and definite injunction. In the case of my body too, those organs that have some liberty and special jurisdiction over themselves at times refuse to obey me, when I fix and bind them to a particular place and hour for the service I need of them. This compulsive and tyrannical prescription offends them; either from fear or spite, they shrink and grow numb.

[3] Once, long ago, I was in a place where it is considered a barbarous discourtesy not to respond to those who pledge you a toast; and, though I was allowed complete freedom, I tried to be convivial, according to the custom of the country, in order to please the ladies of the party. But there was an amusing result. For this threat, and my preparations forcibly to make myself violate my natural habits, so choked my throat that I could not swallow a single drop, and I was unable to drink even the amount I needed for my meal. I found myself full, and my thirst was quenched by the quantity of drink that I had consumed in my thoughts.

[4] This defect is most apparent in those who have the strongest and most active imaginations; yet it is natural, and there is no one who does not feel it in some degree. An excellent archer, who had been condemned to death, was offered his life if he would give some noteworthy proof of his skill. But he refused to try, fearing that the excessive strain on his will might cause him to miss his aim, and that far from saving his life, he would also forfeit the reputation he had acquired as a marksman. A man whose thoughts are elsewhere will not fail to take the same number and length of steps almost to an inch, every time that he walks in a particular place. But if he applies his attention to measuring and counting them, he will find that what he did naturally and by chance, he will not do as accurately by design.

[5] My library, which is a fine one for a country library, is situated at one corner of my house. But if anything occurs to me that I want to look up or write down there, I have to entrust it to some other person for fear that it will escape me merely as I cross my courtyard. If I venture in speaking to wander ever so little from my argument, I never fail to lose it; which is the reason why I keep myself short, concise, and terse in my conversation. I am obliged to call the men who serve me by the names of their offices or their provinces, for I find it very hard to remember a name. I can tell, to be sure, that it has three syllables, that it sounds harsh, and that it begins or ends with a certain letter. And, if I live long enough, I am not sure that I shall not forget my own name, as others have done.

[6] Messala Corvinus was for two years without any trace of memory, and the same is said of George of Trebizond. I often wonder, in my own interest, what kind of life theirs was, and whether, without that faculty, I shall have enough left to support me in some comfort. And when I look closely into it, I fear that this failing, if complete, will destroy all the functions of the soul. 'Memory is, beyond a doubt, the sole receptacle not only of philosophy, but of all that appertains to living and of all the arts.' (Cicero, *Academica*, II, 7.)

Plenus rimarum sum, hac atque illac effluo.
  'I am full of cracks. I leak on every side.' Terence, *Eunuchus, I, ii, 25.*

It has happened to me more than once that I have forgotten the password which three hours ago I had given to, or received from another, or that I have been unable - whatever Cicero may say (*'I have certainly never heard of an old man who forgot where he had buried a treasure.' De Senectute, VII.*) - to remember where I have hidden my purse. If I lock up anything with particular care, I am helping myself to lose it.

[7] Memory is the receptacle and container of learning; mine being so defective, I have no great cause to complain that I know so little. In general, I know the names of the arts and the subjects they treat, but nothing more. I turn over the pages of books; I do not study them. What I retain from them is something that I no longer recognize as another's. All the profit that my mind has made has been from the arguments and ideas that it has imbibed from them. The author, the place, the words, and other facts I immediately forget.

[8] I am so good at forgetting that I forget my own jottings and compositions no less than everything else. People are always quoting me to myself without my noticing it. Anyone who wanted to know where the verses and examples come from that I have accumulated here would leave me at a loss for an answer; and yet I have begged them only at familiar and famous doors and have not been content with their being rich unless they also came from rich and honourable hands; authority and reason are present in equal quantity. It is no great wonder if my book incurs the same fate as other books, and if my memory loses hold of what I write as it does of what I read, of what I give as of what I receive.

FRANCIS BACON

1561 - 1626

From: *The Philosophic Works of Francis Bacon.* Translated by R. C. Ellis and J. Spedding; edited by J. M. Robertson. Published by Routledge, 1905.

English statesman and philosopher of science, Francis Bacon rose by his own efforts to be Lord Keeper of the Great Seal for James I, and fell from power after being convicted of taking a bribe. In his writing Bacon pointed to the practical value of empirical discoveries, e.g., of China and of gunpowder, in contrast to the metaphysical speculation of the medieval schoolmen which had not advanced knowledge beyond that of the ancients. He hoped to enlist the state in organizing a collective enterprise of scientific enquiry for which his works provided a blueprint. He provided a classification of knowledge and a penetrating description of the scientific method. The scientific societies founded in England and France soon after his death are a testament to his influence and foresight.

As part of his account of knowledge Bacon distinguished three types of information obtained by our own efforts: memory (including sensory information) for facts and events; imagination of facts that are not real; and reason which is concerned with general concepts and principles.

Supplementary readings:

Anderson, F. H. (1968). *The Philosophy of Francis Bacon.* Chicago: University of Chicago Press.

Wallace, K. R. (1967). *Francis Bacon on the Nature of Man.* Champaign, IL: University of Illinois Press.

BACON

Table of Contents

Explanation of contents: Bacon's works are divided into books which are in turn divided into numbered aphorisms, or chapters. Paragraph numbers for each excerpt have been added by the editors [in brackets]. Page numbers in the Robertson edition are given in the table of contents.

[1] For example, let the proposed nature be Memory, or that which excites and aids the memory. Constitutive Instances are, order or distribution, which clearly aids the memory; also topics or "places" in artificial memory; which may either be places in the proper sense of the word, as a door, angle, window, and the like; or familiar and known persons; or any other things at pleasure (provided they be placed in a certain order), as animals, vegetables; words too, letters, characters, historical persons, and the like; although some of these are more suitable and convenient than others. Such artificial places help the memory wonderfully, and exalt it far above its natural powers. Again, verse is learnt and remembered more easily than prose. From this group of three instances, viz. order, artificial places, and verse, one species of aid to the memory is constituted. And this species may with propriety be called the cutting off of infinity. For when we try to recollect or call a thing to mind, if we have no prenotion or perception of what we are seeking, we seek and toil and wander here and there, as if in infinite space. Whereas if we have any sure prenotion, infinity is at once cut off, and the memory has not so far to range. Now in the three foregoing instances the prenotion is clear and certain. In the first it must be something which suits the order; in the second it must be an image which bears some relation or conformity to the places fixed; in the third, it must be words that fall into the verse; and thus infinity is cut off. Other instances, again, will give us this second species; that whatever brings the intellectual conception into contact with the sense (which is indeed the method most used in mnemonics) assists the memory. Other instances will give us this third species; that things which make their impression by way of a strong affection, as by inspiring fear, admiration, shame, delight, assist the memory. Other instances will give us this fourth species; that things which are chiefly imprinted when the mind is clear and not occupied with anything else either before or after, as what is learnt in childhood, or what we think of before going to sleep, also things that happen for the first time, dwell longest in the memory. Other instances will give this fifth species; that a multitude of circumstances or points to take hold of aids the memory; as writing with breaks and divisions, reading or reciting aloud. Lastly other instances will give us this sixth species; that things which are waited for and raise the attention dwell longer in the memory than what flies quickly by. Thus, if you read anything over twenty times, you will not learn it by heart so easily as if you were to read it only ten, trying to repeat it between whiles, and when memory failed looking at the book. It appears then that there are six Lesser Forms of aids to the memory; viz. the cutting off of infinity; the reduction of the intellectual to the sensible; impression made on the mind in a state of strong emotion; impression made on the mind disengaged; multitude of points to take hold of; expectation beforehand.

Bacon: De Augmentis Scientiarum, Chapter II

[1] So again, painting revives the memory of a thing by the image of it; has not this been transferred into the art which they call the art of memory?

Division of the Art of Retaining into the doctrine concerning *Helps of Memory,* as doctrine concerning *Memory itself.* Division of the doctrine concerning Memory Itself into *Prenotion* and *Emblem.*

[1] The art of retaining or keeping knowledge I will divide into two parts; namely, the doctrine concerning Helps of Memory, and the doctrine concerning Memory itself. The great help to the memory is *writing*; and it must be taken as a rule that memory without this aid is unequal to matters of much length and accuracy; and that its unwritten evidence ought by no means to be allowed. This is particularly the case in inductive philosophy and the interpretation of nature; for a man might as well attempt to go through the calculations of an Ephemeris in his head without the aid of writing, as to master the interpretation of nature by the natural and naked force of thought and memory, without the help of tables duly arranged. But not to speak of the interpretation of nature, which is a new doctrine, there can hardly be anything more useful even for the old and popular sciences, than a sound help for the memory; that is a good and learned Digest of Common-Places. I am aware indeed that the transferring of the things we read and learn into common-place books is thought by some to be detrimental to learning, as retarding the course of the reader and inviting the memory to take holiday. Nevertheless, as it is but a counterfeit thing in knowledge to be forward and pregnant, except a man be also deep and full, I hold diligence and labour in the entry of common-places to be a matter of great use and support in studying; as that which supplies matter to invention, and contracts the sight of the judgment to a point. But yet it is true that of the methods and frameworks of common-places which I have hitherto seen, there is none of any worth; all of them carrying in their titles merely the face of a school and not of a world; and using vulgar and pedantical divisions, not such as pierce to the pith and heart of things.

[2] For the Memory itself, the inquiry seems hitherto to have been pursued weakly and languidly enough. An art there is indeed extant of it; but it is clear to me that there might be both better precepts for strengthening and enlarging the memory than that art contains, and a better practice of the art itself than that which is received. Not but (if any one chooses to abuse this art for purposes of ostentation) feats can be performed by it that are marvellous and prodigious; but nevertheless it is a barren thing (as now applied) for human uses. At the same time the fault I find with it is not that it destroys and overburdens the natural memory (which is the common objection), but that it is not well contrived for providing assistance to the memory in serious business and affairs. And for my own part (owing perhaps to the life of business I have led) I am ever disposed to make small account of things which make parade of art but are of no use. For the being able to repeat at once and in the same order a great number of names or words upon a single hearing, or to make a number of verses extempore on any subject, or to make a satirical simile of everything that happens, or to turn any serious matter into a jest, or to carry off anything with a contradiction or cavil, or the like, (whereof in the faculties of the mind there is

great store, and such as by device and practice may be exalted to an extreme degree of wonder)--all such things I esteem no more than I do the tricks and antics of clowns and rope-dancers. For they are almost the same things; the one an abuse of the powers of the body, the other of the mind; matters perhaps of strangeness, but of no worthiness.

[3] The Art of Memory is built upon two intentions: Prenotion and Emblem. By Prenotion I mean a kind of cutting off of infinity of search. For when a man desires to recall anything into his memory, if he have no prenotion or perception of that he seeks, he seeks and strives and beats about hither and thither as if in infinite space. But if he have some certain prenotion, this infinity is at once cut off, and the memory ranges in a narrower compass; like the hunting of a deer within an enclosure. And therefore order also manifestly assists the memory; for we have a prenotion that what we are seeking must be something which agrees with order. So again verse is more easily learned by heart than prose; for if we stick at any word, we have a prenotion that it must be such a word as fits the verse. And this prenotion is the principal part of artificial memory. For in artificial memory we have the places digested and prepared beforehand; the images we make extempore according to the occasion. But then we have a prenotion that the image must be one which has some conformity with the place; and this reminds the memory, and in some measure paves the way to the thing we seek. Emblem, on the other hand, reduces intellectual conceptions to sensible images; for an object of sense always strikes the memory more forcibly and is more easily impressed upon it than an object of the intellect; insomuch that even brutes have their memory excited by sensible impressions, never by intellectual ones. And therefore you will more easily remember the image of a hunter pursuing a hare, of an apothecary arranging his boxes, of a pendant making a speech, of a boy repeating verses from memory, of a player acting on the stage, than the mere notions of invention, disposition, elocution, memory, and action. Other things there are (as I said just now) which relate to the help of memory, but the art as it now is consists of the two above stated. But to follow out the particular defects of arts would be from my purpose. So much therefore for the Art of Retaining or Keeping Knowledge.

DAVID HUME

1711-1776

From: *The Philosophical Works of David Hume.* 4 vols. Published by Adam Black, William Tait and Charles Tait, 1886.

David Hume was steered by his parents towards a career in law. Taking a dislike to the subject, he designed his own course of study and began work, at the age of 18, on *A Treatise of Human Nature.* When the book appeared eight years later, it was received with indifference. Hume reformulated his ideas in a series of works, the most important of which is *An Inquiry Concerning Human Understanding*, which first appeared in 1748. His plan was to apply the experimental method of Newton to the British empiricists' study of the human mind. He aimed to produce a truly experimental science of human nature against which rationalist metaphysics could be tested. Hume's interest in memory was part of his general concern with the nature of knowledge. Hume left philosophy and turned his energies to history and economics, in which field he earned the recognition that had been denied him in philosophy.

Supplementary readings:

Ayer, A. J. (1980). *Hume.* New York: Hill & Wang.

Flew, A. G. M. (1961). *Hume's Philosophy of Belief.* Atlantic Highlands, NJ: Humanities Press.

HUME

Table of Contents

Explanation of contents: The excerpts from "A Treatise of Human Nature" are all taken from Book I, Part I, which is divided into sections.   "An Inquiry Concerning Human Understanding" is simply divided into sections.   The excerpt is referred to by section number (large Roman numeral).

Part I: Of Ideas, their Origin, Composition, Connexion,
and Abstraction

Section I: Of the Origin of Our Ideas

All the perceptions of the human mind resolve themselves into two distinct kinds, which I shall call *impressions* and *ideas*. The difference betwixt these consists in the degrees of force and liveliness, with which they strike upon the mind, and make their way into our thought or consciousness. Those perceptions which enter with most force and violence, we may name *impressions*; and, under this name, I comprehend all our sensations, passions, and emotions, as they make their first appearance in the soul. By *ideas*, I mean the faint images of these in thinking and reasoning; such as, for instance, are all the perceptions excited by the present discourse, excepting only those which arise from the sight and touch, and excepting the immediate pleasure or uneasiness it may occasion. I believe it will not be very necessary to employ many words in explaining this distinction. Every one of himself will readily perceive the difference betwixt feeling and thinking. The common degrees of these are easily distinguished; though it is not impossible but, in particular instances, they may very nearly approach to each other. Thus, in sleep, in a fever, in madness, or in any very violent emotions of soul, our ideas may approach to our impressions: as, on the other hand, it sometimes happens, that our impressions are so faint and low, that we cannot distinguish them from our ideas. But, notwithstanding this near resemblance in a few instances, they are in general so very different, that no one can make a scruple to rank them under distinct heads, and assign to each a peculiar name to mark the difference.

There is another division of our perceptions, which it will be convenient to observe, and which extends itself both to our impressions and ideas. This division is into *simple* and *complex*. Simple perceptions, or impressions and ideas, are such as admit of no distinction nor separation. The complex are the contrary to these, and may be distinguished into parts. Though a particular colour, taste and smell, are qualities all united together in this apple, 'tis easy to perceive they are not the same, but are at least distinguishable from each other.

Having, by these divisions, given an order and arrangement to our objects, we may now apply ourselves to consider, with the more accuracy, their qualities and relations. The first circumstance that strikes my eye, is the great resemblance betwixt our impressions and ideas in every other particular, except their degree of force and vivacity. The one seem to be, in a manner, the reflection of the other; so that all the perceptions of the mind are double, and appear both as impressions and ideas. When I shut my eyes, and think of my chamber, the ideas I form are exact representations of the impressions I felt; nor is there any circumstance of the one, which is not to be found in the other. In running over my other perceptions, I find still the same resemblance and representation. Ideas and impressions appear always to correspond to each other. This circumstance seems to me remarkable, and engages my attention for a moment.

171

Upon a more accurate survey I find I have been carried away too far by the first appearance, and that I must make use of the distinction of perceptions into *simple* and *complex*, to limit this general decision, *that all our ideas and impressions are resembling.* I observe that many of our complex ideas never had impressions that corresponded to them, and that many of our complex impressions never are exactly copied in ideas. I can imagine to myself such a city as the New Jerusalem, whose pavement is gold, and walls are rubies, though I never saw any such. I have seen Paris; but shall I affirm I can form such an idea of that city, as will perfectly represent all its streets and houses in their real and just proportions?

I perceive, therefore, that though there is, in general, a great resemblance betwixt our *complex* impressions and ideas, yet the rule is not universally true, that they are exact copies of each other. We may next consider, how the case stands with our *simple* perceptions. After the most accurate examination of which I am capable, I venture to affirm, that the rule here holds without any exception, and that every simple idea has a simple impression, which resembles it, and every simple impression a correspondent idea. That idea of red, which we form in the dark, and that impression, which strikes our eyes in sunshine, differ only in degree, not in nature. That the case is the same with all our simple impressions and ideas, 'tis impossible to prove by a particular enumeration of them. Every one may satisfy himself in this point by running over as many as he pleases. But if any one should deny this universal resemblance, I know no way of convincing him, but by desiring him to show a simple impression that has not a correspondent idea, or a simple idea that has not a correspondent impression. If he does not answer this challenge, as 'tis certain he cannot, we may, from his silence and our own observation, establish our conclusion.

Section II: Division of the Subject

Since it appears, that our simple impressions are prior to their correspondent ideas, and that the exceptions are very rare, method seems to 1require we should examine our impressions before we consider our ideas. Impressions may be divided into two kinds, those of *sensation*, and those of *reflection*. The first kind arises in the soul originally, from unknown causes. The second is derived, in a great measure, from our ideas, and that in the following order. An impression first strikes upon the senses, and makes us perceive heat or cold, thirst or hunger, pleasure or pain, of some kind or other. Of this impression there is a copy taken by the mind, which remains after the impression ceases; and this we call an idea. This idea of pleasure or pain, when it returns upon the soul, produces the new impressions of desire and aversion, hope and fear, which may properly be called impressions of reflection, because derived from it. These again are copied by the memory and imagination, and become ideas; which, perhaps, in their turn, give rise to other impressions and ideas: so that the impressions of reflection are [not] only antecedent to their correspondent ideas, but posterior to those of sensation, and derived from them. The examination of our sensations belongs more to anatomists and natural philosophers than to moral; and, therefore, shall not at present be entered upon. And, as the impressions of reflection, viz. passions, desires, and emotions, which principally deserve our attention, arise mostly from ideas, 'twill be necessary to reverse that method, which at first sight seems most natural; and, in order to explain the nature and principles of the human mind, give a particular account of ideas, before we proceed to impressions. For this reason, I have here chosen to begin with ideas.

Section III: Of the Ideas of the Memory and Imagination

We find, by experience, that when any impression has been present with the mind, it again makes its appearance there as an idea; and this it may do after two different ways: either when, in its new appearance, it retains a considerable degree of its first vivacity, and is somewhat intermediate betwixt an impression and an idea; or when it entirely loses that vivacity, and is a perfect idea. The faculty by which we repeat our impressions in the first manner, is called the *memory*, and the other the *imagination*. 'Tis evident, at first sight, that the ideas of the memory are much more lively and strong than those of the imagination, and that the former faculty paints its objects in more distinct colours, than any which are employed by the latter. When we remember any past event, the idea of it flows in upon the mind in a forcible manner; whereas, in the imagination, the perception is faint and languid, and cannot, without difficulty, be preserved by the mind steady and uniform for any considerable time. Here, then, is a sensible difference betwixt one species of ideas and another. But of this more fully hereafter.

There is another difference betwixt these two kinds of ideas, which is no less evident, namely, that though neither the ideas of the memory nor imagination, neither the lively nor faint ideas, can make their appearance in the mind, unless their correspondent impressions have gone before to prepare the way for them, yet the imagination is not restrained to the same order and form with the original impressions; while the memory is in a manner tied down in that respect, without any power of variation.

'Tis evident, that the memory preserves the original form, in which its objects were presented, and that wherever we depart from it in recollecting any thing, it proceeds from some defect or imperfection in that faculty. An historian may, perhaps, for the more convenient carrying on of his narration, relate an event before another to which it was in fact posterior; but then, he takes notice of this disorder, if he be exact; and, by that means, replaces the idea in its due position. 'Tis the same case in our recollection of those places and persons, with which we were formerly acquainted. The chief exercise of the memory is not to preserve the simple ideas, but their order and position. In short, this principle is supported by such a number of common and vulgar phenomena, that we may spare ourselves the trouble of insisting on it any farther.

The same evidence follows us in our second principle, *of the liberty of the imagination to transpose and change its ideas*. The fables we meet with in poems and romances put this entirely out of question. Nature there is totally confounded, and nothing mentioned but winged horses, fiery dragons, and monstrous giants. Nor will this liberty of the fancy appear strange, when we consider, that all our ideas are copied from our impressions, and that there are not any two impressions which are perfectly inseparable. Not to mention, that this is an evident consequence of the division of ideas into simple and complex. Wherever the imagination perceives a difference among ideas, it can easily produce a separation.

Section IV: Of the Connexion or Association of Ideas

As all simple ideas may be separated by the imagination, and may be united again in what form it pleases, nothing would be more unaccountable than the operations of that faculty, were it not guided by some universal principles, which render it, in some measure, uniform with itself in all times and places. Were ideas entirely loose and unconnected, chance alone would join them; and 'tis impossible the same simple ideas should fall regularly into complex ones (as they commonly do), without some bond of union among them, some associating quality, by which one idea naturally introduces another. This uniting principle among ideas is not to be considered as an inseparable connexion, for that has been already excluded from the imagination: nor yet are we to conclude, that without it the mind cannot join two ideas; for nothing is more free than that faculty: but we are only to regard it as a gentle force, which commonly prevails, and is the cause why, among other things, languages so nearly correspond to each other; Nature, in a manner, pointing out to every one those simple ideas, which are most proper to be united into a complex one. The qualities, from which this association arises, and by which the mind is, after this manner, conveyed from one idea to another, are three, viz. *resemblance, contiguity* in time or place, and *cause* and *effect*.

I believe it will not be very necessary to prove, that these qualities produce an association among ideas, and, upon the appearance of one idea, naturally introduce another. 'Tis plain, that, in the course of our thinking, and in the constant revolution of our ideas, our imagination runs easily from one idea to any other that *resembles* it, and that this quality alone is to the fancy a sufficient bond and association. 'Tis likewise evident, that as the senses, in changing their objects, are necessitated to change them regularly, and take them as they lie *contiguous* to each other, the imagination must, by long custom, acquire the same method of thinking, and run along the parts of space and time in conceiving its objects. As to the connexion that is made by the relation of *cause and effect*, we shall have occasion afterwards to examine it to the bottom, and therefore shall not at present insist upon it. 'Tis sufficient to observe, that there is no relation, which produces a stronger connexion in the fancy, and makes one idea more readily recall another, than the relation of cause and effect betwixt their objects.

That we may understand the full extent of these relations, we must consider, that two objects are connected together in the imagination, not only when the one is immediately resembling, contiguous to, or the cause of the other, but also when there is interposed betwixt them a third object, which bears to both of them any of these relations. This may be carried on to a great length; though, at the same time we may observe, that each remove considerably weakens the relation. Cousins in the fourth degree are connected by *causation,* if I may be allowed to use that term; but not so closely as brothers, much less as child and parent. In general, we may observe, that all the relations of blood depend upon cause and effect, and are esteemed near or remote, according to the number of connecting causes interposed betwixt the persons.

Of the three relations above mentioned this of causation is the most extensive. Two objects may be considered as placed in this relation, as well when one is the cause of any of the actions or motions of the other, as when the former is the cause of the existence of the latter. For as that action or motion is nothing but the object itself, considered in a certain light, and as the object continues the same in all its different situations, 'tis easy to imagine how such an influence of objects upon one another may connect them in the imagination.

We may carry this farther, and remark, not only that two objects are connected by the relation of cause and effect, when the one produces a motion or any action in the other, but also when it has a power of producing it. And this we may observe to be the source of all the relations of interest and duty, by which men influence each other in society, and are placed in the ties of government and subordination. A master is such a one as, by his situation, arising either from force or agreement, has a power of directing in certain particulars the actions of another, whom we call servant. A judge is one, who, in all disputed cases, can fix by his opinion the possession or property of any thing betwixt any members of the society. When a person is possessed of any power, there is no more required to convert it into action, but the exertion of the will; and *that* in every case is considered as possible, and in many as probable; especially in the case of authority, where the obedience of the subject is a pleasure and advantage to the superior.

These are, therefore, the principles of union or cohesion among our simple ideas, and in the imagination supply the place of that inseparable connexion, by which they are united in our memory. Here is a kind of *attraction,* which in the mental world will be found to have as extraordinary effects as in the natural, and to show itself in as many and as various forms. Its effects are every where conspicuous; but, as to its causes, they are mostly unknown, and must be resolved into *original* qualities of human nature, which I pretend not to explain. Nothing is more requisite for a true philosopher, than to restrain the intemperate desire of searching into causes and, having established any doctrine upon a sufficient number of experiments, rest contented with that, when he sees a farther examination would lead him into obscure and uncertain speculations. In that case his inquiry would be much better employed in examining the effects than the causes of his principle.

Section VI: Of Modes and Substances

I would fain ask those philosophers, who found so much of their reasonings on the distinction of substance and accident, and imagine we have clear ideas of each, whether the idea of *substance* be derived from the impressions of sensation or reflection? If it be conveyed to us by our senses, I ask, which of them, and after what manner? If it be perceived by the eyes, it must be a colour; if by the ears, a sound; if by the palate, a taste; and so of the other senses. But I believe none will assert, that substance is either a colour, or sound, or a taste. The idea of substance must therefore be derived from an impression of reflection, if it really exist. But the impressions of reflection resolve themselves into our passions and emotions; none of which can possibly represent a substance. We have, therefore, no idea of substance, distinct from that of a collection of particular qualities, nor have we any other meaning when we either talk or reason concerning it.

The idea of a substance as well as that of a mode, is nothing but a collection of simple ideas, that are united by the imagination, and have a particular name assigned them, by which we are able to recal, either to ourselves or others, that collection. But the difference betwixt these ideas consists in this, that the particular qualities, which form a substance, are commonly referred to an unknown *something,* in which they are supposed to inhere; or granting this fiction should not take place, are at least supposed to be closely and inseparably connected by the relations of contiguity and causation.

Hume: An Inquiry Concerning Human Understanding

Section III: Of the Association of Ideas

It is evident, that there is a principle of connection between the different thoughts or ideas of the mind, and that, in their appearance to the memory or imagination, they introduce each other with a certain degree of method and regularity. In our more serious thinking or discourse, this is so observable, that any particular thought, which breaks in upon the regular tract or chain of ideas, is immediately remarked and rejected. And even in our wildest and most wandering reveries, nay, in our very dreams, we shall find, if we reflect, that the imagination ran not altogether at adventures, but that there was still a connection upheld among the different ideas which succeeded each other. Were the loosest and freest conversation to be transcribed, there would immediately be observed something which connected it in all its transitions. Or where this is wanting, the person who broke the thread of discourse might still inform you, that there had secretly revolved in his mind a succession of thought, which had gradually led him from the subject of conversation. Among different languages, even when we cannot suspect the least connection or communication, it is found, that the words expressive of ideas the most compounded, do yet nearly correspond to each other; a certain proof that the simple ideas comprehended in the compound ones were bound together by some universal principle, which had an equal influence on all mankind.

Though it be too obvious to escape observation, that different ideas are connected together, I do not find that any philosopher has attempted to enumerate or class all the principles of association; a subject, however, that seems worthy of curiosity. To me there appear to be only three principles of connection among ideas, namely, *Resemblance*, *Contiguity* in time or place, and *Cause* or *Effect*.

That these principles serve to connect ideas, will not, I believe, be much doubted. A picture naturally leads our thoughts to the original. The mention of one apartment in a building naturally introduces an inquiry or discourse concerning the others; and if we think of a wound, we can scarcely forbear reflecting on the pain which follows it. But that this enumeration is complete, and that there are no other principles of association except these, may be difficult to prove to the satisfaction of the reader, or even to a man's own satisfaction.

THOMAS REID

1710 - 1796

From: *The Essays on the Intellectual Powers of Man.* Published by M.I.T. Press, 1969.

Thomas Reid, professor of moral philosophy at Glasgow, originated the Scottish school of common sense philosophy. Reid objected that the empiricism of Locke and Hume led to absurd conclusions that defied common sense. For example, the existence of the external world and of other minds was, he held, self evident. Even those philosophers who questioned their existence were obliged to assume a positive answer to their enquiry in order to begin it. A trenchant critic of the views of memory of Locke and Hume, Reid did not propose an account of his own. The school of common sense was influential in the early nineteenth century and affected individual philosophers, e.g., C. S. Pierce, thereafter.

Supplementary readings:

Jones, O. M. (1927). *Empiricism and Intuitionism in Reid's Common Sense Philosophy.* Princeton: Princeton University Press.

Marcel-Lacoste, L. (1982). *Claude Buffier and Thomas Reid: Two Common Sense Philosophers.* Ontario: McGill-Queen's University Press.

THOMAS REID

Table of Contents

The Essays on the Intellectual Powers of Man: Essay III. Concerning Memory

Explanation of contents: Contents are listed by chapter (Roman numeral) and page number in the 1969 edition (Arabic numeral). Page numbers have been added to the text by the editors [in brackets]. All excerpts are from Essay III, Concerning Memory.

[324] In the gradual progress of man, from infancy to maturity, there is a certain order in which his faculties are unfolded, and this seems to be the best order we can follow in treating of them.

The external senses appear first; memory soon follows, which we are now to consider.

It is by memory that we have an immediate knowledge of things past. The senses give us information of things only as they exist in the present moment; and this information, if it were not preserved by memory, would vanish instantly, and leave us as ignorant as if it had never been. Memory must have an object. Every man who remembers must remember something, and that which he remembers is called the object of his remembrance. In this, memory agrees with perception, but differs from sensation, which has no object but the feeling itself.

Every man can distinguish the thing remembered from the remembrance of it. We may remember any thing which we have seen, or heard, or known, or done, or suffered; but the remembrance of it is a particular act of the mind which now exists, and of which we are [325] conscious. To confound these two is an absurdity, which a thinking man could not be led into, but by some false hypothesis which hinders him from reflecting upon the thing which he would explain by it.

In memory we do not find such a train of operations connected by our constitution as in perception. When we perceive an object by our senses, there is, first, some impression made by the object upon the organ of sense, either immediately or by means of some medium. By this an impression is made upon the nerves and brain, in consequence of which we feel some sensation; and that sensation is attended by that conception and belief of the external object which we call perception. These operations are so connected in our constitution, that it is difficult to disjoin them in our conceptions, and to attend to each without confounding it with the others. But in the operations of memory we are free from this embarrassment; they are easily distinguished from all other acts of the mind, and the names which denote them are free from all ambiguity.

The object of memory, or thing remembered, must be something that is past; as the object of perception and of consciousness must be something which is present. What now is, cannot be an object of memory; neither can that which is past and gone be an object of perception or of consciousness.

Memory is always accompanied with the belief of that which we remember, as perception is accompanied with the belief of that which we perceive, and consciousness with the belief of that whereof we are conscious. Perhaps in infancy, or in a disorder of mind, things remembered may be confounded with those which are merely imagined; but in mature years, and in a sound state of mind, every man feels that he must believe what he distinctly remembers, though he can give no other reason of his belief, but that he remembers the thing [326] distinctly; whereas, when he merely imagines a thing ever so distinctly, he has no belief of it upon that account.

This belief, which we have from distinct memory, we account real knowledge, no less certain than if it was grounded on demonstration; no man in his wits calls it in question, or will hear any argument against it. The testimony of witnesses in causes of life and death depends upon it, and all the knowledge of mankind of past events is built on this foundation.

There are cases in which a man's memory is less distinct and determinate, and where he is ready to allow that it may have failed him; but this does not in the least weaken its credit, when it is perfectly distinct.

Memory implies a conception and belief of past duration; for it is impossible that a man should remember a thing distinctly, without believing some interval of duration, more or less, to have passed between the time it happened, and the present moment; and I think it is impossible to show how we could acquire a notion of duration if we had no memory.

Things remembered must be things formerly perceived or known. I remember the transit of Venus over the sun in the year 1769. I must therefore have perceived it at the time it happened, otherwise I could not now remember it. Our first acquaintance with any object of thought cannot be by remembrance. Memory can only produce a continuance or renewal of a former acquaintance with the thing remembered.

The remembrance of a past event is necessarily accompanied with the conviction of our own existence at the time the event happened. I cannot remember a thing that happened a year ago, without a conviction as strong as memory can give, that I, the same identical person who now remember that event, did then exist.

What I have hitherto said concerning memory, I consider as principles, which appear obvious and certain [327] to every man who will take the pains to reflect upon the operations of his own mind. They are facts of which every man must judge by what he feels; and they admit of no other proof but an appeal to every man's own reflection. I shall therefore take them for granted in what follows, and shall first draw some conclusions from them, and then examine the theories of philosophers concerning memory, and concerning duration, and our personal identity, of which we acquire the knowledge by memory.

[328] First, I think it appears that memory is an original faculty given us by the Author of our being, of which we can give no account, but that we are so made.

The knowledge which I have of things past, by my memory, seems to me as unaccountable as an immediate knowledge would be of things to come: and I can give no reason why I should have the one and not the other, but that such is the will of my Maker. I find in my mind a distinct conception, and a firm belief of a series of past events; but how this is produced I know not. I call it memory, but this is only giving a name to it; it is not an account of its cause. I believe most firmly what I distinctly remember; but I can give no reason of this belief. It is the inspiration of the Almighty that gives me this understanding.

When I believe the truth of a mathematical axiom, or of a mathematical proposition, I see that it must be so. Every man who has the same conception of it sees the same. There is a necessary and an evident connection between the subject and the predicate of the proposition; and I have all the evidence to support my belief which I can possibly conceive.

When I believe that I washed my hands and face this morning, there appears no necessity in the truth of this proposition. It might be, or it might not be. A man may distinctly conceive it without believing it at all. How then do I come to believe it? I remember it distinctly. This is all I can say. This remembrance is an act of my mind. it is impossible that this act should be, if the event had not happened. I confess I do not [329] see any necessary connection between the one and the other. If any man can show such a necessary connection, then I think that belief which we have of what we remember will be fairly accounted for; but if this cannot be done, that belief is unaccountable, and we can say no more but that it is the result of our constitution.

Perhaps it may be said, that the experience we have had of the fidelity of memory is a good reason for relying upon its testimony. I deny not that this may be a reason to those who have had this experience, and who reflect upon it. But I believe there are few who ever thought of this reason, or who found any need of it. It must be some very rare occasion that leads a man to have recourse to it; and in those who have done so, the testimony of memory was believed before the experience of its fidelity; and that belief could not be caused by the experience which came after it.

We know some abstract truths, by comparing the terms of the proposition which expresses them, and perceiving some necessary relation or agreement between them. It is thus I know that two and three make five; that the diameters of a circle are all equal. Mr. Locke having discovered this source of knowledge, too rashly concluded that all human knowledge might be derived from it; and in this he has been followed very generally; by Mr. Hume in particular.

But I apprehend, that our knowledge of the existence of things contingent can never be traced to this source. I know that such a thing exists, or did exist. This knowledge cannot be derived from the perception of a necessary agreement between existence and the thing that exists, because there is no such necessary agreement; and therefore no such agreement can be perceived either immediately, or by a chain of reasoning. [330] The thing does not exist necessarily, but by the will and power of him that made it; and there is no contradiction follows from supposing it not to exist.

Whence I think it follows, that our knowledge of the existence of our own thoughts, of the existence of all the material objects about us, and of all past contingencies, must be derived, not from a perception of necessary relations or agreements, but from some other source.

Our Maker has provided other means for giving us the knowledge of these things; means which perfectly answer their end, and produce the effect intended by them. But in what manner they do this, is, I fear, beyond our skill to explain. We know our own thoughts, and the operations of our minds, by a power which we call consciousness: but this is only giving a name to this part of our frame. It does not explain its fabric, nor how it produces in us an irresistible conviction of its informations. We perceive material objects and their sensible qualities by our senses; but how they give us this information, and how they produce our belief in it, we know not. We know many past events by memory; but how it gives this information, I believe, is inexplicable.

It is well known what subtile disputes were held through all the scholastic ages, and are still carried on about the prescience of the Deity. Aristotle had taught, that there can be no certain foreknowledge of things contingent; and in this he has been very generally followed, upon no other grounds, as I apprehend, but that we cannot conceive how such things should be foreknown, and therefore conclude it to be impossible. Hence has arisen an opposition and supposed inconsistency between Divine prescience and human liberty. Some have given up the first in favour of the last, and others have given up the last in order to support the first.

[331] It is remarkable, that these disputants have never apprehended that there is any difficulty in reconciling with liberty the knowledge of what is past, but only of what is future. It is prescience only, and not memory, that is supposed to be hostile to liberty, and hardly reconcileable to it.

Yet I believe the difficulty is perfectly equal in the one case and in the other. I admit, that we cannot account for prescience of the actions of a free agent. But I maintain, that we can as little account for memory of the past actions of a free agent. If any man thinks he can prove that the actions of a free agent cannot be foreknown, he will find the same arguments of equal force to prove that the past actions of a free agent cannot be remembered. It is true, that what is past did certainly exist. It is no less true, that what is future will certainly exist. I know no reasoning from the constitution of the agent, or from his circumstances, that has not equal strength, whether it be applied to his past or to his future actions. The past was, but now is not. The future will be, but now is not. The present is equally connected, or unconnected with both.

The only reason why men have apprehended so great disparity in cases so perfectly like, I take to be this, that the faculty of memory in ourselves convinces us from fact, that it is not impossible that an intelligent being, even a finite being, should have certain knowledge of past actions of free agents, without tracing them from any thing necessarily connected with them. But having no prescience in ourselves corresponding to our memory of what is past, we find great difficulty in admitting it to be possible even in the Supreme Being.

A faculty which we possess in some degree, we easily admit that the Supreme Being may possess in a more perfect degree; but a faculty, which has nothing corresponding [332] to it in our constitution, we will hardly allow to be possible. We are so constituted as to have an intuitive knowledge of many things past; but we have no intuitive knowledge of the future. We might perhaps have been so constituted as to have an intuitive knowledge of the future, but not of the past; nor would this constitution have been more unaccountable than the present, though it might be much more inconvenient. Had this been our constitution, we should have found no difficulty in admitting that the Deity may know all things future, but very much in admitting his knowledge of things that are past.

Our original faculties are all unaccountable. Of these memory is one. He only who made them, comprehends fully how they are made, and how they produce in us, not only a conception, but a firm belief and assurance of things which it concerns us to know.

Reid: Essay III. Concerning Memory

III.333

[333] From the principles laid down in the first chapter of this Essay, I think it appears, that our notion of duration, as well as our belief of it, is got by the faculty of memory. It is essential to every thing remembered that it be something which is past; and we cannot conceive a thing to be past, without conceiving some duration, more or less, between it and the present. As soon, therefore, as we remember any thing, we must have both a notion and a belief of duration. It is necessarily suggested by every operation of our memory; and to that faculty it ought to be ascribed. This is therefore a proper place to consider what is known concerning it.

Duration, extension, and number, are the measures of all things subject to mensuration. When we apply them to finite things which are measured by them, they seem of all things to be the most distinctly conceived, and most within the reach of human understanding.

Extension having three dimensions, has an endless variety of modifications, capable of being accurately defined; and their various relations furnish the human mind with its most ample field of demonstrative reasoning. Duration having only one dimension, has fewer modifications; but these are clearly understood; and their relations admit of measure, proportion, and demonstrative reasoning.

Reid: Essay III. Concerning Memory

IV.340 - 344

[340] I see evidently that identity supposes an uninterrupted continuance of existence. That which has ceased to exist, cannot be the same with that which afterward begins to exist; for this would be to suppose a being to exist after it ceased to exist, and to have had existence before it was produced, which are manifest contradictions. Continued uninterrupted existence is therefore necessarily implied in identity.

Hence we may infer, that identity cannot, in its proper sense, be applied to our pains, our pleasures, our thoughts, or any operation of our minds. The pain felt this day is not the same individual pain which I felt yesterday, though they may be similar in kind and degree, and have the same cause. The same may be said of every feeling, and of every operation of mind. They are all successive in their nature, like time itself, no two moments of which can be the same moment.

It is otherwise with the parts of absolute space. They always are, and were, and will be the same. So far, I think, we proceed upon clear ground in fixing the notion of identity in general. It is perhaps more difficult to ascertain with precision the meaning of personality; but it is not necessary in the present subject: it is sufficient for our purpose to observe, that all mankind place their personality in something that cannot be divided, or consist of parts. A part of a person is a manifest absurdity.

When a man loses his estate, his health, his strength, he is still the same person, and has lost nothing of his personality. If he has a leg or an arm cut off, he is the same person he was before. The amputated member is no part of his person, otherwise it would have a right to a part of his estate, and be liable for a part of his engagements. It would be entitled to a share of his merit and demerit, which is manifestly absurd. A [341] person is something indivisible, and is what Leibnitz calls monad.

My personal identity, therefore, implies the continued existence of that indivisible thing which I call myself. Whatever this self may be, it is something which thinks, and deliberates, and resolves, and acts, and suffers. I am not thought, I am not action, I am not feeling; I am something that thinks, and acts, and suffers. My thoughts, and actions, and feelings, change every moment;

they have no continued, but a successive existence; but that self or I, to which they belong, is permanent, and has the same relation to all the succeeding thoughts, actions and feelings, which I call mine.

Such are the notions that I have of my personal identity. But perhaps it may be said, this may all be fancy without reality. How do you know; what evidence have you, that there is such a permanent self which has a claim to all the thoughts, actions, and feelings, which you call yours?

To this I answer, that the proper evidence I have of all this is remembrance. I remember that twenty years ago I conversed with such a person; I remember several things that passed in that conversation; my memory testifies not only that this was done, but that it was done by me who now remember it. If it was done by me, I must have existed at that time, and continued to exist from that time to the present. If the identical person whom I call myself, had not a part in that conversation, my memory is fallacious; it gives a distinct and positive testimony of what is not true. Every man in his senses believes what he distinctly remembers, and every thing he remembers convinces him that he existed at the time remembered.

Although memory gives the most irresistible evidence of my being the identical person that did such [342] a thing, at such a time, I may have other good evidence of things which befell me, and which I do not remember: I know who bare me, and suckled me, but I do not remember these events.

It may here be observed, though the observation would have been unnecessary, if some great philosophers had not contradicted it, that it is not my remembering any action of mine that makes me to be the person who did it. This remembrance makes me to know assuredly that I did it; but I might have done it, though I did not remember it. That relation to me, which is expressed by saying that I did it, would be the same, though I had not the least remembrance of it. To say that my remembering that I did such a thing, or, as some choose to express it, my being conscious that I did it, makes me to have done it, appears to me as great an absurdity as it would be to say, that my belief that the world was created, made it to be created.

When we pass judgment on the identity of other persons besides ourselves, we proceed upon other grounds, and determine from a variety of circumstances, which sometimes produce the firmest assurance, and sometimes leave room for doubt. The identity of persons has often furnished matter of serious litigation before tribunals of justice. But no man of a sound mind ever doubted of his own identity, as far as he distinctly remembered.

The identity of person is a perfect identity; wherever it is real, it admits of no degrees; and it is impossible that a person should be in part the same, and in part different; because a person is a monad, and is not divisible into parts. The evidence of identity in other persons besides ourselves, does indeed admit of all degrees, from what we account certainty, to the least degree of probability. But still it is true, that the same person is perfectly the same, and cannot be so in part, or in some degree only.

[343] For this cause, I have first considered personal identity, as that which is perfect in its kind, and the natural measure of that which is imperfect.

We probably at first derive our notion of identity from that natural conviction which every man has from the dawn of reason of his own identity and continued existence. The operations of our minds are all successive, and have no continued existence. But the thinking being has a continued existence, and we have an invincible belief, that it remains the same when all its thoughts and operations change.

Our judgments of the identity of objects of sense, seem to be formed much upon the same grounds as our judgments of the identity of other persons besides ourselves.

Wherever we observe great similarity, we are apt to presume identity, if no reason appears to the contrary. Two objects ever so like, when they are perceived at the same time, cannot be the same: but if they are presented to our senses at different times, we are apt to think them the same, merely from their similarity. Whether this be a natural prejudice, or from whatever cause it proceeds, it certainly appears in children from infancy; and, when we grow up, it is confirmed in most instances by experience: for we rarely find two individuals of the same species that are not distinguishable by obvious differences.

A man challenges a thief whom he finds in possession of his horse or his watch, only on similarity. When the watchmaker swears that he sold this watch to such a person, his testimony is grounded on similarity. The testimony of witnesses to the identity of a person is commonly grounded on no other evidence.

Thus it appears, that the evidence we have of our own identity, as far back as we remember, is totally of a different kind from the evidence we have of the identity of other persons, or of objects of sense. The first [344] is grounded on memory, and gives undoubted certainty. The last is grounded on similarity, and on other circumstances, which in many cases are not so decisive as to leave no room for doubt.

It may likewise be observed that the identity of objects of sense is never perfect. All bodies, as they consist of innumerable parts that may be disjoined from them by a great variety of causes, are subject to continual changes of their substance, increasing, diminishing, changing insensibly. When such alterations are gradual, because language could not afford a different name for every different state of such a changeable being, it retains the same name, and is considered as the same thing. Thus we say of an old regiment, that it did such a thing a century ago, though there now is not a man alive who then belonged to it. We say a tree is the same in the seed bed and in the forest. A ship of war, which has successively changed her anchors, her tackle, her sails, her masts, her planks, and her timbers, while she keeps the same name, is the same.

The identity therefore which we ascribe to bodies, whether natural or artificial, is not perfect identity; it is rather something which, for the conveniency of speech, we call identity. It admits of a great change of the subject, providing the change be gradual, sometimes even of a total change. And the changes which in common language are made consistent with identity, differ from those that are thought to destroy it, not in kind, but in number and degree. It has no fixed nature when applied to bodies; and questions about the identity of a body are very often questions about words. But identity, when applied to persons, has no ambiguity, and admits not of degrees, or of more and less: it is the foundation of all rights and obligations, and of all accountableness; and the notion of it is fixed and precise.

Reid: Essay III. Concerning Memory

V.346 - 349

[346] Mr. Locke says, that by reflection he would be understood to mean, "the notice which the mind takes of its own operations, and the manner of them." This, I think, we commonly call consciousness; from which, indeed, we derive all the notions we have of the operations of our own minds; and he often speaks of the operations of our own minds, as the only objects of reflection.

[347] When reflection is taken in this confined sense, to say, that all our ideas are ideas either of sensation or reflection, is to say, that every thing we can conceive is either some object of sense or some operation of our own minds, which is far from being true.

But the word reflection is commonly used in a much more extensive sense; it is applied to many operations of the mind, with more propriety than to that of consciousness. We reflect, when we remember, or call to mind what is past, and survey it with attention. We reflect, when we define, when we distinguish, when we judge, when we reason, whether about things material or intellectual.

When reflection is taken in this sense, which is more common, and therefore more proper than the sense which Mr. Locke has put upon it, it may be justly said to be the only source of all our distinct and accurate notions of things. For, although our first notions of material things are got by the external senses, and our first notions of the operations of our own minds by consciousness, these first notions are neither simple nor clear. Our senses and our consciousness are continually shifting from one object to another: their operations are transient and momentary, and leave no distinct notion of their objects, until they are recalled by memory, examined with attention, and compared with other things.

This reflection is not one power of the mind; it comprehends many; such as recollection, attention, distinguishing, comparing, judging. By these powers

188

our minds are furnished, not only with many simple and original notions, but with all our notions which are accurate and well defined, and which alone are the proper materials of reasoning. Many of these, are neither notions of the objects of sense, nor of the operations of our own minds, and therefore neither ideas of sensation, [348] nor of reflection, in the sense that Mr. Locke gives to reflection. But if any one chooses to call them ideas of reflection, taking the word in the more common and proper sense, I have no objection.

Mr. Locke seems to me to have used the word reflection sometimes in that limited sense which he has given to it in the definition before mentioned, and sometimes to have fallen unawares into the common sense of the word; and by this ambiguity his account of the origin of our ideas is darkened and perplexed.

Having premised these things in general of Mr. Locke's theory of the origin of our ideas or notions, I proceed to some observations on his account of the idea of duration.

"Reflection, he says, upon the train of ideas, which appear one after another in our minds, is that which furnishes us with the idea of succession; and the distance between any two parts of that succession, is that we call duration."

If it be meant that the idea of succession is prior to that of duration, either in time, or in the order of nature, this, I think, is impossible, because succession, as Dr. Price justly observes, presupposes duration, and can in no sense be prior to it; and therefore it would be more proper to derive the idea of succession from that of duration.

But how do we get the idea of succession? It is, says he, by reflecting upon the train of ideas, which appear one after another in our minds.

Reflecting upon the train of ideas can be nothing but remembering it, and giving attention to what our memory testifies concerning it: for if we did not remember it, we could not have a thought about it. So that it is evident, that this reflection includes remembrance, without which there could be no reflection on what is past, and consequently no idea of succession.

[349] It may here be observed, that if we speak strictly and philosophically, no kind of succession can be an object, either of the senses, or of consciousness; because the operations of both are confined to the present point of time, and there can be no succession in a point of time; and on that account the motion of a body, which is a successive change of place, could not be observed by the senses alone without the aid of memory.

As the purposes of conversation make it convenient to extend what is called the present, the same reason [350] leads men to extend the province of sense, and to carry its limit as far back as they carry the present. Thus a man may say, I saw such a person just now; it would be ridiculous to find fault with this way of speaking, because it is authorized by custom, and has a distinct meaning: but if we speak philosophically, the senses do not testify what we saw, but only what we see; what I saw last moment I consider as the testimony of sense, though it is now only the testimony of memory.

There is no necessity in common life of dividing accurately the provinces of sense and of memory; and therefore we assign to sense, not an indivisible point of time, but that small portion of time which we call the present, which has a beginning, a middle, and an end.

Hence it is easy to see, that though in common language we speak with perfect propriety and truth, when we say, that we see a body move, and that motion is an object of sense, yet when as philosophers we distinguish accurately the province of sense from that of memory, we can no more see what is past, though but a moment ago, than we can remember what is present: so that speaking philosophically, it is only by the aid of memory that we discern motion, or any succession whatsoever. We see the present place of the body; we remember the successive advance it made to that place. The first can then only give us a conception of motion, when joined to the last.

[363] The common theory of ideas, that is, of images in the brain, or in the mind, of all the objects of thought, has been very generally applied to account for the faculties of memory and imagination, as well as that of perception by the senses.

The sentiments of the Peripatetics are expressed by Alexander Aphrodisiensis, one of the earliest Greek commentators on Aristotle, in these words, as they are translated by Mr. Harris in his Hermes: "Now what fancy or imagination is, we may explain as follows: we may conceive to be formed within us, from the operations of our senses about sensible objects, some impression, as it were, or picture in our original sensorium, being a relief of that motion caused within us by the external object; a relict, which, when the external object is no longer present, remains, and is still preserved, being, as it were, its image; and which, by being thus preserved, becomes the cause of our having memory. Now such a sort of relict, and as it were impression, they call fancy or imagination."

Another passage from Alcinous, of the doctrines of Plato, chap. 4. shows the agreement of the ancient Platonists and Peripatetics in this theory. "When the form or type of things is imprinted on the mind by the organs of the senses, and so imprinted as not to be deleted by time, but preserved firm and lasting, its preservation is called memory."

Upon this principle Aristotle imputes the shortness of memory in children to this cause, that their brain [364] is too moist and soft to retain impressions made upon it: and the defect of memory in old men he imputes, on the contrary, to the hardness and rigidity of the brain, which hinders its receiving any durable impression.

This ancient theory of the cause of memory is defective in two respects: 1st, if the cause assigned did really exist, it by no means accounts for the phenomenon: and, 2dly, there is no evidence, nor even probability, that that cause exists.

It is probable, that in perception some impression is made upon the brain as well as upon the organ and nerves, because all the nerves terminate in the brain, and because disorders and hurts of the brain are found to affect our powers of perception when the external organ and nerve are sound; but we are totally ignorant of the nature of this impression upon the brain. It can have no resemblance to the object perceived, nor does it in any degree account for that sensation and perception which are consequent upon it. These things have been argued in the second Essay, and shall now be taken for granted, to prevent repetition.

If the impression upon the brain be insufficient to account for the perception of objects that are present, it can as little account for the memory of those that are past.

So that if it were certain, that the impressions made on the brain in perception remain as long as there is any memory of the object; all that could be inferred from this, is, that, by the laws of nature, there is a connection established between that impression, and the remembrance of that object. But how the impression contributes to this remembrance, we should be quite ignorant; it being impossible to discover how thought of any kind should be produced, by an impression on the brain, or upon any part of the body.

[365] To say that this impression is memory, is absurd, if understood literally. If it is only meant that it is the cause of memory, it ought to be shown how it produces this effect, otherwise memory remains as unaccountable as before.

If a philosopher should undertake to account for the force of gunpowder, in the discharge of a musket, and then tell us gravely, that the cause of this phenomenon is the drawing of the trigger, we should not be much wiser by this account. As little are we instructed in the cause of memory, by being told that it is caused by a certain impression on the brain. For, supposing that impression on the brain were as necessary to memory as the drawing of the trigger is to the discharge of the musket, we are still as ignorant as we were how memory is produced; so that, if the cause of memory, assigned by this theory, did really exist, it does not in any degree account for memory.

Another defect in this theory is, that there is no evidence, nor probability, that the cause assigned does exist; that is, that the impression made upon the brain in perception remains after the object is removed.

That impression, whatever be its nature, is caused by the impression made by the object upon the organ of sense, and upon the nerve. Philosophers suppose, without any evidence, that when the object is removed, and the impression upon the organ and nerve ceases, the impression upon the brain continues, and is permanent; that is, that when the cause is removed the effect continues. The brain surely does not appear more fitted to retain an impression than the organ and nerve. But granting that the impression upon the brain continues after its cause is removed, its effects ought to continue while it continues; that is, the sensation and perception should be as permanent as the impression [366] upon the brain, which is supposed to be their cause. But here again the philosopher makes a second supposition, with as little evidence, but of a contrary nature, to wit, that, while the cause remains, the effect ceases.

If this should be granted also, a third must be made, that the same cause, which at first produced sensation and perception, does afterward produce memory; an operation essentially different, both from sensation and perception.

A fourth supposition must be made, that this cause, though it be permanent, does not produce its effect at all times; it must be like an inscription which is sometimes covered with rubbish, and on other occasions made legible: for the memory of things is often interrupted for a long time, and circumstances bring to our recollection what had been long forgotten. After all, many things are remembered which were never perceived by the senses, being no objects of sense, and therefore, which could make no impression upon the brain by means of the senses.

Thus, when philosophers have piled one supposition upon another, as the giants piled the mountains, in order to scale the heavens, all is to no purpose; memory remains unaccountable; and we know as little how we remember things past, as how we are conscious of the present.

But here it is proper to observe, that although impressions upon the brain give no aid in accounting for memory, yet it is very probable, that, in the human frame, memory is dependent on some proper state or temperament of the brain.

Although the furniture of our memory bears no resemblance to any temperament of brain whatsoever, as indeed it is impossible it should; yet nature may have subjected us to this law, that a certain constitution or state of the brain is necessary to memory. That this [367] is really the case, many well known facts lead us to conclude.

It is possible, that, by accurate observation, the proper means may be discovered of preserving that temperament of the brain which is favourable to memory, and of remedying, the disorders of that temperament. This would be a very noble improvement of the medical art. But if it should ever be attained, it would give no aid to understand how one state of the brain assists memory, and another hurts it.

I know certainly, that the impression made upon my hand by the prick of a pin occasions acute pain. But can any philosopher show how this cause produces the effect? The nature of the impression is here perfectly known; but it gives no help to understand how that impression affects the mind; and if we knew as distinctly that state of the brain which causes memory, we should still be as ignorant as before how that state contributes to memory. We might have been so constituted, for any thing that I know, that the prick of a pin in the hand, instead of causing pain, should cause remembrance; nor would that constitution be more unaccountable than the present.

The body and mind operate on each other, according to fixed laws of nature; and it is the business of a philosopher to discover those laws by observation and experiment: but, when he has discovered them, he must rest in them as facts, whose cause is inscrutable to the human understanding.

Reid: Essay III. Concerning Memory

VII.380 - 382

[380] Before we leave this subject of memory, it is proper to take notice of a distinction which Aristotle makes between memory and reminiscence, because the distinction has a real foundation in nature, though in our language, I think, we do not distinguish them by different names.

Memory is a kind of habit which is not always in exercise with regard to things we remember, but is ready to suggest them when there is occasion. The most perfect degree of this habit is, when the thing presents itself to our remembrance spontaneously, and without labour, as often as there is occasion. A second degree is, when the thing is forgotten for a longer or a shorter time, even when there is occasion to [381] remember it, yet at last some incident brings it to mind without any search. A third degree is, when we cast about and search for what we would remember, and so at last find it out. It is this last, I think, which Aristotle calls reminiscence, as distinguished from memory.

Reminiscence, therefore, includes a will to recollect something past, and a search for it. But here a difficulty occurs. It may be said, that what we will to remember we must conceive, as there can be no will without a conception of

193

the thing willed. A will to remember a thing, therefore, seems to imply that we remember it already, and have no occasion to search for it. But this difficulty is easily removed. When we will to remember a thing, we must remember something relating to it, which gives us a relative conception of it; but we may, at the same time, have no conception what the thing is, but only what relation it bears to something else. Thus, I remember that a friend charged me with a commission to be executed at such a place; but I have forgotten what the commission was. By applying my thought to what I remember concerning it, that it was given by such a person, upon such an occasion, in consequence of such a conversation, I am led, in a train of thought, to the very thing I had forgotten, and recollect distinctly what the commission was.

Aristotle says, that brutes have not reminiscence, and this I think is probable; but, says he, they have memory. It cannot, indeed, be doubted but they have something very like to it, and in some instances in a very great degree. A dog knows his master after long absence. A horse will trace back a road he has once gone as accurately as a man; and this is the more strange, that the train of thought which he had in going, must be reversed in his return. It is very [382] like to some prodigious memories we read of, where a person, upon hearing an hundred names, or unconnected words pronounced, can begin at the last, and go backward to the first, without losing or misplacing one. Brutes certainly may learn much from experience, which seems to imply memory.

Yet I see no reason to think that brutes measure time as men do, by days, months, or years, or that they have any distinct knowledge of the interval between things which they remember, or of their distance from the present moment. If we could not record transactions according to their dates, human memory would be something very different from what it is, and perhaps resemble more the memory of brutes.

IMMANUEL KANT

1724-1804

From: *Immanuel Kant's Critique of Pure Reason*. Translated by Norman Kemp Smith. Published by MacMillan & Co. Ltd, London, 1961.

Kant was the son of an East Prussian saddler. He lived his whole life in Konigsberg where he was appointed to the chair in logic and metaphysics at the University of Konigsberg in 1770. At the time of his appointment he started work on the *Critique of Pure Reason*, which appeared in 1781. Clothed in a formal academic architecture which seriously obscures its content, the work addresses the question of what reason can know when it operates "purely," without the assistance of other faculties, such as memory. The central problem of how concepts can be applied to experience was solved by recourse to "schemata," a capacity to form images or models, an idea that has experienced a recent revival in cognitive psychology. The first *Critique* was followed by the *Critique of Practical Reason* and *Critique of Judgment*. In these "critical" works Kant set himself the task of establishing both the authority of science and the autonomy of morals.

Supplementary reading:

Broad, C. D. (1978). *Kant: An Introduction*. Cambridge: Cambridge University Press.

Immanuel Kant

Table of Contents

*Explanation of contents: A single excerpt from Kant's Critique of Pure Reason is
included. Kemp Smith's translation includes page numbers in the German edition which are included here in the text (Arabic numerals), but not in the table of
contents. The passage excerpted was heavily revised by Kant in the second edition. Translations of both versions are included by Kemp Smith. The passage
included here is from the first edition. Kemp Smith indicates this by the "A"
before the page number.*

Chapter II: The Deduction of the Pure Concepts of Understanding

Section 2: The *A Priori* Grounds of the Possibility of Experience

That a concept, although itself neither contained in the concept of possible experience nor consisting of elements of a possible experience, should be produced completely *a priori* and should relate to an object, is altogether contradictory and impossible. For it would then have no content, since no intuition corresponds to it; and intuitions in general, through which objects can be given to us, constitute the field, the whole object, of possible experience. An *a priori* concept which did not relate to experience would be only the logical form of a concept, not the concept itself through which something is thought.

Pure *a priori* concepts, if such exist, cannot indeed contain anything empirical; yet, none the less, they can serve solely as *a priori* conditions of a possible experience. Upon this ground alone can their objective reality rest.

If, therefore, we seek to discover how pure concepts of understanding are possible, we must enquire what are the *a priori* conditions upon which the possibility of experience [A96] rests, and which remain as its underlying grounds when everything empirical is abstracted from appearances. A concept which universally and adequately expresses such a formal and objective condition of experience would be entitled a pure concept of understanding. Certainly, once I am in possession of pure concepts of understanding, I can think objects which may be impossible, or which, though perhaps in themselves possible, cannot be given in any experience. For in the connecting of these concepts something may be omitted which yet necessarily belongs to the condition of a possible experience (as in the concept of a spirit). Or, it may be, pure concepts are extended further than experience can follow (as with the concept of God). But the elements of all modes of *a priori* knowledge, even of capricious and incongruous fictions, though they cannot, indeed, be derived from experience, since in that case they would not be knowledge *a priori*, must none the less always contain the pure *a priori* conditions of a possible experience and of an empirical object. Otherwise nothing would be thought through them, and they themselves, being without data, could never arise even in thought.

The concepts which thus contain *a priori* the pure thought involved in every experience, we find in the categories. If we [A97] can prove that by their means alone an object can be thought, this will be a sufficient deduction of them, and will justify their objective validity. But since in such a thought more than simply the faculty of thought, the understanding, is brought into play, and since this faculty itself, as a faculty of knowledge that is meant to relate to objects, calls for explanation in regard to the possibility of such relation, we must first of all consider, not in their empirical but in their transcendental constitution, the subjective sources which form the *a priori* foundation of the possibility of experience.

If each representation were completely foreign to every other, standing apart in isolation, no such thing as knowledge would ever arise. For knowledge is [essentially] a whole in which representations stand compared and connected. As sense contains a manifold in its intuition, I ascribe to it a synopsis. But to such synopsis a synthesis must always correspond; receptivity can make knowledge possible only when combined with spontaneity. Now this spontaneity is the ground of a threefold synthesis which must necessarily be found in all knowledge; namely, the apprehension of representations as modifications of the mind in intuition, their reproduction in imagination, and their recognition in a concept. These point to three subjective sources of knowledge which make possible the understanding itself--and consequently all experience as [A98] its empirical product.

Preliminary Remark

The deduction of the categories is a matter of such extreme difficulty, compelling us to penetrate so deeply into the first grounds of the possibility of our knowledge in general, that in order to avoid the elaborateness of a complete theory, and yet at the same time to omit nothing in so indispensable an enquiry, I have found it advisable in the four following passages rather to prepare than to instruct the reader. Systematic exposition of these elements of the understanding is first given in Section 3, immediately following. The reader must not therefore be deterred by obscurities in these earlier sections. They are unavoidable in an enterprise never before attempted. They will, as I trust, in the section referred to, finally give way to complete insight.

1. The Synthesis of Apprehension in Intuition

Whatever the origin of our representations, whether they are due to the influence of outer things, or are produced through inner causes, whether they arise *a priori*, or being appearances have an empirical origin, they must all, as modifications of the mind, belong to inner sense. All our knowledge [A99] is thus finally subject to time, the formal condition of inner sense. In it they must all be ordered, connected, and brought into relation. This is a general observation which, throughout what follows, must be borne in mind as being quite fundamental.

Every intuition contains in itself a manifold which can be represented as a manifold only in so far as the mind distinguishes the time in the sequence of one impression upon another; for each representation, in so far as it is contained in a single moment, can never be anything but absolute unity. In order that unity of intuition may arise out of this manifold (as is required in the representation of space) it must first be run through, and held together. This act I name the synthesis of apprehension, because it is directed immediately upon intuition, which does indeed offer a manifold, but a manifold which can never be represented as a manifold, and as contained in a single representation, save in virtue of such a synthesis.

This synthesis of apprehension must also be exercised *a priori*, that is, in respect of representations which are not empirical. For without it we should never have *a priori* the representations either of space or of time. They can be produced [A100] only through the synthesis of the manifold which sensibility presents in its original receptivity. We have thus a pure synthesis of apprehension.

2. The Synthesis of Reproduction in Imagination

It is a merely empirical law, that representations which have often followed or accompanied one another finally become associated, and so are set in a relation whereby, even in the absence of the object, one of these representations can, in accordance with a fixed rule, bring about a transition of the mind to the other. But this law of reproduction presupposes that appearances are themselves actually subject to such a rule, and that in the manifold of these representations a coexistence or sequence takes place in conformity with certain rules. Otherwise our empirical imagination would never find opportunity for exercise appropriate to its powers, and so would remain concealed within the mind as a dead and to us unknown faculty. If cinnabar were sometimes red, sometimes black, sometimes light, sometimes heavy, if a man changed sometimes into this and sometimes into that animal form, if the country on the longest day were sometimes covered with [A101] fruit, sometimes with ice and snow, my empirical imagination would never find opportunity when representing red colour to bring to mind heavy cinnabar. Nor could there be an empirical synthesis of reproduction, if a certain name were sometimes given to this, sometimes to that object, or were one and the same thing named sometimes in one way, sometimes in another, independently of any rule to which appearances are in themselves subject.

There must then be something which, as the *a priori* ground of a necessary synthetic unity of appearances, makes their reproduction possible. What that something is we soon discover, when we reflect that appearances are not things in themselves, but are the mere play of our representations, and in the end reduce to determinations of inner sense. For if we can show that even our purest *a priori* intuitions yield no knowledge, save in so far as they contain a combination of the manifold such as renders a thoroughgoing synthesis of reproduction possible, then this synthesis of imagination is likewise grounded, antecedently to all experience, upon *a priori* principles; and we must assume a pure transcendental synthesis of imagination as conditioning the very possibility of all experience. For experience as such necessarily presupposes the reproducibility of appearances. When [A102] I seek to draw a line in thought, or to think of the time from one noon to another, or even to represent to myself some particular number, obviously the various manifold representations that are involved must be apprehended by me in thought one after the other. But if I were always to drop out of thought the preceding representations (the first parts of the line, the antecedent parts of the time period, or the units in the order represented), and did not reproduce them while advancing to those that follow, a complete representation would never be obtained: none of the above-mentioned thoughts, not even the purest and most elementary representations of space and time, could arise.

The synthesis of apprehension is thus inseparably bound up with the synthesis of reproduction. And as the former constitutes the transcendental ground of the possibility of all modes of knowledge whatsoever--of those that are pure *a priori* no less than of those that are empirical--the reproductive synthesis of the imagination is to be counted among the transcendental acts of the mind. We shall therefore entitle this faculty the transcendental faculty of imagination.

3. The Synthesis of Recognition in a Concept [A103]

If we were not conscious that what we think is the same as what we thought a moment before, all reproduction in the series of representations would be useless. For it would in its present state be a new representation which would not in any way belong to the act whereby it was to be gradually generated. The manifold of the representation would never, therefore, form a whole, since it would lack that unity which only consciousness can impart to it. If, in counting, I forget that the units, which now hover before me, have been added to one another in succession, I should never know that a total is being produced through this successive addition of unit to unit, and so would remain ignorant of the number. For the concept of the number is nothing but the consciousness of this unity of synthesis.

The word 'concept' might of itself suggest this remark. For this unitary consciousness is what combines the manifold, successively intuited, and thereupon also reproduced, into one representation. This consciousness may often be only faint, so that we do not connect it with the act itself, that is, not in any direct manner with the generation of the representation, [A104] but only with the outcome [that which is thereby represented]. But notwithstanding these variations, such consciousness, however indistinct, must always be present; without it, concepts, and therewith knowledge of objects, are altogether impossible.

At this point we must make clear to ourselves what we mean by the expression 'an object of representations'. We have stated above that appearances are themselves nothing but sensible representations, which, as such and in themselves, must not be taken as objects capable of existing outside our power of representation. What, then, is to be understood when we speak of an object corresponding to, and consequently also distinct from, our knowledge? It is easily seen that this object must be thought only as something general $= x$, since outside our knowledge we have nothing which we could set over against this knowledge as corresponding to it.

Now we find that our thought of the relation of all knowledge to its object carries with it an element of necessity; the object is viewed as that which prevents our modes of knowledge from being haphazard or arbitrary, and which determines them *a priori* in some definite fashion. For in so far as they are to relate to an object, they must necessarily agree with one another, that is, must possess that unity which [A105] constitutes the concept of an object.

But it is clear that, since we have to deal only with the manifold of our representations, and since that x (the object) which corresponds to them is nothing to us -- being, as it is, something that has to be distinct from all our representations -- the unity which the object makes necessary can be nothing else than the formal unity of consciousness in the synthesis of the manifold of representations. It is only when we have thus produced synthetic unity in the manifold of intuition that we are in a position to say that we know the object. But this unity is impossible if the intuition cannot be generated in accordance with a rule by means of such a function of synthesis as makes the reproduction of the manifold *a priori* necessary, and renders possible a concept in which it is united. Thus we think a triangle as an object, in that we are conscious of the combination of three straight lines according to a rule by which such an intuition can always be represented. This *unity of rule* determines all the manifold, and limits it to conditions which make unity of apperception possible. The concept of this unity is the representation of the object $= x$, which I think through the predicates, above mentioned, of a triangle.

All knowledge demands a concept, though that concept [A106] may, indeed, be quite imperfect or obscure. But a concept is always, as regards its form, something universal which serves as a rule. The concept of body, for instance, as the unity of the manifold which is thought through it, serves as a rule in our knowledge of outer appearances. But it can be a rule for intuitions only in so far as it represents in any given appearances the necessary reproduction of their manifold, and thereby the synthetic unity in our consciousness of them. The concept of body, in the perception of something outside us, necessitates the representation of extension, and therewith representations of impenetrability, shape, etc.

All necessity, without exception, is grounded in a transcendental condition. There must, therefore, be a transcendental ground of the unity of consciousness in the synthesis of the manifold of all our intuitions, and consequently also of the concepts of objects in general, and so of all objects of experience, a ground without which it would be impossible to think any object for our intuitions; for this object is no more than that something, the concept of which expresses such a necessity of synthesis.

This original and transcendental condition is no other [A107] than *transcendental apperception*. Consciousness of self according to the determinations of our state in inner perception is merely empirical, and always changing. No fixed and abiding self can present itself in this flux of inner appearances. Such consciousness is usually named *inner sense*, or *empirical apperception*. What has *necessarily* to be represented as numerically identical cannot be thought as such through empirical data. To render such a transcendental presupposition valid, there must be a condition which precedes all experience, and which makes experience itself possible.

201

There can be in us no modes of knowledge, no connection or unity of one mode of knowledge with another, without that unity of consciousness which precedes all data of intuitions, and by relation to which representation of objects is alone possible. This pure original unchangeable consciousness I shall name *transcendental apperception*. That it deserves this name is clear from the fact that even the purest objective unity, namely, that of the *a priori* concepts (space and time), is only possible through relation of the intuitions to such unity of consciousness. The numerical unity of this apperception is thus the *a priori* ground of all concepts, just as the manifoldness of space and time is the *a priori* ground of the intuitions of sensibility.

[A108] This transcendental unity of apperception forms out of all possible appearances, which can stand alongside one another in one experience, a connection of all these representations according to laws. For this unity of consciousness would be impossible if the mind in knowledge of the manifold could not become conscious of the identity of function whereby it synthetically combines it in one knowledge. The original and necessary consciousness of the identity of the self is thus at the same time a consciousness of an equally necessary unity of the synthesis of all appearances according to concepts, that is, according to rules, which not only make them necessarily reproducible but also in so doing determine an object for their intuition, that is, the concept of something wherein they are necessarily interconnected. For the mind could never think its identity in the manifoldness of its representations, and indeed think this identity *a priori*, if it did not have before its eyes the identity of its act, whereby it subordinates all synthesis of apprehension (which is empirical) to a transcendental unity, thereby rendering possible their interconnection according to *a priori* rules.

Now, also, we are in a position to determine more adequately our concept of an *object* in general. All representations have, as representations, their object, and can themselves in turn become objects of other representations. Appearances are the sole objects which can be given to us immediately, and [A109] that in them which relates immediately to the object is called intuition. But these appearances are not things in themselves; they are only representations, which in turn have their object--an object which cannot itself be intuited by us, and which may, therefore, be named the non-empirical, that is, transcendental object = x.

The pure concept of this transcendental object, which in reality throughout all our knowledge is always one and the same, is what can alone confer upon all our empirical concepts in general relation to an object, that is, objective reality. This concept cannot contain any determinate intuition, and therefore refers only to that unity which must be met with in any manifold of knowledge which stands in relation to an object. This relation is nothing but the necessary unity of consciousness, and therefore also of the synthesis of the manifold, through a common function of the mind, which combines it in one representation. Since this unity must be regarded as necessary *a priori*--otherwise knowledge would be without an object--the relation to a transcendental object, that is, the objective reality of our empirical knowledge, rests [A110] on the transcendental law, that all appearances, in so far as through them objects are to be given to us, must stand under those *a priori* rules of synthetical unity whereby the inter-relating of these appearances in empirical intuition is alone possible. In other words, appearances in experience must stand under the conditions of the necessary unity of apperception, just as in mere intuition they must be subject to the formal conditions of space and of time. Only thus can any knowledge become possible at all.

4. Preliminary Explanation of the Possibility of the Categories, as Knowledge *a priori*

There is one single experience in which all perceptions are represented as in thoroughgoing and orderly connection, just as there is only one space and one time in which all modes of appearance and all relation of being or not being occur. When we speak of different experiences, we can refer only to the various perceptions, all of which, as such, belong to one and the same general experience. This thoroughgoing synthetic unity of perceptions is indeed the form of experience; it is nothing else than the synthetic unity of appearances in accordance with concepts.

[A111] Unity of synthesis according to empirical concepts would be altogether accidental, if these latter were not based on a transcendental ground of unity. Otherwise it would be possible for appearances to crowd in upon the soul, and yet to be such as would never allow of experience. Since connection in accordance with universal and necessary laws would be lacking, all relation of knowledge to objects would fall away. The appearances might, indeed, constitute intuition without thought, but not knowledge; and consequently would be for us as good as nothing.

The *a priori* conditions of a possible experience in general are at the same time conditions of the possibility of objects of experience. Now I maintain that the categories, above cited, are nothing but the conditions of thought in a possible experience, just as space and time are the conditions of intuition for that same experience. They are fundamental concepts by which we think objects in general for appearances, and have therefore *a priori* objective validity. This is exactly what we desired to prove.

But the possibility, indeed the necessity, of these categories rests on the relation in which our entire sensibility, and with it all possible appearances, stand to original apperception. In original apperception everything must necessarily conform to the conditions of the thoroughgoing unity of self-consciousness, that is, to the universal functions of synthesis, [A112] namely, of that synthesis according to concepts in which alone apperception can demonstrate *a priori* its complete and necessary identity. Thus the concept of a cause is nothing but a synthesis (of that which follows in the time-series, with other appearances) *according to concepts;* and without such unity, which has its *a priori* rule, and which subjects the appearances to itself, no thoroughgoing, universal, and therefore necessary, unity of consciousness would be met with in the manifold of perceptions. These perceptions would not then belong to any experience, consequently would be without an object, merely a blind play of representations, less even than a dream.

All attempts to derive these pure concepts of understanding from experience, and so to ascribe to them a merely empirical origin, are entirely vain and useless. I need not insist upon the fact that, for instance, the concept of a cause involves the character of necessity, which no experience can yield. Experience does indeed show that one appearance customarily follows upon another, but not that this sequence is necessary, nor that we can argue *a priori* and with complete universality from the antecedent, viewed as a condition, to the consequent. But as regards the empirical rule of *association*, which we must postulate throughout when we assert that everything in the series of events is so subject to rule that nothing ever [A113] happens save in so far as something precedes it on which it universally follows--upon what, I ask, does this rule, as a law of nature, rest? How is this association itself possible? The ground of the possibility of the association of the manifold, so far as it lies in the object, is named the *affinity* of the manifold. I therefore ask, how are we to make comprehensible to ourselves the thoroughgoing affinity of appearances, whereby they stand and *must* stand under unchanging laws?

On my principles it is easily explicable. All possible appearances, as representations, belong to the totality of a possible self-consciousness. But as self-consciousness is a transcendental representation, numerical identity is inseparable from it, and is *a priori* certain. For nothing can come to our knowledge save in terms of this original apperception. Now, since this identity must necessarily enter into the synthesis of all the manifold of appearances, so far as the synthesis is to yield empirical knowledge, the appearances are subject to *a priori* conditions, with which the synthesis of their apprehension must be in complete accordance. The representation of a universal condition according to which a certain manifold can be posited in uniform fashion is called a *rule*, and, when it *must* be so posited, a *law*. Thus all appearances stand in [A114] thoroughgoing connection according to necessary laws, and therefore in a transcendental affinity, of which the empirical is a mere consequence.

That nature should direct itself according to our subjective ground of apperception, and should indeed depend upon it in respect of its conformity to law, sounds very strange and absurd. But when we consider that this nature is not a thing in itself but is merely an aggregate of appearances, so many representations of the mind, we shall not be surprised that we can discover it only in the radical faculty of all our knowledge, namely, in transcendental apperception, in that unity on account of which alone it can be entitled object of all possible experience, that is nature. Nor shall we be surprised that just for this very reason this unity can be known *a priori*, and therefore as necessary. Were the unity given in itself independently of the first sources of our thought, this would never be possible. We should not then know of any source from which we could obtain the synthetic propositions asserting such a universal unity of nature. For they would then have to be derived from the objects of nature themselves; and as this could take place only empirically, none but a merely accidental unity could be obtained, which would fall far short of the necessary interconnection that we have in mind when we speak of nature.

[A115] Section 3: The Relation of the Understanding to Objects in General, and the Possibility of Knowing Them *A Priori*

What we have expounded separately and singly in the preceding section, we shall now present in systematic interconnection. There are three subjective sources of knowledge upon which rests the possibility of experience in general and of knowledge of its objects -- *sense, imagination*, and *apperception*. Each of these can be viewed as empirical, namely, in its application to given appearances. But all of them are likewise *a priori* elements or foundations, which make this empirical employment itself possible. *Sense* represents appearances empirically in *perception, imagination* in *association* (and reproduction), *apperception* in the *empirical consciousness* of the identity of the reproduced representations with the appearances whereby they were given, that is, in recognition.

But all perceptions are grounded *a priori* in pure intuition (in time, the form of their inner intuition as representations), association in pure synthesis of imagination, and empirical [A116] consciousness in pure apperception, that is, in the thoroughgoing identity of the self in all possible representations.

If, now, we desire to follow up the inner ground of this connection of the representations to the point upon which they have all to converge in order that they may therein for the first time acquire the unity of knowledge necessary for a possible experience, we must begin with pure apperception. Intuitions are nothing to us, and do not in the least concern us if they cannot be taken up into consciousness, in which they may participate either directly or indirectly. In this way alone is any knowledge possible. We are conscious *a priori* of the complete identity of the self in respect of all representations which can ever belong to our knowledge, as being a necessary condition of the possibility of all representations. For in me they can represent something only in so far as they belong with all others to one consciousness, and therefore must be at least capable of being so connected. This principle holds *a priori*, and may be called the transcendental principle of the *unity* of all that is manifold in our representations, and consequently also in intuition. Since this unity of the manifold in one subject is synthetic, pure apperception [A117] supplies a principle of the synthetic unity of the manifold in all possible intuition.

SAMUEL ROGERS

1763 - 1855

(with an Addendum by Robert Merry)

From: *The Pleasures of Memory*. First published in 1792; republished in 1805 by Daniel Johnson with an Addendum, *The Pains of Memory* by Robert Merry.

Samuel Rogers began publishing at 17 and achieved literary success at age 29 with *The Pleasures of Memory* and became a popular figure in London society. He inherited his father's bank and continued to write poetry which was well regarded by his contemporaries. Rogers' poem is based on a clear conception of memory which is spelled out in two prose sections which are reproduced here, together with a few stanzas of his poem and the poem of Robert Merry.

SAMUEL ROGERS

Table of Contents

The Pleasures of Memory

Explanation of contents: The two prose passages "Analysis of the First Part" and "Analysis of the Second Part" are referred to by page number in the 1805 edition. The pages of "Analysis of the First Part" are numbered with small Roman numerals, "Analysis of the Second Part" with Arabic numerals. Rogers' verse is referred to by line numbers which appear in the 1805 edition. The lines of Merry's verse are not numbered and are referred to by page number in the 1805 edition.

Rogers: The Pleasures of Memory

Analysis of the First Part, pages ix - xii

[ix] The Poem begins with the description of an obscure village, and of the pleasing melancholy which it excites on being revisited after a long absence. This mixed sensation is an effect of the memory. From an effect we naturally ascend to the cause; and the subject proposed is then unfolded with an investigation of the nature and leading principles of this faculty.

[x] It is evident that there is a continued succession of ideas in the mind, and that they introduce each other with a certain degree of regularity. Their complexion depends greatly on the different perceptions of pleasure and pain which we receive through the medium of sense; and, in return, they have a considerable influence on the animal economy.

They are sometimes excited by sensible objects and sometimes by an internal operation of the mind. Of the former species is most probably the memory of brutes; and its many sources of pleasure to them, as well as to ourselves, are considered in the First Part. The latter is the most perfect degree of memory, and forms the subject of the Second.

[xi] When ideas have any relation whatever, they are attractive of each other in the mind; and the perception of any object naturally leads to the idea of another which was connected with it either in time or place, or which can be compared or contrasted with it. Hence arises our attachment to inanimate objects; hence also, in some degree, the love of our country, and the emotion with which we contemplate the celebrated scenes of antiquity. Hence a picture directs our thoughts to the original: and, as cold and darkness suggest forcibly the ideas of heat and light, he, who feels the infirmities of age, dwells most on whatever reminds him of the vigour and vivacity of his youth.

[xii] The associating principle, as here employed, is no less conducive to virtue than to happiness; and, as such, it frequently discovers itself in the most tumultuous scenes of life. It addresses our finer feelings, and gives exercise to every mild and generous propensity.

Not confined to man, it extends through all animated nature; and its effects are peculiarly striking in the domestic tribes.

Part I, lines 7 - 36

Thee, in whose hand the keys of science dwell,
The pensive portress of her holly cell;
Whose constant vigils chase the chilling damp
Oblivion steals upon her vestal lamp.   [10]

The friends of reason, and the guides of youth,
Whose language breath'd the eloquence of truth;
Whose life, beyond perceptive wisdom, taught
The great in conduct, and the pure in thought;
These still exist, by thee to fame consign'd,   [15]
Still speak and act, the models of mankind.

From thee sweet hope her airy colouring draws;
And fancy's flights are subject to thy laws.
From thee that bosom spring of rapture flows,
Which only virtue, tranquil virtue, knows.   [20]

When joy's bright sun has shed his even ray,
And hope's delusive meteors cease to play;
When clouds on clouds the smiling prospect close,
Still thro' the gloom thy star serenely glows;
Like yon'fair orb, she gilds the brow of night   [25]
With the mild magic of reflected light.

The beauteous maid, that bids the world adieu,
Oft of that world will snatch a fond review;
Oft at the shrine neglect her beads, to trace
Some social scene, some dear, familiar face,   [30]
Forgot, when first a father's stern controul
Chas'd the gay visions of her opening soul:
And ere, with iron tongue, the vesper bell,
Bursts thro' the cypress walk, the convent cell,
Oft will her warm and wayward heart revive,   [35]
To love and joy still tremblingly alive;

Rogers: The Pleasures of Memory

Part I, lines 231 - 248

And hence the charm historic scenes impart:
Hence Tiber awes, and Avon melts the heart.
Aerial forms, in Tempe's classic vale,

Glance thro' the gloom, and whisper in the gale;
In wild Vaucluse with love and Laura dwell,   [235]
And watch and weep in Eloisa's cell.
'Twas ever thus. As now at Virgil's tomb,
We bless the shade, and bid the verdure bloom:
So Tully paus'd, amid the wrecks of time,
On the rude stone to trace the truth sublime;   [240]
When at his feet, in honour'd dust disclos'd,
The immortal sage of Syracuse repos'd.
And as his youth in sweet delusion hung,
Where once a Plato taught, a Pindar sung;
Who now but meets him musing, when he roves   [245]
His ruin'd Tusculan's romantic groves?
In Rome's great forum, who but hears him roll
His moral thunders o'er the subject soul?

Rogers: The Pleasures of Memory

Part I, lines 342 - 355

Hark! the bee winds her small but mellow horn,
Blithe to salute the sunny smile of morn.
O'er thymy downs she bends her busy course,
And many a stream allures her to its source.   [345]
'Tis noon, 'tis night. That eye so finely wrought,
Beyond the search of sense, the soar of thought,
Now vainly asks the scenes she left behind;
Its orb so full, its vision so confin'd!
Who guides the patient pilgrim to her cell?   [350]
Who bids her soul with conscious triumph swell?
With conscious truth retrace the mazy clue
Of varied scents, that charm'd her as she flew?
Hail, memory, hail! thy universal reign
Guards the least link of being's glorious chain.   [355]

Rogers: The Pleasures of Memory

Analysis of the Second Part, pages 41 - 44

[41] THE Memory has hitherto acted only in subservience to the senses, and so far man is not eminently distinguished from other animals: but, with respect to man, she has a higher province; and is often busily employed, when excited by no external cause whatever. She preserves, for his use, the treasures of art and science, history and philosophy. [42] She colours all the prospects of life: for 'we can only anticipate the future, by concluding what is possible from what is past.' On her agency depends every effusion of the fancy, whose boldest effort can only compound or transpose, augment or diminish the materials which she has collected and retained.

210

When the first emotions of despair have subsided, and sorrow has softened into melancholy, she amuses with a retrospect of innocent pleasures, and inspires that noble confidence which results from the consciousness of having acted well. When sleep has suspended the organs of sense from their office, she not only supplies the mind with images, but assists in their combination. [43] And even in madness itself, when the soul is resigned over to the tyranny of a distempered imagination, she revives past perceptions, and awakens that train of thought which was formerly most familiar.

Nor are we pleased only with a review of the brighter passages of life; events, the most distressing in their immediate consequences, are often cherished in remembrance with a degree of enthusiasm.

But the world and its occupations give a mechanical impulse to the passions, which is not very favourable to the indulgence of this feeling. It is in a calm and well regulated mind that the memory [44] is most perfect; and solitude is here best sphere of action. With this sentiment is introduced a tale, illustrative of her influence in solitude, sickness and sorrow. And the subject having now been considered, so far as it relates to man and the animal world, the poem concludes with a conjecture, that superior beings are blest with a nobler exercise of this faculty.

Rogers: The Pleasures of Memory

Part II, lines 1 - 6

Sweet memory, wafted by thy gentle gale,   [1]
Oft up the tide of time I turn my sail,
To view the fairy haunts of long lost hours,
Blest with far greener shades, far fresher flowers.

Ages and climes remote to thee impart
What charms in genius, and refines in art;

Part II, lines 417 - 442

To meet the changes time and chance present,
With modest dignity and calm content.
When thy last breath, ere nature sunk to rest,
Thy meek submission to thy God express'd;   [420]
When thy last look, ere thought and feeling fled,
A mingled gleam of hope and triumph shed;
What to thy soul its glad assurance gave,
Its hope in death, its triumph o'er the grave?
The sweet remembrance of unblemish'd youth,   [425]
The inspiring voice of innocence and truth!

211

Hail, memory, hail! in thy exhaustless mine,
From age to age unnumber'd treasures shine!
Thought and her shadowy brood thy call obey,
And place and time are subject to thy sway!   [430]
Thy pleasures most we feel, when most alone;
The only pleasures we can call our own.
Lighter than air, hope's summer visions die,
If but a fleeting cloud obscure the sky;
If but a beam of sober reason play,   [435]
Lo, fancy's fairy frost work melts away!
But can the wiles of art, the grasp of power,
Snatch the rich relics of a well spent hour?
These, when the trembling spirit wings her flight,
Pour round her path a stream of living light;   [440]
And gild those pure and perfect realms of rest,
Where virtue triumphs, and her sons are blest!

The Pains of Memory (by Robert Merry)

Pages 96 - 97

When gather'd thunders burst, abrupt, and loud,   [96]
And midnight lightning leaps from cloud to cloud.
Or rends, with forceful, momentary stroke,
The ivied turret, and the giant oak;
Can faint remembrance of meridian mirth,
Bedeck with visionary charms the earth;
Renew the season when each wak'ning flow'r
Lifted its leaves to drink the morning show'r;
Dispel the gloom, the fi'ry storm remove,
Gem the wide vault, and animate the grove?
The fond illusions could but feebly show,
The colours scarce appear, or faintly glow;
Fix'd would the sad realities remain,
And memory waste her vaunted stores in vain.
Alas! all inefficient is her pow'r,
To cheer, by what is past, the present hour;
For ev'ry good gone by, each transport o'er,   [97]
She may regret, but never can restore.
Yet shall her fest'ring touch corrode the heart,
Compel the subjugated tear to start:
She calls grim phantoms, from the shad'wy deep,
And sends her furies forth to torture sleep:
The lapse of time, the strength of reason dares,
And with fresh rage her straining rack prepares.

THOMAS BROWN

1778 - 1820

From: *Lectures on the Philosophy of the Human Mind.* Nineteenth edition published by William Tegg & Co: London, 1858.

Thomas Brown held the chair in moral philosophy at Edinburg University. His zeal for simplification contributed to the popularity of his lectures which, when published after his death, rapidly went through many editions. He shared with Thomas Reid and the Scottish school of common sense philosophy a reliance on intuitive truths. His analysis of consciousness led him to the view that conciousness is not, as others maintained, a separate faculty, but is the sum of other faculties. Introspective examination of mental events is thus retrospective rather than introspective.

Supplementary readings:

McCosh, J. (1875). *The Scottish Philosophy.* New York: Robert Carter & Bros.

Robinson, D. S. (1961). *The Story of Scottish Philosophy.* New York: Exposition Press.

THOMAS BROWN

Table of Contents

Explanation of contents: Brown's lectures are numbered with Roman numerals. Paragraph numbers have been added by the editors [in brackets].

Lecture XL. 1 - 4

Reasons for Preferring the Term *Suggestion*, to the
Phrase *Association of Ideas*

[1] The latter part of my Lecture of yesterday, Gentlemen, was employed in illustrating a distinction which seems to me of great consequence in its applications to the whole theory of the intellectual phenomena, the distinction of the trains of our thought from other trains of which we are accustomed to speak, in this most important circumstance, that, in our mental sequences, the one feeling which precedes and induces another feeling, does not, necessarily, on that account, give place to it; but may continue in that virtual sense of combination, as applied to the phenomena of the mind, of which I have often spoken, to coexist with the new feeling which it excites, outlasting it, perhaps, and many other feelings to which, during its permanence, it may have given rise. I pointed out to you how important this circumstance in our mental constitution is to us, in various ways; to our intellectual acquirements; since, without it, there could be no continued meditation, but only a hurrying confusion of image after image, in wilder irregularity than in the wildest of our dreams; and to our virtue and happiness, since, by allowing the coexistence and condensation of various feelings in one complex emotion, it furnishes the chief source of the delight of those moral affections which it is at once our happiness to feel, and our virtue to obey.

[2] After these remarks on a distinction which it appears to me of essential importance to make, I proceed to the consideration of a question of still more importance in the theory of our trains of thought, at least in the light in which these have been commonly regarded by philosophers. Its importance in this respect, is, however, I must confess, its principal attraction; and it will require from you a little more attention and patience than the greater number of the discussions which have recently engaged us.

[3] Before entering on this particular part of my Course, which treats of the phenomena commonly classed together under the general term *association of ideas*, I remarked the error of this seeming limitation to our ideas, of a tendency which is common to them with all our other feelings; and at the same time mentioned, that there were other reasons afterwards to be stated, which led me to prefer to this phrase a term more strictly indicative of the simple fact of the rise of certain states or affections of the mind, after certain other states or affections of mind; unwilling as I was to alter, without some urgent motives, a phrase which the universal language of philosophers, and even the popular language on this most popular part of intellectual philosophy, might be considered almost as having fully and finally established. The term which I preferred, as most strictly expressive of the simple fact of the mere antecedence of one feeling, and sequence of another feeling, was *suggestion*; and instead, therefore, of inquiring into the laws of association, I inquired into the general circumstance on which suggestion depends. In the course of our discussions, indeed, I have continued sometimes to avail myself, as you must have remarked, of the more

familiar phrase association. But I have done this only in cases in which the use of it appeared without danger, or at least when any misconception that might arise from it, was sufficiently obviated, by the use of the corresponding term suggestion, as explaining and restricting its meaning. The examination of the question on which we are about to enter will show the reason which chiefly led me to the preference of the one of these terms to the other; and though, as I have already said, the discussion is not of a kind that admits of pleasing illustration, I trust that you are sufficiently impressed with the paramount importance in science of the useful to the agreeable, or rather, that the useful is itself agreeable to you, by the mere circumstance of its utility.

[4] That, when two objects have been perceived by us in immediate succession, the presence of the one will often suggest the other,--though this second object, or a similar external cause, be not present,--it is that great fact of association or suggestion, which we must admit, whatever opinion we may form with respect to its nature, or whatever name we may give to it. But when the former of these two objects first suggests the conception of the latter, in the absence of this latter, and at a considerable interval of time after the first coexistence of the two perceptions, or their first proximity to each other, we may inquire whether the suggestion be the consequence of a law or general tendency of the mind, first operating at that moment of the suggestion itself;--or the consequence of another earlier law of mind, distinct from that of the mere perception itself, but operating at the time when both objects were originally perceived together, whether, during the original perception of the two objects, at the period long preceding the first suggestion of one by the other, there was, beside the simple perception of each, some other intellectual process or operation, by which a union might be supposed to be formed of the two conceptions in all their future recurrences,--or, simply, whether such be not the natural constitution of the mind, that one affection of it succeeds another affection of it, and that the successions occur in a certain order; in short, whether the laws that regulate the recurrence be laws of association, in the strictest sense of that word, as expressive of some former connecting process, or merely laws of suggestion, as expressive of the simple tendency of the mind, in the very moment in which it is affected in a certain manner, to exist immediately afterwards in a certain different state.

Brown: Lecture XL. 14 - 16

[14] Proceeding, accordingly, on the general belief of distinct tribes of suggestions, in our inquiry into the evidence which the phenomena afford of a previous influence of association, let us take for an example, then, a case of contrast, in which the perception or conception of one object suggests immediately the conception of some other object, of which the qualities are so dissimilar, as to be absolutely opposite to those qualities which we are perceiving or conceiving at the moment.

[15] The first sight of a person, of stature remarkably beyond the common size, is sufficient, in many cases, to bring instantly before us, in concep-

tion, the form of some one, with whom we may happen to be acquainted, of stature as remarkably low. In consequence of what law of mind does this suggestion take place?

[16] If we say merely that such is the nature of the mind that it is not affected by external objects alone, but that the state or affection of mind which we call a conception or idea of an object, in whatever manner excited, may give immediate rise to other ideas, of which no external cause at the moment exists before us; that one idea, however, does not suggest indifferently any other idea, but only such as have some peculiar relation to itself; that there is a considerable variety of such relations, resemblance, contiguity, and others; and that of this variety of relations, according to which ideas may spontaneously suggest each other, contrast is one;--we deliver an accurate statement of the facts, and of the whole facts; and whatever goes beyond this, to some earlier mysterious process of union,--even though it could, by a skilful effort of ingenuity, be reconciled with the phenomena,--must still be a supposition only; for, if we trust the evidence of our consciousness, which affords the only evidence, we have no knowledge of any intermediate process that can have the name of association, but simply of the original perceptions, and the subsequent suggestion. Of this the slightest retrospect will convince any one. It is to our consciousness, then, at the time of the perception and the time of the suggestion that we must look. Now, all of which we are conscious at the time of perception might be precisely the same, though there were no memory whatever after perception ceases, or though, in remembrance, there were no such order of suggestions afterwards, as is supposed to justify the supposition of some pre-existing association, but, on the contrary, the utmost irregularity and confusion. Our consciousness during perception, is thus far from indicating any process of association; and all of which we are conscious at the time of the suggestion itself, is the mere succession of one feeling to another, not certainly of any prior process on which this suggestion has depended. The laws of suggestion, then, as opposed to what may be called association,--or, in other words, the circumstances which seem to regulate the spontaneous successions of our ideas, without reference to any former intellectual process, except the simple primary perceptions from which all our corresponding conceptions are derived,--form a legitimate theory, being a perfect generalization of the known facts, without a single circumstance assumed. To these laws, which require no prior union of that which suggests with that which is suggested, the particular case which we are considering is easily referable, being one of the very cases comprehended in the generalization. The sight of a gigantic stranger brings before us the image of our diminutive friend; because such is the nature of the mind, that,--in whatever manner the primary ideas may have been induced, and though there may never have been any coexistence or immediate succession of them before,--opposites, by the very circumstance of their opposition, suggest opposites. It is as much a law of mind that one perception or conception shall introduce, as it were spontaneously the conception of some similar object,--or of one so dissimilar as to be contrasted with it,--or of one which formerly succeeded it,--or of one in some other way related to it,--and that it shall introduce such relative conceptions alone as it is a law of mind that the influence of light on the retina, and thus indirectly on the sensorium, shall be followed by the sensation of vision and not

of sound; and, however mysterious and inexplicable the one process may be, it is not more inexplicable than the other. It is as little necessary to the suggestion that there should be any prior union or association of ideas, as, to vision, that there should be any mysterious connexion of the organ with light, at some period prior to that in which light itself first acted on the organ, and the visual sensation was its consequence. As soon as the presence of the rays of light at the retina has produced a certain affection of the sensorium, in that very moment the mind begins to exist in the state which constitutes the sensation of colour;--as soon as a certain perception or conception has arisen, the mind begins to exist in the state which constitutes what is said to be some associate conception. Any prior connexion or association is as little necessary in the one of these cases as in the other. All that is prior, is not any process connecting light with the organ, or the conception of a giant with the conception of a dwarf, but only certain original susceptibilities of the mind by which it is formed, to have in the one case some one of the sensations of vision when light is at the retina,--in the other case to have, in certain circumstances, the conception of a dwarf as immediately consecutive to that of a giant.

Brown: Lecture XL. 26 - 27

[26] You will now then, I hope, perceive,--or, I flatter myself, may already have perceived, without the necessity of so much repetition of the argument,-- the reasons which led me to prefer the term *suggestion* to *association*, as a more accurate general term for all the spontaneous successions of our thought; since, by making the suggestion itself to depend on an association or combination of ideas prior to it, we should not merely have assumed the reality of process, of which we have no consciousness whatever, but should have excluded, by the impossibility of such previous combination, many of the most important classes of suggestions,--every suggestion that arises from the relations of objects which we perceive for the first time, and, indeed, every suggestion that does not belong, in the strictest sense, to Mr. Hume's single class of *contiguity in time.*

[27] That our suggestions do not follow each other loosely and confusedly, is no proof of prior associations of mind, but merely of the general constitutional tendency of the mind, to exist, successively, in states that have certain relations to each other. There is nothing in the nature of our original perceptions, which could enable us to infer this regularity and limitation of our subsequent trains of thought. We learn these from experience alone; and experience does not teach us, that there is any such intervening process of mysterious union, as is supposed, but only, that when the mind has been affected in a certain manner, so as to have one perception or conception, it is, successively, and of itself, affected in certain other manners, so as to have other relative conceptions. If the association of ideas be understood to mean nothing more than this succession of ideas arising without an external cause, and involving no prior union of the ideas suggesting and suggested,--nor, in short, any influence previous to that which operates at the moment of the suggestion itself, though it would certainly, with this limited meaning, (which excludes what

218

is commonly meant by the term association,) be a very awkward phrase,--still, if it were always understood in this limited sense alone, it might be used with safety. But, in this sense,--the only sense in which it can be used without error,--it must always be remembered, that the association of ideas denotes as much the successions of ideas of objects which never have existed together before, as the successions of ideas of objects which have been perceived together,--that there are not two separate mental processes, therefore, following perception, and necessary to the succession,--one by which ideas are primarily associated, and another by which they are subsequently suggested,--but that the association is, in truth, only another word for the fact of the suggestion itself. All this, however, being admitted, it may perhaps be said,--what advantage is to be gained from the use of a simpler term, or even from the more accurate distinction which such a term denotes?

Brown: Lecture XLI. 1 - 35

Reduction of Certain Supposed Faculties to Simple Suggestion, -- I. Conception, -- II. Memory

[1] Gentlemen, my last Lecture was employed in considering the nature of that tendency of the mind, by which it exists, successively in the states which constitute the variety of our conceptions, in our trains of thought; my object being to ascertain whether this tendency depend on any previous intellectual process, constituting what has been termed a union or association of ideas, or, simply on the relations of the conceptions themselves, at the moment of suggestion, without any previous union or association whatever, of the idea or other feeling which suggests, with the idea or other feeling which is suggested. I explained to you the reasons which seem to lead us, in every case, in which conception follows conception, in trains that have a sort of wild regularity, to look back to the past, for some mysterious associations of our ideas, by which this regular confusion of their successions may be explained; though, in the phenomena themselves, there is no evidence of any such association, or earlier connecting process of any kind, all of which we are conscious being merely the original perception and the subsequent suggestion.

[2] It is, in a great measure, I remarked, in consequence of obscure notions, entertained with respect to this supposed association of ideas, as something prior and necessary to the actual operation of the simple principle of spontaneous suggestion, that the phenomena of this simple principle of the mind have been referred to various intellectual powers, from the impossibility of finding, in many cases, any source of prior association, and the consequent necessity of inventing some new power for the production of phenomena, which seemed not to be reducible to suggestion, or to differ from its common forms, merely because we had encumbered the simple process of suggestion with unnecessary and false conditions.

[3] My next object, then, will be to show, how truly that variety of powers, thus unnecessarily, and, therefore, unphilosophically devised, are reducible to

the principle of simple suggestion; or, at least, to this simple principle, in combination with some of those other principles, which I pointed out, as parts of our mental constitution, in my arrangement of the phenomena of the mind.

[4] It will be of advantage, however, previously, to take a slight retrospect of the principal points which may be considered as established, with respect to simple suggestion; that we may see more clearly what it is, from which the other supposed powers are said to be different.

[5] In the first place, we can have no doubt of the general fact of suggestion, that conception follows conception, in our trains of thought, without any recurrence of the external objects, which, as perceived, originally gave occasion to them.

[6] As little can we doubt that these conceptions, as internal states of the mind, independent of any immediate influence of external things, do not follow each other loosely but according to a certain general relation, or number of relations, which constitute what I have termed the primary laws of suggestion, and which exercise their influence variously, in different persons, and at different times, according to circumstances, which, as modifying the former, I have denominated secondary laws of suggestion.

[7] In the third place, we have seen that they do not follow each other merely, the suggesting idea giving immediate place to the suggested; but that various conceptions, which arise at different moments, may coexist, and form one compound feeling, in the same manner as various perceptions, that arise together, or different moments, may coexist, and form one compound feeling of another species,--all that complexity of forms and colours, for example, which gives a whole world of wonders at once to our vision, or those choral sounds which flow mingled from innumerable vibrations that exist together, without confusion, in the small aperture of the ear, and in a single moment fill the soul with a thousand harmonies, as if, in the perception of so many coexisting sounds, it had a separate sense for every separate voice, and could exist, with a strange diffusive consciousness, in a simultaneous variety of states.

[8] Lastly, we have seen that no previous association, or former connecting process, of any kind, is necessary for suggestion,--that we have no consciousness of any intermediate process between the primary perception and the subsequent suggestion, and that we are not merely without the slightest consciousness of a process, which is thus gratuitously supposed, but that there are innumerable phenomena which it is not very easy to reconcile with the supposition, on any view of it, and which certainly, at least, cannot be reconciled with it, on that view of the primary laws of suggestion, which the assertors of a distinct specific Faculty of Association have been accustomed to take.

[9] Let us now, then, apply the knowledge which we have thus acquired, and proceed to consider some of those forms of suggestion, which have been ranked as indistinct intellectual powers.

[10] That, which its greater simplicity leads me to consider first, is what has been termed by philosophers the *Power of Conception,* which has been defined, the power that enables us to form a notion of an absent object of perception, or of some previous feeling of the mind. The definition of the supposed power is sufficiently intelligible; but is there reason to add the power thus defined, to our other mental functions, as a distinct and peculiar faculty?

[11] That we have a certain mental power or susceptibility by which, in accordance with this definition, the perception of one object may excite the notion of some absent object, is unquestionably true. But this is the very function which is meant by the power of suggestion itself, when stripped of the illusion as to prior association; and if the conception be separated from the suggestion, nothing will remain to constitute the power of suggestion, which is only another name for the same power. I enter, for example, an apartment in my friend's house during his long absence from home; I see his flute, or the work of some favourite author lying on his table. The mere sight of either of these awakes instantly my conception of my friend, though, at the moment, he might have been absent from my thought. I see him again present. If I look at the volume, I almost think that I hear him arguing strenuously for the merits of his favourite, as in those evenings of social contention when we have brought poets and philosophers to war against poets and philosophers. If I look at the flute, I feel instantly a similar illusion. I hear him again animating it with his very touch,--breathing into it what might almost, without a metaphor, be said to be the breath of life,--and giving it not utterance merely but eloquence. In these cases of simple suggestion, it is said the successive mental states which constitute the notions of my friend himself, of the arguments which I again seem to hear and combat, of the melodies that silently enchant me,--are conceptions indicating, therefore, a power of the mind from which they arise, that, in reference to the effects produced by it, may be called the power of conception. But if they arise from a peculiar power of conception,--and if there be a power of association or suggestion which is also concerned, how are these powers to be distinguished, and what part of the process is it which we owe to this latter power? If there were no suggestion of my friend, it is very evident that there could be no conception of my friend; and if there were no conception of him, it would be absurd to speak of a suggestion in which nothing was suggested. Whether we use the term suggestion or association in this case is of no consequence. Nothing more can be accurately meant by either term, in reference to the example which I have used, than the tendency of my mind, after existing in the state which constitutes the perception of the flute or volume, and of the room in which I observe it, to exist immediately afterwards in that different state which constitutes the conception of my friend. The laws of suggestion or association are merely the general circumstances according to which conceptions or certain other feelings arise. There is not, in any case of suggestion, both a suggestion and a conception, more than there is, in any case of vision, both a vision and a sight. What one glance is to the capacity of vision one conception is to the capacity of suggestion. We may see innumerable objects in succession; we may conceive innumerable objects in succession. But we see them because we are susceptible of vision; we conceive them because we have that susceptibility of spontaneous suggestion by which conceptions arise after each

other in regular trains.

[12] This duplication of a single power, to account for the production of a single state of mind, appears to me a very striking example of the influence of that misconception with respect to association, which I occupied so much of your time in attempting to dissipate. If association and suggestion had been considered as exactly synonymous, implying merely the succession of one state of mind to another state of mind, without any mysterious process of union of the two feelings prior to the suggestion, the attention of inquirers would, in this just and simple view, have been fixed on the single moment of the suggestion itself:--and I cannot think that any philosopher would, in this case, have contended for two powers, as operating together at the very same moment, in the production of the very same conception; but that one capacity would have been regarded as sufficient for this one simple effect, whether it were termed, with more immediate reference to the secondary feeling that is the effect, the power of conception, or, with more immediate reference to the primary feeling which precedes it as its cause, the power of suggestion or association. It is very different, however, when the conception--the one simple effect produced--is made to depend not merely on the tendency of the mind to exist in that state at the particular moment at which the conception arises, but on some process of association, which may have operated at a considerable interval before; for in that case the process of association, which is supposed to have taken place at one period, must itself imply one power or function of the mind, and the actual suggestion, or rise of the conception, at an interval afterwards, some different power or function.

[13] With respect to the supposed intellectual power of conception, then, as distinct from the intellectual power of association or suggestion, we may very safely conclude, that the belief of this is founded merely on a mistake as to the nature of association;--that the power of suggestion and the power of conception are the same, both being only that particular susceptibility of the mind from which, in certain circumstances, conceptions arise,--or at least, that if the power of conception differs from the more general power of suggestion, it differs from it only as a part differs from the whole,--as the power of taking a single step differs from the power of traversing a whole field,--the power of drawing a single breath from the general power of respiration,--the moral susceptibility by which we are capable of forming one charitable purpose from that almost divine universality of benevolence, in a whole virtuous life, to which every moment is either some exertion for good or some wish for good, which comprehends within its sphere of action, that has no limits but physical impossibility, every being whom it can instruct or amend, or relieve or gladden, and, in its sphere of generous desire, all that is beyond the limits of its power of benefiting.

[14] The next supposed intellectual power to which I would call your attention, is the power of memory.

[15] In treating of our suggestions, and consequently, as you have seen, of our conceptions, which are only parts of the suggested series, I have, at the

same time, treated of our remembrances, or, at least, of the more important part of our remembrances, because our remembrances are nothing more than conceptions united with the notion of a certain relation of time. They are conceptions of the past, felt as conceptions of the past,--that is to say, felt as having a certain relation of antecedence to our present feeling. The remembrance is not a simple but a complex state of mind; and all which is necessary to reduce a remembrance to a mere conception, is to separate from it a part of the complexity,--that part of it which constitutes the notion of a certain relation of antecedence. We are conscious of our present feeling whatever it may be; for this is, in truth, only another name for our consciousness itself. The moment of present time, at which we are thus conscious, is a bright point, ever moving, and yet, as it were, ever fixed, which divides the darkness of the future from the twilight of the past. It is, in short, what Cowley terms the whole of human life,--

> "A weak isthmus, that doth proudly rise
> Up betwixt two eternities."

The present moment, then, though ever fleeting, is to us, as it were, a fixed point; and it is a point which guides us in the most important of our measurements, in our retrospects of the past, and our hopes of the future. The particular feeling of any moment before the present, as it rises again in our mind, would be a simple conception, if we did not think of it, either immediately or indirectly, in relation to some other feeling earlier or later. It becomes a remembrance when we combine with it this feeling of relation--the relation which constitutes our notion of time; for time, as far as we are capable of understanding it, or rather of feeling it, is nothing more than the varieties of this felt relation, which, in reference to one of the subjects of the relation, we distinguish by the word *before*,--in reference to the other, by the word *after*. It is a relation, I may remark, which we feel nearly in the same manner as we feel the relation which bodies bear to each other, as coexisting in space. We say of a house, that it is two miles from a particular village, half a mile from the river, a mile from the bridge, with a feeling of relation very similar to that with which we say of one event, that it occurred a month ago,--of another event, that it occurred in the memorable year of our first going to school,--of another, that it happened in our infancy. There is some point to which, in estimating distance of space, we refer the objects which we measure, as there is a point of time in the present moment, or in some event which we have before learned to consider thus relatively, to which, directly or indirectly, we refer the events of which we speak as past or future, or more or less recent.

[16] If we had been incapable of considering more than two events together, we probably never should have invented the word *time*, but should have contented ourselves with simpler words, expressive of the simple relation of the two. But we are capable of considering a variety of events, all of which are felt by us to bear to that state of mind which constitutes our present consciousness, some relation of priority or subsequence, which they seem to us to bear also reciprocally to each other; and the varieties of this relation oblige us to invent a general term for expressing them all. This general word, invented by us or expressing all the varieties of priority and subsequence, is *time*,--a word,

therefore, which expresses no actual reality, but only relations that are felt by us in the objects of our conception. To think of time is not to think of any thing existing of itself, for time is not a thing but a relation; it is only to have some conceptions of objects which we regard as prior and subsequent; and, without the conception of objects of some kind, as subjects of the relation of priority and subsequence, it is as little possible for us to imagine any time, as to imagine brightness or dimness without a single ray of light,--proportional magnitude without any dimensions,--or any other relation without any other subject. When the notion of time, then, is combined with any of our conceptions, as in memory, all which is combined with the simple conception is the feeling of a certain relation. To be capable of remembering, in short, we must have a capacity of the feelings which we term *relations*, and a capacity of the feelings which we term *conceptions*, that may be the subjects of the relations; but with these two powers no other is requisite,--no power of memory distinct from the conception and relation which that complex term denotes.

[17] When I say that time, as far as we are capable of understanding it, is nothing more than a certain felt relation of certain conceptions of our own mind, I am sufficiently aware of the necessity of this qualifying clause with respect to the limits of our understanding, and of the truth of the very striking remark of St. Austin on this most obscure subject, that he knew well what time was till he was asked about it, and that then he knew nothing of it:--"Quid ergo est tempus? Quis hoc facile explicuerit? Si nemo a me quaerat, scio. Si quaerenti explicare vetim, nescio."

[18] It is truly one of those subjects which, instead of growing clearer as we gaze upon it, grows more obscure beneath our very gaze. All of which we can be said to be conscious, is certainly the present moment alone. But of that complex state of mind which forms to us the present moment, there are parts which impress us irresistibly, and beyond all the power of scepticism, with the relation which, as I have already said, we term *priority*, in reference to the one, and *succession* or *subsequence* in reference to the other; time, as felt by us, being this relation of the two, and nothing more. It is not because we have a previous notion of time that we regard objects as prior and posterior, more than we regard objects as large or small, because we have a previous notion of magnitude; but time, as a general word, is significant to us merely of the felt varieties of the relation of priority and subsequence, as magnitude is a general word, expressive of the felt varieties of comparative dimensions.

[19] But I have already dwelt too long on a point, which I may very probably have made darker to you than it was before; but which, impressed as I am with the truth of St. Austin's remark, I scarcely can venture to flatter myself with the hope of having made much more distinctly conceivable by you.

[20] Obscure as the relation of priority and succession may be, however, which is all that mingles with conception in our remembrance, it is still only a certain relation; and the feeling of this relation does not imply any peculiar power, generically distinct from that which perceives other relations, whether clear or obscure; unless, indeed, we should be inclined to invent a separate

name of some new faculty of the mind for every relation with which the mind can be impressed, in the almost infinite variety of these feelings. Memory, therefore, is not a distinct intellectual faculty, but is merely conception or suggestion combined with the feeling of a particular relation,--the relation to which we give the name of priority, a feeling that is not essential, indeed, to the accompanying conception itself, but that admits of being combined with it, in the same manner as the relation of place, or any other relation, admits of being combined with other conceptions or perceptions. It cannot be denied, for example, that, in the darkness of the night, after an interval of many years, and at the distance probably of many thousand miles, we have the faculty of conceiving, or of beholding again, almost with the same vividness as when we trod its steep ascent, the mountain which we have been accustomed perhaps to ascend in our boyhood, for the pleasure of looking down, from its topmost rock, with a sort of pride at the height which we had mastered. To behold mentally this eminence again, without any feeling of the relation of past time, is to have only a conception of the mountain. We cannot think of the mountain itself, however, even for a few moments, without thinking also of the scene which we have been accustomed to survey from it,--the humbler hills around, that served only to make the valley between appear lower than we should otherwise have conceived it to be, and to make us feel still more proudly the height which we had attained,--the scattered villages,--the woods, the streams, in various directions, mingling and resting in the motionless expanse of the lake. By comprehending gradually more of these objects in our mental view, we have widened our conception, indeed, but it is still a conception only; and we are not said to exercise any power distinct from that of conception or suggestion. Yet we cannot thus conceive the landscape as a whole, without feeling various relations which its parts bear to each other in space, as near or distant, high or low,--the wood hanging over the village,--the spire gleaming through the trees,--the brook hurrying down to the mill, and the narrow pathway by its side. These relations, which give unity to the scene, are relations of space only, and they do not hinder our complex feeling from being denominated simply a conception. So far, then, no new power is said to be concerned. If, however, in addition to all these local relations, we introduce but a single relation of time,--the thought of the most trifling circumstance which occurred when we last ascended the same mountain, and beheld the same scene,--though this new part of the complex feeling have risen, according to the same exact laws of suggestion, as the conception of the mere scene, the conception is then instantly said to indicate a new power, and what was before a conception is a conception no longer. In one sense, indeed, there is truly the operation of a new power, for there is a new relation most certainly felt; and every relation felt implies a power or susceptibility in the mind of feeling this relation. But the relations of coexistence in space are not less relations than those of succession in time; and both or neither, therefore, when coexisting with our conceptions, should be said to indicate a new intellectual faculty.

[21] The state of mind, in memory, is, as I have already said, a complex one,--a conception, and a feeling of relation. But it admits of very easy analysis into these two parts, and, therefore, does not require the supposition of any new power to comprehend it, more than the complex state of mind, which results

from the combination of the simple sensations of warmth and fragrance, requires the supposition of a new power to comprehend it, distinct from the separate senses to which the elementary feelings, if existing alone, would be referred. The conception, which forms one element of the remembrance, is referable to the capacity of simple suggestion, which we have been considering; the feeling of the relation of priority, which forms the other element of the remembrance, is referable, like all our other feelings of relation, to the capacity of relative suggestion, which we are afterwards to consider. It is merely as this relation of priority is or is not felt, that the state of mind, in which there is pictured some absent object or past feeling, has the name of a conception or the name of a remembrance; and that part of the complex whole, which is a mere conception, does not differ from the common products of suggestion, but, as we have seen, in treating of our conceptions in general, is merely a particular form, or result, of that general power of suggestion, which gives a second being to the whole shadowy train of our thought. Indeed, since one of the relations, according to which association or suggestion is said to take place, is, by every writer who treats of the laws of association, allowed to be that of priority, or former succession in time, it would surely have been a very singular arrangement, if the conceptions, arising according to this very relation, were to be held as not fairly referable to the class to which they have previously been ascribed; and that what renders them associate should be itself the very cause, for which, and for which alone, they are to be excluded from the class of associations.

[22] Simple memory, then, it appears, is nothing more than a particular suggestion, combined with the feeling of the relation of priority, and all the conceptions, therefore, which it involves, arise according to the laws which regulate suggestion in general. The same resemblances, contrasts, contiguities, give rise to our conceptions of objects, whether we do or do not consider those objects in the relation of priority, which they bear to our present feeling, or to any other event. In journeying along a road which I have never passed before, some form of the varying landscape may recal to me the scenery around the home which I have left; and it suggests it equally by its mere resemblance, whether it recal it to me as a simple picture, or remind me, at the same time, that it is the very home which I have left, and that, as many weeks have intervened since I saw it, many weeks are likely also to pass before I see it again.

[23] In simple memory, then, it will be allowed, that conception follows conception by the ordinary laws of suggestion, as much as in those conceptions to which we do not attach, that is to say, with which there is not combined, any notion of time. But there is a species of memory, which is said to be under our control,--that memory combined with desire of remembering something forgotten, to which we commonly give the name of recollection. We will the existence of certain ideas, it is said, and they arise in consequence of our volition; though, assuredly, to will any idea, is to know what we will, and therefore to be conscious of that very idea, which we surely need not desire to know, when we already know it, so well as to will its actual existence.

[24] The contradiction implied in this direct volition of any particular idea, is, indeed, so manifest, that the assertion of such a direct power over the

course of our thought is now pretty generally abandoned. But still it is affirmed, with at least equal incongruity, that we have it in our power to will certain conceptions indirectly, and that there is, therefore, a species of memory which is not mere suggestion, but follows, in part, at least, other laws. This indirect volition however, as I have shown in some paragraphs of my Essay on Cause and Effect, is only another form of that very direct volition of ideas, the absurdity of which it is introduced to obviate. Thus, if I wish to remember a piece of news which was communicated to me by a friend, it is acknowledged, indeed, that I cannot will the conception of this immediately and directly, since that would be to know it already; but I am said to have the power of calling up such ideas as I know to have coexisted with it, the place at which the news was told me, the person who told it, and various circumstances of our conversation, at the same time; and this supposed power of calling up such relative ideas, is that indirect power over our course of thought which we are said to possess. But, surely, if these ideas of the circumstances that formerly accompanied the event which I wish to remember, arise, of themselves, to the mind, according to the simple course of suggestion, there is not even indirect volition in the parts of the spontaneous train; and, if they do not arise of themselves, but are separately willed, there is then as direct volition, and consequently as much absurdity, involved in this calling up of the person, the place, and the other accompanying circumstances, as in calling up the very conception itself, which is the object of all this search. In either case, we must be supposed to will to know that, of which the will to know it implies the knowledge. The only difference is, that, instead of one direct volition, which is acknowledged, or which must be acknowledged to be absurd, we have now many separate direct volitions, and have consequently multiplied the inconsistency which we wished to avoid. The true and simple theory of the recollection is to be found in the permanence of the desire, and the natural spontaneous course of suggestion. I do not call up the ideas of the person and the place; but these, by their relations to the desire which I feel, arise uncalled; and when these have arisen, the suggestion of some part of the conversation at that place, and with that person, is a very natural effect of this mere conception of the person and of the place. If that particular part of the discourse be thus simply suggested, which I wished to remember, my object is gained, and my desire, of course, ceases; if not, my desire still continuing, and being itself now more strongly, because more recently associated with the conceptions of the person and the place, keeps them constantly before me, till, in the variety of suggestions to which they spontaneously give rise, I either obtain, at last, the remembrance which I wish, or, by some new suggestion, am led into a new channel of thought, and forget altogether that there was any thing which I wished to remember. What is termed voluntary recollection then, whether direct or indirect, is nothing more than the coexistence of some vague and indistinct desire with our simple trains of suggestion.

[25] It is a complex feeling, or series of feelings, of which the continued desire, and a variety of successive relative conceptions, are parts; but the coexistence of the train of conceptions, with an unsatisfied desire, though a complex state of mind, is not the exercise of any new power, distinct from the elementary powers or feelings which compose it. We have only to perform our

mental analysis, as in any other complex phenomenon of the mind, and the elements instantly appear.

[26] Such, then, is memory, not a simple affection of the mind, the result of a peculiar power, but a combination of two elementary feelings, the more important of which is to be traced to the laws of simple suggestion, while the other element is referable to a power that is afterwards to be considered by us.

[27] In my remarks on the secondary laws of suggestion, I considered, very fully, those circumstances which diversify the general power of suggestion, in different individuals, and which thus give occasion to all the varieties of conception or remembrance, in individuals, to whom the mere primary laws of suggestion may be supposed to have been nearly equal. It will not be necessary for me, therefore, to revert to these at present, as explanatory of the varieties of memory; since the same secondary laws, which diversify our suggestions as mere conceptions, without any notion of priority combined with them, diversify them, in like manner, when the notion of this relation is combined with them.

[28] In estimating the power of memory, however, in those striking diversities of it which appear in different individuals, I must warn you against an error into which you may naturally fall, if you pay attention chiefly to the more obvious suggestions, which arise and display themselves in the common intercourse of life. It is in this way, that a good memory, which is, in itself, so essential an accompaniment of profound and accurate judgment, has fallen into a sort of proverbial disrepute, as if unfriendly to judgment, or indicative of a defect in this nobler part of our intellectual constitution. In the cases, however, which have led to this very erroneous remark, it is not the quantity, if I may so express it, of the power of memory, but the peculiar species of it, that, by the sort of connexions which it involves, presents itself to us more readily, and seems more absurd, merely by coming thus more frequently before our view.

[29] What we are too ready to consider, exclusively as memory, is the suggestion which takes place, according to the mere relations of contiguity in time and place, of the very objects themselves, without regard to the conceptions, which arise, in our trains of thought, by the same power of spontaneous suggestion, but which arise according to other relations, and which, therefore, we never think of ascribing to the same simple power. It is not a good memory, in its best sense, as a rich and retentive store of conceptions, that is unfriendly to intellectual excellence, poetic or philosophic, but a memory of which the predominant tendency is to suggest objects or images which existed before in this very order, in which, as objects or images, they existed before, according to the merely imitative relations of contiguity. The richer the memory, and consequently the greater the number of images that may arise to the poet, and of powers and effects that may arise to the philosopher, the more copious, in both cases, will be the suggestions of analogy, which constitute poetic invention or philosophic discovery,--and the more copious the suggestions of analogy may be, the richer and more diversified, it is evident, must be the inventive power of the mind. It is the quality of memory, then, as suggesting objects in their old and familiar sequences of contiguity, not the quantity of the store of sugges-

tions that is unfriendly to genius, though, as I before remarked, this very difference of quality may, to superficial observers, seem like a difference of the quantity of the actual power.

[30] It is in common conversation chiefly that we judge of the excellence of the memory of others, and that we feel our own defects of it,--and the species of relation which forms by far the more important tie of things, in ordinary discourse, is that of previous contiguity. We talk of things which happened at certain times, and in certain places; and he who remembers these best, seems to us to have the best memory, though the other more important species of suggestion, according to analogy, may, in his mind, be wholly unproductive, and though no greater number of images, therefore, may be stored in it, and no greater number of spontaneous suggestions arise; but, on the contrary, perhaps, far fewer than in the more philosophic minds, whose admirable inventions and discoveries, as we term them, we admire, but whose supposed bad memories, which are in truth only different modifications of the same principle of suggestion, we lament.

[31] The most ignorant of the vulgar, in describing a single event, pour out a number of suggestions of contiguity, which may astonish us indeed, though they are a proof not that they remember more, but only that their prevailing suggestions take place, according to one almost exclusive relation. It is impossible to listen to a narrative of the most simple event, by one of the common people who are unaccustomed to pay much attention to events but as they occur together, without being struck with a readiness of suggestion of innumerable petty circumstances which might seem like superiority of memory, if we did not take into account the comparatively small number of their suggestions of a different class. They do not truly remember more than others, but their memory is different in quality from the memory of others. Suggestions arise in their minds which do not arise in other minds; but there is at least an equal number of suggestions that arise in the minds of others, of which their minds, in the same circumstances, would be wholly unsusceptible. Yet still, as I have said, to common observers, their memory will appear quick and retentive, in a peculiar and far surpassing degree. How many trifling facts, for example, does Mrs. Quickly heap together to force upon Sir John Falstaff's remembrance his promise of marriage. The passage is quoted by Lord Kames, as a very lively illustration of the species of recollections of a vulgar mind.

[32] "In the minds of some persons, thoughts and circumstances crowd upon each other by the slightest connexions. I ascribe this to a bluntness in the discerning faculty; for a person who cannot accurately distinguish between a slight connexion and one that is more intimate is equally affected by each: such a person must necessarily have a great flow of ideas, because they are introduced by any relation indifferently; and the slighter relations, being without number, furnish ideas without end. This doctrine is, in a lively manner, illustrated by Shakspeare:--

Falstaff. What is the gross sum that I owe thee?

Hostess. Marry, if thou wert an honest man, thyself and thy money too. Thou didst swear to me on a parcel-gilt goblet, sitting in my Dolphin-chamber, at the round table, by a sea-coal fire, on Wednesday in Whitsun-week, when the Prince broke thy head for likening him to a singing man of Windsor; thou didst swear to me then, as I was washing thy wound, to marry me, and make me my lady thy wife. Canst thou deny it? Did not Goodwife Keech, the butcher's wife, come in then, and call me Gossip Quickly? coming in to borrow a mess of vinegar; telling us she had a good dish of prawns; whereby thou didst desire to eat some; whereby I told thee they were ill for a green wound. And didst not thou, when she was gone down stairs, desire me to be no more so familiarity with such poor people, saying, that ere long they should call me madam? And didst thou not kiss me, and bid me fetch thee thirty shillings? I put thee now to thy book oath, deny it if thou canst.—Second Part, Henry IV. Act 2, Scene 2.

[33] "On the other hand, a man of accurate judgment cannot have a great flow of ideas; because the slighter relations, making no figure in his mind, have no power to introduce ideas. And hence it is, that accurate judgment is not friendly to declamation or copious eloquence. This reasoning is confirmed by experience; for it is a noted observation, That a great or comprehensive memory is seldom connected with a good judgment."

[34] It is not from any defect of memory, as Lord Kames thinks, that fewer of the ideas which prevail in common conversation, arise to a mind of accurate judgment; but because the prevailing tendencies to suggestion, in such a mind, are of a species that have little relation to the dates, &c. of the occurrences that are the ordinary topics of familiar discourse. The memory differs in quality, not in quantity; or, at least, the defect of these ordinary topics is not itself a proof that the general power of suggestion is less vigorous.

[35] In the case of extemporary eloquence, indeed, the flow of mere words may be more copious in him who is not accustomed to dwell on the permanent relations of objects, but on the slighter circumstances of perception and local connexion. Yet this is far from proving that the memory of such a person, which implies much more than the recurrence of verbal signs, is less comprehensive; on the contrary, there is every reason to suppose, that, unless probably in a few very extraordinary cases, which are as little to be taken into account, in a general estimate of this kind, as the form and functions of monsters in a physiological inquiry, the whole series of suggestions, of which a profound and discriminating mind is capable, is greater, upon the whole, than the number of those which rise so readily to the mind of a superficial thinker. The great difference is, that the wealth of the one is composed merely of those smaller pieces which are in continual request, and therefore brought more frequently to view,--while the abundance of the other consists chiefly in those more precious coins, which are rather deposited than carried about for current use, but which, when brought forward, exhibit a magnificence of wealth, to which the petty counters of the multitude are comparatively insignificant.

Reduction of Certain Supposed Mental Faculties to
Simple Suggestion. -- III. Imagination

[5] Nor is it only intellectual wealth which we thus acquire and preserve; it is by our remembrances that we are truly moral beings, because we owe to them the very conception of every thing which can be the object of morality. Without them there could be no esteem, no gratification for kindness received, no compassion for those who are in sorrow, no love of what is honourable and benevolent. How many of our purest affections might we trace, through a long series of reciprocal kindnesses, to the earliest years of our boyhood--to the field of our sports--to the nursery--to the very cradle in which our smile answered only still fonder smiles that hung ceaseless around it! The Greeks, in their Theogony, by a happy allegorical illustration of the importance of this principle, to all the exercises of fancy and the understanding, fabled the Muses to be Daughters of Memory. They might, with equal truth, have given the same parentage to the Virtues.

WILLIAM H. BURNHAM

1855 - 1941 A.D.

From: Memory, Historically and Experimentally Considered. By William H. Burnham. Published in the *American Journal of Psychology*, 1888, 2, 39-90, 255-270, 431-464, 566-622.

William H. Burnham was born in Dunbarton, New Hampshire. He received his bachelor's degree from Harvard in 1882 and his doctorate from Johns Hopkins in 1888. Subsequently, he taught at Clark University until his retirement in 1926. Burnham is best remembered for his work on human memory, especially his superb history of memory, of which the conclusion is included here.

Table of Contents

Memory, Historically and Experimentally Considered

Explanation of contents: Burnham's article is divided into sections of which the last is reprinted here. Paragraph numbers [in brackets] have been added by the editors .

XIII.1 - 2

Conclusion

[1] Whether or not we agree with Emerson that all men may be divided into Platonists and Aristotelians, the various theories of memory studied naturally divide into two series--one begun by Plato, the other by Aristotle--the former transcendental, the latter physiological and empirical in its tendency. Plato, the Neo-Platonists, St. Augustine, Leibnitz regard memory as an act of the soul, limited, perhaps, by physiological processes, but not dependent upon them. Sensation may furnish memory the data in great part, yet memory belongs not to the sensory but to the intellectual part of the mind. On the other hand, according to Aristotle, Thomas Aquinas, Hobbes, Condillac, Bonnet, and others (making allowance for differences of opinion due to their individual systems), memory belongs to the sensory side of the mind. The images of memory and the imagination are the relics of former sensations. The sensations were due originally to physiological processes. The reproduced images depend upon physiological processes, weaker, but not essentially different from the original ones.

[2] The theories of memory that we have studied may be of little value in themselves, but they form a part of the data necessary for a complete study of the psychology of memory. These theories were formed very much as we form our theories to-day, i.e., by generalization from observed facts--with less of scientific rigor probably, with the usual coloring of the thinker's mental environment, and with the peculiar ornaments of the individual apperception. But, if "million-eyed observation" is better than the observation of any one man, if the experience of the race is more trustworthy than that of the individual, then a theory, though worthless as such, may be valuable because containing, however obscurely, a record of the observation and experience of the times when it was formed. Most of all, however, a theory, worthless in itself, may be valuable as an instance of the working of the human mind before one of the greatest problems of psychology. A great number of such instances may prove valuable for psychological study in the same way as the myths of savage tribes and the records of childlife.

APPENDIX

Sources on the History of Memory

For those who want to delve more deeply into the history of memory we provide the following information about source material.

Primary Sources

Primary sources include the works, letters, and papers of scholars and sourcebooks cataloging or excerpting these materials. The availability of the work of a particular scholar depends on his or her importance in the eyes of earlier generations. For those scholars whose collected works have been published the task of the historical researcher is greatly simplified. Many of the scholars included in this collection fall into this category. For scholars whose work has not been collected the task of uncovering material is considerably more arduous.

Useful information on how to locate primary sources may be found in Bagg (1973). Also the staff at the Archive of Psychology in Akron, Ohio, will answer queries about original source materials. Once the material is located, there come the problems of interpreting it. A useful discussion of issues of interpretation can be found in Crutchfield and Krech (1963).

Memory in Historical Perspective is the first sourcebook devoted to memory before Ebbinghaus. Sourcebooks on more general psychological topics also include some materials on memory, e.g., Herrnstein & Boring, 1965; Rand, 1912; Sahakian, 1970). More general source books that include information about memory include Adler's (1952) *Great Ideas: A Synopticon of Great Books of the Western World.*

Secondary Sources

There are several general histories of memory: Burnham (1888), Cohen (1980), Middleton (1888), Marshall and Fryer (1978), Murray (1976). Of these Burnham's is by far the most complete. General accounts are also available in some encyclopedias, e.g., Encyclopaedia Britannica (Mitchell, 1911), and the Catholic Encyclopaedia (Lansberg, 1967).

Histories written from a specific theoretical perspective include the following: from the associative perspective - Warren (1921), Anderson and Bower (1973); from a trace theory perspective - Gomulicki (1953); from a cognitive perspective - Beare (1906); at least two histories have been written from a philosophical perspective: Edgell (1924), Shoemaker (1967). Several histories of mnemonics have been written; these include Higbee (1979), Hoffman and Senter (1978), Paivio (1971), Paivio and Desrochers (1981), and Rawles (1978). A detailed history of the art of memory has been written by Yates (1966). There is history of memory in the oral tradition (Natopoulos, 1938) and there are two histories of mnemonists (Atkinson, 1912; Brown and Deffenbacher, 1975).

Several histories have been written which focus on just one particular author on memory: Vives (Murray, 1976); Wundt (Scheerer, 1980); Ebbinghaus (Hoffman, Bringmann, Bamberg & Klein, 1987); Ebbinghaus and Semon (Schacter, Eich and Tulving, 1978; Schacter, 1982); and Giordano Bruno (Yates, 1964). A search of the literature will reveal other biographies in addition to these.

The history of the impact of Ebbinghaus' work on the study of memory is described in several works (Postman, 1968; Shakow, 1930; Woodworth, 1909) and in general texts on the history of psychology (e.g., Boring, 1950; Flugel, 1933; Murray, 1976). A brief but excellent review is given by Schacter (1982) in his book on Semon.

In addition to these histories there are a small number of bibliographies dealing with memory: Adler (1952), Wozniak (1984), and Young (1961).

REFERENCES

(References for the *supplementary readings* for each writer are given in the text and are not repeated here)

Adler, M. J. (1952). *The Great Ideas: A Synopticon of Great Books of the Western World*. Chicago: Encyclopedia Britannica.

Anderson, J. R., & Bower, G. H. (1973). *Human Associative Memory*. Hillsdale, NJ: Erbaum.

Anonymous (incorrectly attributed to Cicero) (1954). *(Cicero) Ad G. Herennium de Ratione Dicendi*. Harry Caplan, Trans. Loeb Classical Library. London: William Heinemann.

Aquinas, T. (1953). *Truth*. Vol. 2, Questions X-XX. J. V. McGlynn, Trans. Chicago: Henry Regnery.

Aquinas, T. (1961). *Commentary on the Metaphysics of Aristotle*. J. P. Rowan, Trans. Chicago: Henry Regnery.

Aquinas, T. (1964). *Summa Theologiae*. T. Gilby, K. Foster, & L. Bright, Trans. and Eds. London: Blackfriars, in conjunction with McGraw-Hill, New York, and Eyre & Spottiswoode, London.

Aristophanes (1962). The Clouds. In *Aristophanes: Works*. B. B. Rogers, Trans. The Loeb Classical Library. London: William Heinemann.

Aristotle (1928-1952). *The Works of Aristotle Translated into English,* Vols. 1 - 12. W. D. Ross, Ed. Oxford: Oxford University Press.

Atkinson, W. W. (1912). *Memory: How to Develop, Train, and Use It*. Holyoke, MA: The Elizabeth Towne Co.

Augustine, St. (1955). *Augustine: Confessions and Enchiridion*. A. C. Outler, Ed. and Trans. Library of the Christian Classics, Vol. VII. Philadelphia: Westminster Press.

Augustine, St. (1955). *Augustine: Later Works*. J. Burnaby, Ed. and Trans. Library of the Christian Classics, Vol. VIII. Philadelphia: Westminster Press.

Bacon, F. (1905). *The Philosophic Works of Francis Bacon*. John M. Robertson, Ed. (Reprinted from translations by R. C. Ellis and J. Spedding.) London: George Routledge and Sons.

Bagg, R. A. (1973). Annotated bibliographic sources in the history of psychology. In M. Henle, J. Jaynes, & J. J. Sullivan (Eds.), *Historical Conceptions of Psychology*. New York: Springer Publishing Company.

Bahrick, H. P. (1985). The laboratory and the ecology: Supplementary sources of data for memory research. The Third George A. Tallars Conference on Memory and Aging. Cape Cod, Massachusetts.

Beare, J. I. (1906). *Greek Theories of Elementary Cognition*. London: Oxford University Press.

Boring, E. G. (1950). *A History of Experimental Psychology*. New York: Appleton-Century-Crofts.

Bower, G. (1967). A multicomponent theory of the memory trace. In K. W. Spence & J. T. Spence (Eds.) *Advances in Learning and Motivation*, Vol. 1. New York: Academic Press.

Brown, E., & Deffenbacher, K. (1975). Forgotten mnemonists. *Journal of the History of the Behavioral Sciences, 11*, 342-349.

Brown, T. (1858). *Lectures on the Philosophy of the Human Mind*. 19th ed. London: William Tegg & Co.

Burnham, W. H. (1888). Memory, historically and experimentally considered. *American Journal of Psychology, 2*, 39-90, 225-270, 431-464, 566-622.

Capella, M. (1977). *Martianus Capella and the Seven Liberal Arts*. Vol. II, *The Marriage of Philology and Mercury*. W. H. Stahle & R. Johnson with E. L. Burge, Trans. New York: Columbia University Press.

Cicero (1942). *De Oratore*. E. W. Sutton, Trans. Loeb Classical Library. London: William Heinemann.

Cicero (1927). *Tusculan Disputations*. J. E. King, Trans. Loeb Classical Library. London: William Heinemann.

Cohen, J. (1980). *The Lineaments of Mind*. Oxford: W. H. Freeman.

Cole, R. A., & Rudnicky, A. I. (1983). What's new in speech perception? The research and ideas of William Chandler Bagley, 1874-1946. *Psychological Review, 90*, 94-101.

Craik, F. I. M., & Lockhart, R. S. (1972). Levels of processing: A framework for memory research. *Journal of Verbal Learning and Verbal Behavior, 11*, 671-684.

Crutchfield, R. S., and Krech, D. (1963). Some guides to the understanding of the history of psychology. In L. Postman (Ed.), *Psychology in the Making*. New York: Alfred A. Knopf.

da Vinci, L. (1981). *The Literary Works of Leonardo da Vinci*, Vols. 1-2. Jean Paul Richter, Ed. London: Phaidon Press.

Ebbinghaus, H. (1885). *Uber das Gedachtnis: Untersuchugen zur experimentellan Psychologie.* Leipzig: Dunker & Humbolt, 1885. Translated by H. A. Ruger & C. E. Byssenine as *Memory: A Contribution to Experimental Psychology.* New York: Dover, 1913.

Ebbinghaus, H. (1908). *Abris der Psychologie.* Leipzig: Dunker & Humbolt. Translated by M. Meyer as *Psychology: An Elementary Textbook.* Boston: Heath, 1908.

Edgell, B. (1924). Historical outline of the treatment of memory by philosophic writers from Hobbs to Spencer. In B. Edgell (Ed.), *Theories of Memory.* Oxford: Clarendon Press.

Edmonds, J. M., Ed. and Trans. (1927). *Lyra Graeca.* Vol. III, *Other Scolia.* Loeb Classical Library. London: William Heinemann.

Flugel, J. C. (1933). *A Hundred Years of Psychology.* London: Duckworth.

Gomulicki, B. R. (1953). History of the trace theory. In B. R. Gomulicki (Ed.), *The Development and Present Status of the Trace Theory of Memory.* Cambridge: Cambridge University Press.

Herrmann, D. J. (1982). The semantic-episodic distinction and the history of long-term memory typologies. *Bulletin of the Psychonomic Society, 20,* 207-210.

Herrmann, D. J., & Chaffin, R. (1987). Memory before Ebbinghaus. In D. Gorfein & R. R. Hoffman (Eds.), *Learning and Memory: The Ebbinghaus Centennial Conference.* Hillsdale, NJ: Erlbaum.

Herrnstein, R. J., & Boring, E. G. (1965). *A Source Book in the History of Psychology.* Harvard University Press: Cambridge, MA.

Hesiod (1959). *Hesiod.* R. Lattimore, Trans. Ann Arbor, MI: University of Michigan Press.

Higbee, K. L. (1979). Recent research on visual mnemonics: Historical roots and educational fruits. *Review of Educational Research, 49,* 611-629.

Hoffman, R. R., Bringmann, W., Bamberg, M., & Klein, R. (1987). Some historical observations on Ebbinghaus. In D. Gorfein & R. R. Hoffman (Eds.), *Learning and Memory: The Ebbinghaus Centennial Conference.* Hillsdale, NJ: Erlbaum.

Hoffman, R. R., & Senter, R. J. (1978). Recent history of psychology: Mnemonic techniques and the psycholinguistic revolution. *Psychological Record, 28,* 3-15.

Hume, D. (1951). *The Philosophical Works of David Hume.* 4 vols. Published by Adam Black, William Tait and Charles Tait, 1886.

Kant, I. (1961). *Immanuel Kant's Critique of Pure Reason.* N. Kemp Smith, Trans. London: MacMillan.

Lansberg, H. (1967). Memory in ancient and medieval thought. In *New Catholic Encyclopaedia,* Vol. IX, pp. 643-644. San Francisco: McGraw-Hill.

Marshall, J. C., & Fryer, D. M. (1978). Speak, Memory! An introduction to some historical studies of remembering and forgetting. In M. M. Gruneberg & P. Morris (Eds.), *Aspects of Memory.* London: Methuen.

Middleton, A. E. (1888). *Memory Systems: New and Old.* New York: G. S. Fellows.

Mill, J. (1829). *Analysis of the Phenomena of the Human Mind.* London: Baldwin & Cradock.

Mitchell, J. M. (1911). Mnemonics. In *Encyclopaedia Britannica,* Vol. 18. Cambridge: Cambridge University Press.

Montaigne, Michel Eyquem de (1958). *Essays.* J. M. Cohen, Trans. Harmondsworth: Penguin.

Murray, D. J. (1976). Research on memory in the nineteenth century. *Canadian Journal of Psychology,* 1976, *30,* 201-220.

Natopoulos, J. A. (1938). Mnemosyne in oral literature. *Transactions of the American Philosophical Association,* *69,* 465-493.

Paivio, A., & Desrochers, A. (1981). Mnemonic techniques in second language learning. *Journal of Educational Psychology,* *73,* 780-795.

Paivio, A. (1969). Mental imagery in associative learning and memory. *Psychological Review, 76,* 241-263.

Paivio, A. (1971). *Imagery and Verbal Processes.* New York: Holt, Rinehart and Winston.

Patrick, G. T. W. (1888). A further study of Heraclitus. *American Journal of Psychology, 1,* 557-690.

Plato (1953). *The Dialogues of Plato.* 4th ed. B. Jowett, Trans. Oxford: Clarendon Press.

Pliny the Elder (1952). *Natural History,* Vol. II. Loeb Classical Library. London: William Heinemann.

239

Postman, L. (1968). Hermann Ebbinghaus. *American Psychologist, 23,* 149-157.

Quintillian (1921). *The Institutio Oratoria of Quintillian.* H. E. Butler, Trans. Loeb Classical Library. London: William Heinemann.

Rand, B., Ed. (1912). *The Classical Psychologists.* Boston: Houghton Mifflin.

Rawles, R. E. (1978). The past and present of mnemotechny. In M. Gruneberg, P. E. Morris, & R. N. Sykes (Eds.), *Practical Aspects of Memory.* London: Academic Press.

Reid, T. (1969). *The Essays on the Intellectual Powers of Man.* Introduction by B. A. Brody. Cambridge, MA: M.I.T. Press.

Rogers, S. (1805). *The Pleasures of Memory: In Two Parts to Which Are Added the Pains of Memory.* Portland, England: Daniel Johnson.

Sahakian, W. S. (1970). *Psychology of Learning.* Chicago: Markham Publishing Company.

Schacter, D. L. (1982). *Stranger behind the Engram.* Hillsdale, NJ: Erlbaum.

Schacter, D. L., Eich, J. E., & Tulving, E. (1978). Richard Semon's theory of memory. *Journal of Verbal Learning and Verbal Behavior, 17,* 721-743.

Scheerer, E. (1980). Wilhelm Wundt's psychology of memory. *Psychological Research, 42,* 135-155.

Shakow, D. (1930). Hermann Ebbinghaus. *American Journal of Psychology, 62,* 505-518.

Shiffrin, R. M. (1970). Memory search. In D. Norman (Ed.), *Models of Human Memory.* New York: Academic Press.

Shoemaker, S. (1967). Memory. In P. Edwards (Ed.), *Encyclopedia of Philosophy.* New York: Macmillan.

Sorabji, R. (1972). *Aristotle on Memory.* London: Gerald Duckworth and Company, 1972.

Tulving, E. (1972). Episodic and semantic memory. In E. Tulving & W. Donaldson (Eds.), *Organization of Memory.* New York: Academic Press.

Tulving, E. (1983). *Elements of Episodic Memory.* New York: Oxford University Press.

Underwood, B. J. (1969). Attributes of memory. *Psychological Review, 76,* 559-576.

Warren, H. C. (1921). *A History of Association Psychology*. New York: Scribner.

Watson, R. I. (1960). The history of psychology: A neglected area. *American Psychologist, 15,* 251-255.

Wickens, D. D. (1970). Encoding categories of words: An empirical approach to memory. *Psychological Review, 77,* 1-15.

Woodworth, R. S. (1909). Hermann Ebbinghaus. *Journal of Philosophy, Psychology, and Scientific Method, 6,* 253-256.

Wozniak, R. H. (1984). A brief history of serial publication in psychology. In D. V. Osier & R. H. Wozniak (Eds.), *A Century of Serial Publications in Psychology. 1850-1950: An International Bibliography*. Millwood, NY: Kraus International.

Yates, F. A. (1964). *Giordano Bruno and the Hermetic Tradition*. Chicago: University of Chicago Press.

Yates, F. A. (1966). *The Art of Memory*. London: Routledge & Kegan Paul.

Young, M. N. (1961). *Bibliography of Memory*. Philadelphia: Chilton Co.

SUBJECT INDEX

The subject index uses current terminology from the field of human memory to describe the topics discussed in the writings. The keyword index, which follows, lists terms used by the writers themselves.

KEYWORD INDEX

The keyword index lists terms used in the writings with a minimum of interpretation by the editors. Related forms of a word, e.g., plural and past tense forms, are not listed separately.

NAME INDEX

Adler, 234, 235
Anderson, 164, 235
Aquinas, 2, 5, 7, 18, 128, 129, 131,
    233
Aristophanes, 2, 6, 22
Aristotle, 2, 5, 6, 7, 18, 25, 56, 81,
    105, 128, 131-6, 141-3,
    146-8, 151-5, 179, 183,
    190, 191, 193, 194, 233
Atkinson, 235
Augustine, 2, 5, 7, 12, 18, 110, 111,
    121, 122, 128, 132-42, 145,
    147-9, 151, 233
Averroes, 144
Avicenna, 134, 144, 146

Bacon, 2, 5, 7, 13, 161, 164-6
Bagg, 234
Bahrick, 1
Beare, 16, 235
Bonnet, 233
Boring, 4, 6, 234, 235
Bower, 5, 235
Brown, 2, 5, 7, 19, 213, 214, 235
Bruno, 7, 235
Burnham, 2, 16, 232, 234

Chaffin, 6
Cicero, 2, 3, 5, 7, 11, 75, 83, 94, 96,
    99, 100, 101, 124, 132,
    133, 153, 163
Cohen, 161, 234
Cole, 4
Condillac, 233
Craik, 5
Crutchfield, 4, 6, 234

Deffenbacher, 235
Descartes, 161

Ebbinghaus, 1-7, 16, 234, 235
Edgell, 16, 235
Eich, 235

Flugel, 235
Fryer, 5, 6, 16, 234

Gomulicki, 235

Heraclitus, 2, 6, 21
Herennius (ad Herennium), 7, 83-6
Herrmann, 5, 6
Herrnstein, 234
Hesiod, 2, 6, 7, 19
Higbee, 235
Hintzman, 7
Hobbes, 233
Hoffman, 235
Homer, 19, 44, 81
Hume, 2, 7, 14, 169, 178, 182, 218

James, 5, 164

Kant, 2, 7, 15, 195, 196
Krech, 4, 6, 234

Leibnitz, 185, 233
Leonardo da Vinci, 2, 157-160
Locke, 178, 182, 188, 189
Lockhart, 5

Merry, 7, 206, 207, 212
Middleton, 234
Mill, James, 5
Mitchell, 16, 234
Montaigne, 2, 161
Murray, 5, 16, 234, 235

Natopoulos, 235

Paivio, 5
Plato, 2, 3, 6, 7, 18, 23, 25, 56, 76,
    80, 98, 105, 191, 210, 233
Pliny, 2, 92
Plotinus, 2, 105

Quintillian, 2, 3, 5, 7, 94, 95

Ramus, 7
Rand, 234
Rawles, 235
Reid, 2, 5, 7, 178, 179, 213
Rogers, 2, 7, 22, 206, 207

253

This series reports new developments in all areas of psychological research—quickly, informally, and professionally. The types of research considered for publication include preliminary drafts of original papers and monographs; technical reports of high quality and broad interest; award winning theses; reports of conferences of exceptional interest, focused on a single topic. The timeliness of the manuscript is more important than its form. The publication of *Recent Research in Psychology* is intended to serve the international psychological community. Springer-Verlag can offer a wide distribution of documents and reports which would otherwise have a restricted audience. Once published and copyrighted, these reports can be documented in the scientific literature.

Manuscript
Manuscripts should not be less than 100 and preferably not more than 500 pages in length. Since they are reproduced by a photographic process, they must be typed with extreme care. Manuscripts submitted should be clean originals with few corrections or errors. Special symbols not on the typewriter should be inserted by hand in indelible black ink. The typescript is reduced slightly in size during reproduction with best results being obtained if each page is kept within the limit of 15.6 x 26.5 cm (6⅛ x 10½ inches). On request, the publisher will supply special paper with the typing area outlined. All authors are free to use the material in other publications.

Manuscripts should be sent to Psychology Editorial, Springer-Verlag New York Inc., 175 Fifth Avenue, New York, New York 10010 USA or Psychology Editorial, Springer-Verlag, Tiergartenstrasse 17, D-6900 Heidelberg 1, Federal Republic of Germany.

ISBN 0-387-96705-2
ISBN 3-540-96705-2

DATE DUE